T0320472

Method of Systems Potential (MSP) Applications in Economics:

Emerging Research and Opportunities

Grigorii Pushnoi
Independent Researcher, Russia

A volume in the Advances in Finance, Accounting, and Economics (AFAE) Book Series

www.igi-global.com

Published in the United States of America by
  IGI Global
  Business Science Reference (an imprint of IGI Global)
  701 E. Chocolate Avenue
  Hershey PA 17033
  Tel: 717-533-8845
  Fax: 717-533-8661
  E-mail: cust@igi-global.com
  Web site: http://www.igi-global.com

Library of Congress Cataloging-in-Publication Data

Names: Pushnoi, Grigorii, 1960- author.
Title: Method of systems potential (MSP) applications in economics : emerging
  research and opportunities / by Grigorii Pushnoi.
Description: Hershey : Business Science Reference, [2017]
Identifiers: LCCN 2016055826| ISBN 9781522521709 (hardcover) | ISBN
  9781522521716 (ebook)
Subjects: LCSH: Economics--Mathematical models. | Self-organizing systems.
Classification: LCC HB135 .P874 2017 | DDC 330.01/51--dc23 LC record available at https://lccn.loc.gov/2016055826

This book is published in the IGI Global book series Advances in Finance, Accounting, and Economics (AFAE) (ISSN: 2327-5677; eISSN: 2327-5685)

British Cataloguing in Publication Data
A Cataloguing in Publication record for this book is available from the British Library.

Advances in Finance, Accounting, and Economics (AFAE) Book Series

ISSN:2327-5677
EISSN:2327-5685

Editor-in-Chief: Ahmed Driouchi, Al Akhawayn University, Morocco

MISSION

In our changing economic and business environment, it is important to consider the financial changes occurring internationally as well as within individual organizations and business environments. Understanding these changes as well as the factors that influence them is crucial in preparing for our financial future and ensuring economic sustainability and growth.

The **Advances in Finance, Accounting, and Economics (AFAE)** book series aims to publish comprehensive and informative titles in all areas of economics and economic theory, finance, and accounting to assist in advancing the available knowledge and providing for further research development in these dynamic fields.

COVERAGE

- Economic Theory
- Managerial Accounting
- Macroeconomics
- Bankruptcy
- Entrepreneurship in Accounting and Finance
- Applied Finance
- Economic Indices and Quantitative Economic Methods
- Wages and Employment
- Microfinance
- Public Finance

IGI Global is currently accepting manuscripts for publication within this series. To submit a proposal for a volume in this series, please contact our Acquisition Editors at Acquisitions@igi-global.com or visit: http://www.igi-global.com/publish/.

Titles in this Series

For a list of additional titles in this series, please visit:
http://www.igi-global.com/book-series/advances-finance-accounting-economics/73685

Measuring Sustainable Development and Green Investments in Contemporary Economies
Mihai Mieila (Valahia University of Târgovişte Romania)
Business Science Reference • ©2017 • 250pp • H/C (ISBN: 9781522520818) • US $170.00

Handbook of Research on Unemployment and Labor Market Sustainability in the Era...
Füsun Yenilmez (Eskişehir Osmangazi University, Turkey) and Esin Kılıç (Eskişehir Osmangazi University, Turkey)
Business Science Reference • ©2017 • 474pp • H/C (ISBN: 9781522520085) • US $245.00

Business Infrastructure for Sustainability in Developing Economies
Nilanjan Ray (Netaji Mahavidyalaya, India)
Business Science Reference • ©2017 • 343pp • H/C (ISBN: 9781522520412) • US $190.00

Applied Behavioral Economics Research and Trends
Rodica Ianole (University of Bucharest, Romania)
Business Science Reference • ©2017 • 255pp • H/C (ISBN: 9781522518266) • US $160.00

Value Relevance of Accounting Information in Capital Markets
Marianne Ojo (George Mason University, USA) and Jeanette Van Akkeren (QUT School of Accountancy, Australia)
Business Science Reference • ©2017 • 323pp • H/C (ISBN: 9781522519003) • US $205.00

Handbook of Research on the EU's Role and Representation in the G20 Political...
Abdulkadir Isik (Namik Kemal University, Turkey)
Business Science Reference • ©2017 • 429pp • H/C (ISBN: 9781522508564) • US $310.00

Examining the Role of National Promotional Banks in the European Economy...
Iustina Alina Boitan (Bucharest University of Economic Studies, Romania)
Business Science Reference • ©2017 • 184pp • H/C (ISBN: 9781522518457) • US $120.00

For an enitre list of titles in this series, please visit:
http://www.igi-global.com/book-series/advances-finance-accounting-economics/73685

www.igi-global.com

701 East Chocolate Avenue, Hershey, PA 17033, USA
Tel: 717-533-8845 x100 • Fax: 717-533-8661
E-Mail: cust@igi-global.com • www.igi-global.com

Table of Contents

Preface

This book summarizes the main findings of explorations devoted to so-called Method of Systems Potential (MSP). This is new Method for the modelling of Complex Adaptive Systems (CAS). Traditionally Multi-Agent Modelling (MAM) is used for the modelling of Complex Adaptive Systems. Macroscopic properties of system are explored via multiple run of computer program.

This method of modelling is based on the principle "down-up": from interacting agents to macroscopic properties of the system. My Method of Systems Potential describes complex adaptive system as a holistic system which evolves on the basis of some simple and almost trivial macroscopic regulative algorithms. The Method of Systems Potential is based on "up-down" principle: from properties of holistic system to properties of adaptive agents. Method of Systems Potential treats complex adaptive system both as ensemble of interacting adaptive agents and as the self-contained adaptive agent of other complex adaptive system of higher level.

The first paper devoted to this topic was published in 2003 in the Proceedings of the 21st International Conference of the System Dynamics Society (Pushnoi, 2003). System Dynamics explores complex systems by special schemas describing the processes within a system as flows of resources, of information, and so on. Although traditional schemas of system dynamics (flows and stocks) are used in this paper to describe the function of complex systems, the scope of this paper is broader than that of standard system dynamics. Later I named this method as the "Method of Systems Potential" (MSP).

My path of discovering and formulating the main principles of this Method was long and difficult. When I was a student of the Physics Department at the Leningrad State University I was interested in a mathematical formalization of dialectic laws. Very dissimilar structures such as organisms, ecosystems, social and economic systems, enterprises and so on which spontaneously appear in nature and in society evolve on the basis of the general principles which were described by Georg Wilhelm Friedrich Hegel in his famous philosophical treatises "Phenomenology of Mind" (1807), "Science of Logic"

(1812; 1813; 1816, "Doctrine of Being" was revised 1831 and "Encyclope-dia of the Philosophical Sciences" (1817)). The curriculum at the Physics Department didn't include detailed studying of philosophy. Therefore I was engaged in self-education in the field of philosophy and some other subjects in addition to education in physics. It was in the 1980s right before the deep transformation of the USSR. My first attempt of formulating the laws of dialectics was made at that time.

Sometimes I open a desk drawer, I take in hands my old notebook which has turned yellow from time, and I remember a clear day in May many years ago when, after long searches and failures the main principles of the Method were eventually found and written down in this notebook.

The basic notions ("potential of a system", "conditions of realization of this potential", "efficiency of the system", "density of conditions") and basic principles of the Method were formulated at the end of the 1980s. Dramatic events in the life of my country, deep in crisis in the 1990s, did not leave opportunities for further research. This time was extremely difficult, and now I think that the experience of survival during the 1990s became some kind of a practical check for the basic ideas of this Method. My work in St. Petersburg enterprises as a manager, a director, and a financial analyst gave me opportunities to observe a situation of origin, prosperity and episodic deep structural transformations of the business structures. The analysis of the causes of sudden crises which happen even to apparently successful organizations led me to the conclusion that basic principles of Method are actually working.

Practical life experience accumulated during 1990s helped me to de-velop this Method in details. At the beginning of the 2000s I began to look for similarities of this Method to methods in those fields of science which explore complex systems: system dynamics, synergetics, chaos and complex-ity, complex nonlinear systems, dynamical systems, and complex adaptive systems. Solid qualifications in the fields of physics and mathematics helped me to formulate the basic principles in mathematical form.

The main ideas which are the cornerstones of this new method of model-ing are quite simple and almost trivial but the conclusions following from these simple trivial ideas are diverse and absolutely unexpected. I treat the Method of Systems Potential as an attempt to formulate the most general and fundamental laws which govern by the complex systems spontaneously appearing in nature and in society. The Method can be treated also as an attempt to formulate laws of dialectics as laws of development of complex adaptive systems. I doubt it can possibly be completed but I think that the main and the most essential laws of dialectics can be described as features of dynamics and of the structure of the complex evolving systems.

The Method describes complex systems via very abstract concepts: the "potential of a system" (its adaptive capacity), the "conditions of realization", a conditions providing realization of "potential", the process of realization, an application of adaptive capacity in adaptive activity, and the "realized potential", a part of "potential" which is exploited in adaptive activity of a system. These are the basic concepts of the Method. Other notions, such as the "efficiency" of a system and the "density of conditions" follow from the basic MSP-notions. "Efficiency" of a complex adaptive system is the rate of exploitation of accumulated "potential". "Efficiency" is equal to "realized potential" per "entire potential" ratio. "Density of conditions" is quantity of "conditions" per unit of "potential". The detailed description of concepts and discussion of logical schema of the Method is given in papers Pushnoi (2004a, 2006, 2010, 2014), Pushnoi and Bonser (2008). The application of the Method in economics is considered in papers Pushnoi (2004a, 2004b, 2005, 2010, 2014), Pushnoi and Bonser (2008).

The significant progress in a research of macroscopic properties of complex adaptive systems has been made after emergence of powerful computers. Modern computers and special software opened the possibility for exploration of complex adaptive systems via computer simulation of multi-agent models. There is already a huge amount of literature devoted to multi-agent models. Multi-agent models are being created for exploration of very dissimilar real objects: ecosystems, markets, social structures, organizations of various type and so on. Although these are absolutely different multi-agent models the macroscopic dynamical properties of these models are often almost identical. Episodic jumps in macro-indices, cyclic dynamics, inverse power law for probability distribution function are the typical features of multi-agent models.

For example Kephart (2002) in the paper devoted to agent-based models of markets noticed that dissimilar models of market economy demonstrate the identical macroscopic properties; the sudden jumps and cyclic changes in dynamics of macro-indices. He concluded that the reason of universal macroscopic dynamics is due to fundamental characteristics of market economy as a complex adaptive system.

... we have analyzed and simulated several different market models. Several phenomena appear to be quite generic: not only are they observed in many different scenarios, but their root causes appear to be very basic and general. (Kephart, 2002; p.7211)

Among the multi-agent models imitating the dynamics of real complex adaptive systems, there are models within which the system episodically changes the mode of functioning (work mode). It is macroscopic phenomenon which is explained by the change in configuration of the so-called "fitness landscape". In multi-agent models adaptive agents seek the most profitable fitness peak in the fitness landscape. Each agent moves gradually in the direction of a fitness peak in its fitness landscape. But the changes in the fitness landscape interfere with this motion, sooner or later. and reorient the agent into a new direction to a new peak.

This reorientation of agent interrupts the stability of trajectories of motion of other agents which in turn find more attractive peaks in fitness landscape.

A burst of activity of agents in their search for new attractive peaks changes radically the configuration of the fitness landscapes. Avalanche-like processes of reorientation of agents towards new peaks is switching the system as a whole onto a new work mode. Episodic switching of the system from one work mode to another creates a discontinuous cycle in macroscopic dynamics of the system.

For instance, Hommes's (2002) model of financial markets displays the four-phase cycles in which phases of high volatility alternate with phases of low volatility. The sharp changes in the index of volatility exist due to switching of the system onto the new work mode. Each switching changes the configuration of the system. After a new reconfiguration the process repeats itself. The length of smooth phases is not constant. This model displays the dynamics of stochastic discontinuous cycles consisting of two stages with a gradual change in the macro-index and two catastrophe-like switches of the system from one work mode to another. Epstein's (2002) Model of Civil Violence also demonstrates dynamics of stochastic discontinuous cycles in tension index (Epstein, 2002, Fig. 8, p. 7247). The jumps are caused by avalanche-like transitions of agents from the inactive state (patience) to an active state (rebellion) and vice versa.

Intermittent dynamics and sudden sharp jumps in macro-indices are typical features of the dynamics of multi-agent systems with adaptive agents. Statistics of jumps often points to phenomenon of self-organized criticality (SOC) if the probability distribution function satisfies the inverse-power law. Multi-agent models imitate the behaviour of real complex adaptive systems. Obvious identity of macroscopic dynamic properties of very dissimilar complex adaptive systems apparently indicates the existence of some general macroscopic laws which regulate the development of such systems.

Sornette (2002) notes that:

We live on a planet and in society with intermittent dynamics rather than a state of equilibrium... Evolution is probably characterized by phases of quasistasis interrupted by episodic bursts of activity and destruction. (p.2522)

The Method of Systems Potential explains these identical macroscopic dynamic properties of very dissimilar complex adaptive systems as the action of general regulative algorithms which determine dynamics of the system at a macroscopic level. The Method of Systems Potential considers so-called MSP-systems i.e. the systems which are functioning in accordance with the general principles of this Method. The MSP-system is a pure mathematical object and some procedure of interpretation must be added in order that the general mathematical scheme can be applied to real objects such as economic systems for example.

The Method uses very simple ideas. According to this Method there are three basic algorithms which are regulating the dynamics of complex system as a whole.

1. Each real complex system has some potential for development but the realization of the potential via the activity of the system depends upon available conditions. As a rule only some part of the potential is used up in current activity of the system. This part of the potential is called the realized potential of the system. The other part of the potential is not used up in the activity of the system. This is unrealized potential. Realized potential grows and gets stronger due to application in practice. Unrealized potential weakens and degrades. There is a huge set of examples which confirm the simple regulative algorithm in our life. Training and exercise as we know, develops the applied abilities. Abilities which aren't applied for a long time die off. In economy the entities which stand idle degrade (the old equipment becomes useless and depreciates). On the contrary, the functioning enterprises increase productive power. The French zoologist Jean Baptist Lamarck (1744-1829) believed that a similar principle regulates the development of organs in living beings (Lamarck, 1809). Therefore we treat this general principle as the modern formulation of one of Lamarck's laws.

2. The second regulative adaptive algorithm describes how the activity of a system and the impact of random destructive factors influence conditions of realization of potential. Conditions increase due to activity and degenerate due to the influence of random factors. The destructive impact of random factors can be treated as an action of the general law of the growth of entropy. For example in economy the fixed capital of plants

grows due to production of investment goods (productive activity) and depreciates due to aging and degradation of equipment (the growth of entropy). The Lamarck's Law and the Principle of Entropy are evidence of the simple regulative algorithms which characterize the development of any real complex systems at utmost abstract level.

3. Complex adaptive systems consist of multitude of adaptive agents which interact with each other. In addition to the previously noted one more additional algorithm works in these systems. This is the algorithm which stabilizes the temporary equilibrium state of complex adaptive systems. The process of homeostasis in biological, cellular and economic systems are well known examples of the action of this algorithm in real complex adaptive systems.

The Method of Systems Potential describes mathematically the actions of these regulative adaptive algorithms. The Method assumes that basic notions of the Method such as the potential and the conditions of realization can be described in terms of definite quantities i.e. as some mathematical variables. Regulative algorithms in this case can be formalized as some equations for these variables. A dynamical system consisting of these equations can be explored by mathematical methods. After mathematical interpretation of the MSP as a dynamical system of equations, it turned out that the above mentioned simple and almost trivial regulative algorithms generate very complex dynamics with discontinuous cycles and episodic sudden jumps. This is a remarkable fact.

The efficiency of the MSP-system (realized potential per entire potential ratio) is changing cyclically. Each cycle consists of two stages of gradual growth and two jumps upwards and downwards. Statistics of jumps in efficiency of the system in some cases demonstrate an inverse-power law for the probability distribution function. Thus, the MSP-system demonstrates all the basic features of the macroscopic dynamics observed in many real complex adaptive systems and in many multi-agent models of these systems.

Some interpretational rules are necessary in order to apply the Method for the exploration of real complex adaptive systems. It is not a simple task. The basic notions of the Method are very abstract. Although such concepts as "potential" and "conditions of realization" often can be found in speeches of economists and politicians, it is difficult to decipher, to give the exact definition for these concepts. Therefore the interpretation of MSP-notions is a special task which requires deep analysis of information about the factors which promote or slow down the development of the system.

This book contains both a short introduction into the Method of Systems Potential and applications of this Method in economics. I tried to simplify material where it was possible, and excluded long calculations and purely mathematical nuances which can be interesting only to professional mathematicians. The readers who are interested in mathematical aspects can be addressed to my earlier publications: Pushnoi (2003; 2014), Pushnoi and Bonser (2008), and Pushnoi (2004a; 2006). To make material more easily understood I used illustrations which visually explain often quite complex results in a mathematical sense. The main body of the text is devoted to application of the Method in economics. I used findings from my papers devoted to application of the Method in economic analysis: Pushnoi (2004a; 2004b; 2005; 2010). The fifth chapter contains new unpublished material about MSP-systems with variable parameters.

The content of this book is structured as follows:

Introduction contains a short introduction into the Method of Systems Potential: the basic notions and principles. Although this chapter contains a brief description of the interrelation between agent-based modelling and MSP-modelling of complex adaptive systems I would advise the readers who are interested in the general philosophical aspects of the Method to examine earlier published works where this subject was considered in more details. Chapter 1 is mainly devoted to the formulation of the basic principles of the Method. This chapter describes a pure mathematical object, the MSP-system: definitions of variables, formalization of macroscopic adaptive algorithms, and a description of the dynamical system of equations. The solution of MSP-equations is provided but all calculations are omitted.

MSP-Model of the Economic Complex Adaptive System discusses how the MSP-approach can be used in economics. This chapter summarizes information which is used for the right choice of interpretational rules. Economy is considered as a complex adaptive system which consists of a multitude of interacting agents: firms, organizations, enterprises and so on. Analysis of the basic economic concepts and approaches in economic modelling definitely helped me to choose the main interpretation rules for applying the MSP-model for the exploration of the economy.

MSP-variables and MSP-parameters are interpreted as well-known economic indices and rates.

"Potential" of the Economic Complex Adaptive System (ECAS) is economic potential i.e. economic capacity. "Economic potential" can be measured by "maximum output" which is the output of an economic system with full utilization of all available production resources, their optimal allocation and optimal factor prices.

"Conditions of realization" depend upon many factors. Intuitively this notion is connected with stock of capital, investment conditions, and the economic legislation in the country. Capital is the main driving force for productive utilization of available resources: labor, land, plant, and knowledge in the modern economy. A definite amount of capital must be advanced in order to combine (and to transform) the potential forces of the labor, machines, land, and technologies into the real production. Therefore the capital is the main index which characterizes volume of "conditions of realization" in modern economy.

"Realized economic potential" is the same as exploited economic potential. Productive activity of economic agents (firms, entrepreneurs etc.) in the economy is proportional to "realized economic potential". Consequently the notion of "output" in economics can be used as the quantitative measure of employed (realized) economic potential.

The "efficiency of an economic system" can be described by an economic index capacity utilization rate: actual per maximal (or potential) output ratio.

"Density of conditions" is a variable which equals quantity of "conditions" divided into magnitude of "potential".

After the interpretation of basic MSP-notions in the sense of economic variables and parameters we can treat MSP-equations as the equations of a new economic model, MSP-model of Economic Complex Adaptive System (MSP-model of ECAS). All mathematical findings obtained for MSP-systems (chapter 1) can be interpreted as properties of economic system. However this is only the first step in the formulation of the MSP-model which could be applied in practice. Some additional specification of this Model is necessary in order for MSP-model of ECAS to be used in practical calculations. The second and third chapters describe general, fundamental properties of the MSP-model of ECAS without a specification of this model.

The Main properties of the MSP-ECAS-Model: Application to the European Economy considers the properties of ECAS. According to the MSP-model the economy develops cyclically. The efficiency of an economic system changes cyclically. The cycle consists of two stages of the gradual growth of efficiency and two jumps upwards and downwards. Each cycle can be graphed in the plane "density of conditions" vs. "efficiency". The trajectory of a system in this plane depicts a loop which consists of two "evolutionary branches" (upper and lower) and of two vertical pieces connecting these evolutionary branches. A system moves clockwise along this trajectory. It is convenient to use the following names: 1) a jump downwards – the "crisis", 2) a jump upwards – the "revival", 3) a phase of the gradual development along the lower evolutionary branch – the "depression" and 4) a stage of the gradual development along the upper evolutionary branch – the "prosperity". The MSP-model predicts existence of an interrelation between "efficiency" and "density of conditions". This interrelation determines non-trivial economic correlations between the productivity of capital and the capacity utilization rate in the MSP-model of ECAS. The MSP-model of ECAS, after specification, predicts the existence of non-trivial interrelations between the productivity of labor and the productivity of capital and between capital intensity and the productivity of labor. These theoretical dependencies are hidden because various stochastic factors perpetually influence the system so that the parameters of the economic system can change during the course of time. However, if we graph the data about the productivity of capital, capital intensity and the productivity of labor in various countries and for various years then the distribution of these data must show the existence of theoretical dependencies if these dependencies actually exist. Italian economist Paolo Giussani (2004) in the paper "Capitale Fisso e Guruismo" has presented annual data about productivity of labor, productivity of capital, and capital intensity for 118 countries in the period of 1963-2000 (Penn World Tables). He represented these data in two figures: capital intensity versus labor productivity (Fig. 3) and productivity of capital versus labor productivity (Fig.4). Giussani's statistical distributions confirm the theoretical predictions of the MSP-model. We have reproduced his results using modern stylized facts: World Penn Tables, version 9.0, Bank Database, and database Knoema. MSP- interrelation predictions between productivity of labor and productivity of capital and between capital intensity and productivity of labor are confirmed very well. We obtained a theoretical dependence between the productivity of labor and the productivity of capital in the European economy in the period of 1950-2014. This dependence is confirmed by stylized facts perfectly (Figure. 29, chapter 2).

The Great Depression of the 1930s Demonstrates Crisis and Depression of a Prolonged Evolutionary Cycle contains an application of the MSP-model to stylized facts for the U.S. economy during of years 1909-1949 (Solow's (1957) and Kendrick's (1961) data about the U.S. economy). Specification of the MSP-model consists in the choice of mathematical dependencies for the output and the maximal output as functions of production factors (labor, capital, technologies and etc.). The following two assumptions were used for specification of the Model: (1) output and maximal output are Cobb-Douglas production functions which depend on labor, capital and total factor productivity (so-called Solow' technological factor), (2) the growth of maximal total factor productivity can be mathematically described as an exponential function.

The MSP-model of ECAS predicts the existence of evolutionary cycles. However the actual dynamics of economy is forming not only under the influence of general regulative MSP-algorithms but also under the influence of various random factors. Therefore a pure picture of evolutionary cycles in the real economic dynamics is a rare event. Stochastic internal and external shocks perpetually interfere with this picture. But there are situations when the evolutionary cycle in its pure form is visualized as the main trend of changes. These are situations when the long-term equilibrium-state suddenly and sharply changes. In this case the dynamics of the economic system demonstrates the typical picture of an evolutionary cycle. The period of "Great Depression" in 1930s and the Second World War is obviously the period of deep transformations in the U.S. economic system. The long-term equilibrium state of the U.S. economic system was changing rapidly during this period and therefore productivity of capital was growing. Solow' (1957) and Kendrick' (1961) data about American economy were used for calculation of efficiency and density of conditions in the U.S. economic system before and after "Black Tuesday". The economic system in 1929-1945 demonstrates a typical picture of an evolutionary cycle in the relationship between "density of conditions" and "efficiency." Productivity of capital, as the MSP-model predicts, actually grows under the logistic law. The phenomenon "Great Depression" of the 1930s is a unique example which illustrates undoubtedly the existence of evolutionary branches predicted in the MSP-model of ECAS. The depth of crisis in 1930s was strengthened by a rapid shift of the long-term equilibrium point of the economic system. Simultaneously this change in the long-term equilibrium influenced productivity of capital in the U.S. economy. Logistic growth of productivity of capital during 1933-1945 was due to change of the long-term equilibrium of the U.S. economic system.

MSP-Systems With Variable Parameters is devoted to generalization of the MSP-model for the case of variable MSP-parameters. We consider in this chapter a new, second version of MSP-model. Standard MSP-equations in this version can be obtained from the principle of maximization of some criteria, the so-called "goal-function", if MSP-parameters satisfy some new equations. The MSP-model with variable parameters is mathematically a much more complex theory than the standard MSP-model with constant parameters. However this model is more realistic because the parameters of real complex adaptive systems change. Mathematical exploration of this Model finds that the differences between old and new model aren't that large. Qualitatively, the new model is similar to the standard MSP-model. Although the equations for evolutionary branches in the new model differ the geometric shape of schedules is almost identical. Therefore the dynamical properties of this model are qualitatively almost identical with the standard model. At the same time the new model allows us to find the efficiency and density of conditions of the MSP-system via parameters of this system. Moreover these parameters are interconnected by some equations. Standard interpretation of MSP-variables and MSP-parameters is used in order to apply the new model in economics. Economic stylized facts for the U.S economic system (1950-2014) (database of the U.S. Bureau of Economic Analysis) confirm predictions of the new version of the MSP-model. Calculation of efficiency and density of conditions confirm the existence of evolutionary branches.

The new model explains (and describes) the crisis of 2008-2009 years. According to the new version of the MSP-model the development of an economic system can be depicted as the movement along a surface which depicts the stabilizing function. In the new version of MSP-model the role of stochastic impacts in dynamics of the system is not negligible. Therefore the system influenced by stochastic shocks wanders along a "plateau of stability" on the surface of a stabilizing function. The "plateau of stability" is limited by the barriers which restrict the system from leaving the plateau. In 2007 the U.S. economic system overcame one of the barriers of limiting "plateau of stability" for the first time ever. However the rate of growth of GDP and the share of investment in GDP for the area located outside of this barrier are very small. Therefore as soon as the economic system gets into the area located behind the barrier the rate of growth of economy and share of investment in GDP rapidly falls. This is the situation of a deep crisis.

Other non-trivial results of the new version of MSP-model concerns the behaviour of the "goal-function" of the U.S. economic system. The goal-function is a kind of criteria of optimalization for the economic system. The goal-function grows with time during almost the entire period of 1950-2013. This function decreases only during years of crisis 2008-2009. According to MSP-modelling the crisis of 2008-2009 qualitatively differs from any other crisis of this period (1950-2013) because the goal-function begins to fall for the first time ever. According to analysis of other historical data the similar fall of the goal-function was observed only in 1930-1932 years at the beginning of "Great Depression".

Conclusion contains a brief overview of possible applications of the Method in other areas of systems research and of unsolved yet problems of the Method.

I think that this book will be interesting to the wide audience. Our world consists of tremendous number of interconnected "complex adaptive systems". The methods of complex adaptive systems are applied widely in various fields of science and management: in economy, ecology, biology, linguistics, sociology and others fields. There is a gap in our understanding of how the microscopic and macroscopic properties of the complex adaptive systems are interconnected (Pacheco, 2016). On one hand there is a huge and constantly growing literature devoted to studying of multi-agent systems which consist of multitude of interacting adaptive agents. On the other hand, macroscopic properties of these systems are often qualitatively similar, indicating existence of some universal macroscopic adaptive regulators operating in these systems. This is similar to what takes place in statistical physics and thermodynamics where the ensemble of the interacting molecules is described either as statistical ensemble (at the micro-level) or as thermodynamic system which is characterized by the set of interconnected macroscopic parameters, such as pressure, temperature, an enthalpy, entropy, chemical potential, etc. (macroscopic approach). We still don't know as microscopic and macroscopic properties of complex adaptive systems are interconnected. Multi-agent modelling (microscopic approach) and Method of Systems Potential, MSP (macroscopic approach) are two complementary methods for the description of complex adaptive systems.

I didn't attempt to give the detailed description of all findings in the field of the complex adaptive systems in this book. Foundations of this subject (CAS) can be found, for example, in the following books and papers: Lansing (2003), Miller and Scott (2007), Yang and Shan (2008), Bruno et al. (2016).

The content of this book is focused mainly on the description of macroscopic approach to the modelling of CAS and on the applications of this approach in economics. It is important to note that according to this approach the macroscopic dynamics of CAS is regulated, most likely, by the universal principles which describe the action of evolutionary laws of Lamarck (so-called Lamarckian evolution) in real complex adaptive systems: ecosystems, socio-economic systems, linguistic systems and so on. The description, discussion and mathematical formulation of these universal principles acting at the macroscopic level in very dissimilar real complex adaptive systems, I suppose, will be interested both for students and for experts in these fields. The potential readers of this book specializing in economics, both in general theory and in economic modelling, will find a discussion how the macroscopic approach to the modelling of complex adaptive systems can be successfully applied for the analysis of the real economic complex adaptive systems. The book contains description of new economic model (MSP-ECAS model) in two versions (with constant and variable economic parameters). Application of this Model to the European economy and to the economy of the United

States quantitatively explains the phenomenon of Great Depression in 1930s and stylized facts about productivity of capital, productivity of labor, and capital intensity during 1950-2014 years. Economic historians and experts in the field of the economic modelling, I suppose, find these findings interesting. I hope that the book can be useful also for experts in the field of mathematical biology, biomathematics, econophysics, and philosophers specializing in Hegel's dialectics.

REFERENCES

Bruno, B., Faggini, M., & Parziale, A. (2016). Complexity modelling in economics: The state of the art. *Economic Thought*, *5*(2), 29–43.

Epstein, J. M. (2002). Modeling civil violence: an agent-based computational approach. *Proceedings of the National Academy of Sciences of the U.S.* Washington, DC: National Academy of Sciences. doi:10.1073/pnas.092080199

Giussani, P. (2004). *Capitale Fisso e Guruismo*. Retrieved July 18, 2005, from: http://www.countdownnet.info/archivio/analisi/altro/326.pdf

Hegel, G. W. F. (1807). *Phänomenologie des Geistes. Academic Press.*

Hegel, G. W. F. (1817). Enzyklopädie der philosophischen Wissenschaften. Academic Press.

Hegel, G. W. F. (1812, 1813, 1816). Wissenschaft der Logik. Academic Press.

Hommes, C. H. (2002). Modeling the stylized facts in finance through simple nonlinear adaptive systems. *Proceedings of the National Academy of Sciences of the U.S.* Washington, DC: National Academy of Sciences. doi:10.1073/pnas.082080399

Kendrick, J. W. (1961). *Productivity trends in the United States*. Princeton, NJ: The National Bureau of Economic Research (NBER), General Series, No.71.

Kephart, J. O. (2002). Software agents and the route to the information economy. *Proceedings of the National Academy of Sciences of the U.S.* Washington, DC: National Academy of Sciences. doi:10.1073/pnas.082080499

Lamarck, J. B. (1809). Philosophie zoologique. Paris: Macmillan.

Lansing, J. S. (2003). Complex adaptive systems. *Annual Review of Anthropology*, *32*(1), 183–204. doi:10.1146/annurev.anthro.32.061002.093440

Miller, J. H., & Scott, E. P. (2007). *Complex adaptive systems: an introduction to computational models of social life*. Princeton University Press.

Pacheco, J. M. (2016). Linking individual to collective behaviorin complex adaptive networks. In C. Gershenson, T. Froes, J. M. Siqueiros, W. Aguilar, E. J. Isquierdo, & H. Sayama (Eds.), *Proceedings of the ALife 2016, the Fifteenth International Conference on the Synthesis and Simulation of Living Systems,* (p. 19). Cancun, Mexico: Latin America.

Pushnoi, G. S. (2003). Dynamics of a system as a process of realization of its "potential". *Proceedings of*, (July), 20–24.

Pushnoi, G. S. (2004a, November). Application of Method of Systems Potential for Analysis of Economic System Evolution. *The Second Internet Conference on Evolutionary Economics and Econophysics.* Yekaterinburg: International A. Bogdanov Institute.

Pushnoi, G. S. (2004b, November). *The Business Cycle Model on the Basis of Method of Systems Potential.The Second Internet Conference on Evolutionary Economics and Econophysics.* Ekaterinburg, Russia: International A. Bogdanov Institute.

Pushnoi, G. S. (2005, April). Long-term and short-term dynamics of the Economic System on the basis of Systems Potential Method. *The Third Internet Conference on Evolutionary Economics and Econophysics.* Ekaterinburg, Russia: International A. Bogdanov Institute.

Pushnoi, G. S. (2006). *Method of systems potential and evolutionary cycles*. Retrieved October 11, 2016 from: http://www.socintegrum.ru/msp06_1.pdf

Pushnoi, G. S. (2010). *Crisis as Reconfiguration of the Economic Complex Adaptive System.* AAAI Fall CAS Simposium.

Pushnoi, G. S. (2014). Method of system's potential as holistic approach for CAS-modelling. In M. Khosrow-Pour (Ed.), *Encyclopedia of Information Science and and Technology* (3rd ed.; pp. 7180–7191). Hershey, PA: IGI-Publishing.

Pushnoi, G. S., & Bonser, G. L. (2008). Method of systems potential as "top-bottom" technique of the complex adaptive systems modelling. In A. Yang & Y. Shan (Eds.), *Intelligent Complex Adaptive Systems* (pp. 26–73). Hershey, PA: IGI-Publishing. doi:10.4018/978-1-59904-717-1.ch002

Solow, R. M. (1957). Technical change and production function. *The Review of Economics and Statistics*, *39*(3), 312–320. doi:10.2307/1926047

Sornette, D. (2002). Predictability of catastrophic events: Material rupture, earthquakes, turbulence, financial crashes, and human birth. *Proceedings of the National Academy of Sciences of the U.S.* Washington, DC: National Academy of Sciences.

Yang, A., & Shan, Y. (Eds.). (2008). *Intelligent Complex Adaptive Systems*. Hershey, PA: IGI-Publishing. doi:10.4018/978-1-59904-717-1

Acknowledgment

I dedicate this book to my mother, who was helping me many years. I thank my friends Marina and Wayne Bonser, and also Roy Rocca for their input into translation of this book from Russian. I thank of my friend, Dr. Viktor Pokolodin (forum "Socintegrum") for the support and discussion of my researches. I am grateful to Dr. Aleksandr Fradkov for valuable discussion of the main ideas of the Method.

Introduction

COMPLEX ADAPTIVE SYSTEMS: BRIEF OVERVIEW

There is no special scientific discipline such as "complex adaptive systems" (CAS) in the theory of systems. This term unifies various systems which consist of interacting adaptive agents which are connected by nonlinear interactions into the complex network (Perez (2008); Wallis (2008)). Holland (1992) gives the following definition of CAS:

A Complex Adaptive System (CAS) is a dynamic network of many agents (which may represent cells, species, individuals, firms, nations) acting in parallel, constantly acting and reacting to what the other agents are doing. The control of a CAS tends to be highly dispersed and decentralized. If there is to be any coherent behavior in the system, it has to arise from competition and cooperation among the agents themselves. The overall behavior of the system is the result of a huge number of decisions made every moment by many individual agents.

"Agent-based" (or "multi-agent") models are used most often for simulation and investigation of complex adaptive systems. Economy is the system which consists of many real "agents" (organizations, firms, enterprises). They interact with each other via complex corporative networks and market institutions.

There is a long history of application of complex adaptive systems in economics. Walras (1874a; 1874b) has formulated the basic principles of general equilibrium in economy in 1874. Possibly, it was the historically first description of economy as a complex nonlinear system. If we omit ideological aspects of Marx' (1867, 1885, 1894) "Das Kapital" this book is one more attempt to describe economy as the complex system which consists of interacting economic agents: "workers", "capitalists", "landowners". Russian mathematical economist Vladimir Dmitriev (1898-1902) and American economist Wassiliy Leontief (1868-1913) independently from each other created the basis of modern "input-output model" of economy which describes interaction of different industries ("agents") via flows of goods and money. Neumann and Morgenstern (1944) suggested considering the economy as a game of economic agents which attempt to maximize gain (revenue, profit). It is necessary to note that researches in economics stimulated development of new directions in pure mathematical theory of complex nonlinear systems: "theory of catastrophes", "theory of nonlinear dynamic systems", "chaos theory" and others.

Some notions (such as "adaptation", "adaptive agents", "fitness landscape" and others) of the modern complex adaptive systems initially were used in evolutionary mathematical biology as conceptual tools for mathematical researches and modeling of evolutionary processes (Wright, S. (1932), Kauffman (1993)). Evolutionary process was modeling as motion of "agents" along "fitness landscape" in direction to the closest "fitness peak". Structure of "fitness landscape" depends on properties of agents and their positions on landscape.

Idea about "fitness landscape" was generalized for the case of any ensemble consisting of interacting adaptive agents. Agents are seeking some optimal position with maximal "gain" (analogue of "fitness peak") within environment (analogue of "fitness landscape"). Adaptive search of agents is regulated by adaptive rules which formalize Darwinian laws of evolution (struggle for survival). Each adaptive agent seeks position with maximal gain ("fitness", "profit", "income" and so on). Consequently the system of interacting agents as a whole also seeks a maximum of total "gain". Behavior of separate agents and dynamics of multi-agent system are interconnected. Exactly because of each agent within CAS looks for its own benefit all system in general also behaves as the adaptive agent maximizes the total "gain".

Principles of "maximization" (or of optimization) of some criteria ("utility", "profit", "income", "output", "welfare") are in the basis of many modern economic models. There are two big directions in economics. Microeconomics describes the behavior of separate economic agents (consumers, entrepreneurs, firms and so on). Macroeconomics describes the dynamics of the economy as a whole. There are many macroscopic models which are formulated as dynamic systems of nonlinear equations for macrovariables (gross domestic product, the total income, aggregate stock of capital and so on). Principles of optimization are used for finding of equation describing the dynamics of an economic system as a whole. Microeconomic models describe the behavior of individual economic agents interacting via market transactions. The consumer decision-making models (CDM in "consumer theory") describe the actions of consumers on the different markets (see for example overview in Milner and Rosenstreich (2013). "Producer theory" in microeconomics describes the behavior of "producers" seeking the maximal profit or other gain. Both "consumer theory" and "producer theory" describe adaptive search of individual economic agents in market economy. The structure of markets (prices and volumes of transactions) depends on behavior of economic agents (of "consumers" and "producers").

The economic multi-agent system consisting of consumers and producers interacting via markets can be conceptualized as the Economic Complex Adaptive

System (ECAS). The general principles regulating the dynamics and properties of complex adaptive systems are working also in the economic system.

The detailed studying of multi-agent systems arose only recently became possible due to the development of powerful computers. Principles of modeling were formulated in 1990-s (Gell-Mann (1994), Holland (1992, 1995), Arthur et al. (1997)).

Agent-based computational economics (ACE) creates computer models of systems which consist of interacting adaptive economic agents. Tracking the dynamics of many agent-based models became possible because of the progress of computers and software. An experience accumulated in research of these systems revealed surprising universality of properties of macroscopic dynamics. Very dissimilar agent-based systems nevertheless demonstrated similar macroscopic properties, the so-called "emergent properties" of complex adaptive systems:

1. Phenomenon of "punctuated equilibrium",
2. Alternation of gradual change and sudden jumps of macrovariables,
3. Episodic bursts of avalanche-like changes of structure of the system (reconfigurations of CAS),
4. Phenomenon of "self-organized criticality" (inverse-power law for statistical distribution of reconfiguration scale),
5. Phenomenon of "self-organized instability" of long-term equilibrium state,
6. Cyclical dynamics of macroscopic variables with catastrophic jumps (often four-phases discontinuous cycles).

For example Kephart (2002) indicates:

Typical price trajectory consists of linear drops punctuated by sharp discontinuities up or down. These discontinuities coincide with quick shifts by all sellers to a new set of product parameters... Although the intuitive explanations for the sudden price or price/product discontinuities differ considerably across the various models, there is a generic mathematical principle that explains why this behaviour is so ubiquitous and provides insight into how broadly it might occur in real agent markets of the future. Mathematically, the phenomenon occurs in situations where the underlying profit landscape contains multiple peaks. Competition among sellers collectively drives the price vector in such a way that each seller is forced down a peak in its profit landscape, although its individual motion carries it up the peak. At some point, a seller will find it best to abandon its current peak and make a discontinuous jump to another peak in its landscape. This discontinuous shift in the price vector suddenly places all other sellers at a different point in their own profit landscapes. If the next seller to move finds itself near a new peak in its landscape, it will make an incremental shift in its price and hence in the price vector; otherwise, it will respond with yet another radical shift. (Kephart, 2002; p.7211)

There are many CAS-models which demonstrate at macroscopic level these universal "emergent properties" (for example, Hommes's (2002) model of financial markets, Epstein' (2002) Model of Civil Violence, Westerhoff and Franke' (2012) models for economic policy design, Erlingsson' et al. (2013) model of a credit network economy and so on).

The general methods developed in the field of CAS-modeling are successfully used in research of many real complex adaptive systems.

METHOD OF SYSTEMS POTENTIAL AS HOLISTIC APPROACH IN CAS-MODELLING

There are two opposite directions in the modelling of complex adaptive systems (CAS-modelling):

1. **Agent-Based Modeling (ABM or AB-Modeling):** Macroscopic properties of a system as a whole emerge as aggregate outcome of interactions between agents. As a rule, if we model a real system (market, finance, economy and so on), behavior of agents is regulated by Darwin's laws of evolution (struggle for survival, search for maximal gain) i. e. each agent seeks the most favorable niche in environment which guarantees him the maximal gain ("fitness", "profit", "income" and so on). This is "down-up" approach for CAS-modeling, starting from the interaction of a multitude of "agents" to revealing the "emergent properties" of the system. Computer simulations of AB-models of real systems (such as stock markets, socio-economic and ecological systems) and data of real systems' evolution indicate that very dissimilar systems demonstrate the same emergent properties. Pushnoi (2008) considers a set; points out a sequence of "emergent properties" which are meeting most often in AB-models:
    a. *Universal Emergent properties:*
        i.   *Punctuated equilibrium.*
        ii. *Self-organized criticality.*
        iii. *Superposition of deterministic and stochastic patterns in macroscopic dynamics.*
        iv. *Discontinuous cycles.*
        v.   *Catastrophic jumps.*
        vi. *Self-affine dynamics of macro-indices.*
        vii. *Power law for avalanche-size distribution.*

viii. *Perpetual renewal of configuration.*

ix. *Creation of hierarchical fractal-like structure in course of evolution.*

x. *Episodic sudden reconfigurations of CAS-structure. (p. 27)*

There is remarkable peculiarity: the closer the AB-model is to its real prototype, the more clearly these general macroscopic properties are appear. Such similarity of macroscopic properties of very dissimilar models can be explained on the basis of holistic approach in CAS-modeling.

2. **Method of Systems Potential (MSP):** Postulates the existence of macroscopic algorithms of adaptation acting at the level of a system as a whole. As universal emergent properties of CAS do not depend on its internal structure or on specific features of the agents's adaptive behavior in a specific model, these properties are inherent in CAS as a holistic System. These universal macroscopic properties of CAS are result of macroscopic adaptive algorithms acting at the level of holistic system. MSP is holistic approach for CAS-modelling. The basic ideas and notions of this approach (MSP-approach) were formulated in 2003 (Pushnoi, 2003) and later were developed in series of publications (Pushnoi, 2008; 2011; 2014). According to MSP-approach the evolution of real complex adaptive systems which consist of multitude of interacting real adaptive agents is regulated by Lamarck's evolution laws. Computer models of real systems mimic real macroscopic dynamics and for this reason these models display above listed universal macroscopic properties.

The existence of macroscopic adaptive algorithms acting at the level of holistic system is reliably established fact. For example, "living systems" (organisms) are capable of maintaining homeostatic balance. They accumulate useful experience and maximize own gain in big game under the name "life". There are two types of equilibrium states for such systems: (1) short-term (temporary) equilibrium where the system attempts be perpetually and (2) long-term equilibrium which is attractor for the system in the long-run. Economic systems also demonstrate the existence of two types of equilibrium. The first type is equilibrium which regulates current dynamics of a system via process of small oscillations in prices and sells, and the second one is an attractor of the economic system, so-called the global equilibrium state. Gell-Mann (1994, p. 17), Holland (1995, p. 127), Arthur et al. (1997, p. 157), McMillan (2004, p. 103) all noted the existence of macroscopic adaptive algorithms working at the level of the system as a whole. For example, such systems are accumulate information about the environment, use this information in adaptive activity and adjust itself proceeding from the efficiency of resultant gain. One may say that any real CAS accumulates the useful adaptive experience through the process of adaptive activity and applies the accumulated experience as the tool of survival.

MSP generalizes Lamarck's ideas about influence of activity onto the development of organs. Lamarck (1809) stated that "a more frequent and continuous use of any organ gradually strengthens, develops and enlarges that organ, and gives it a power proportional to the length of time it has been so used; while the permanent disuse of any organ imperceptibly weakens and deteriorates it, and progressively diminishes its functional capacity, until it finally disappears" (p.113). MSP takes Lamarck's law and applies it for adaptive abilities (for "functional capacities") i. e. spreads this law not only for organs of "living systems" but as general principle acting in relation of any macroscopic adaptive abilities of real complex adaptive systems.

Lamarck's law describes the influence of adaptive activity of the system onto the development of adaptive abilities. The abilities which are applied in adaptive activity of the system are developing and strengthening and the abilities which are not applied in adaptive activity of the system are degenerating. A summary of the abilities which are applied in adaptive activity is the "realized potential" of the system. Abilities which are not applying in adaptive activity of the system form the "nonrealized potential" of the system. Let's introduce terms and mathematical interrelations which formalize the Lamarck's laws acting at the level of multi-agent system as a whole.

MSP describes macroscopic adaptive process within CAS using terms which formalize Lamarck's ideas about evolution: (1) the "potential of CAS", i. e. the stock of adaptive abilities of a system and (2) the "conditions for realization" of "potential"[1].

D1 - MSP-System: The complex adaptive system which evolves (as a whole) according to Lamarck's laws generalized for the case of multi-agent systems which evolve as a holistic structures similar to organisms which consist of interacting cells.

D2 - "Potential" of MSP-System (Φ): Of CAS is the aggregate adaptive ability (functional capacity) of CAS. "Potential" "summarizes" multitude of adaptive abilities of agents and so-called "synergetic effect" of a system as a whole.

D3 - "Conditions of (for) Realization" in MSP-System (U): Summarize all factors which help and promote application (realization) of "potential" in useful adaptive activity. These factors are usually depend on peculiarities of agent's environment (for example, "competitive pressure" or abundance of resources).

D4 - "Realized Potential" of MSP-System (Φ_R): Part of "potential" which is applied in adaptive activity of the CAS.

D5 - "Nonrealized Potential" of MSP-System (Φ_D): Part of "potential" which is not applied in adaptive activity of the CAS.

MSP describes long-term development of the system using these three macro-scopic variables. MSP assumes that these MSP-variables can be quantitatively measured, and each triplet $\left(U; \Phi; \Phi_R\right)$ consequently can be depictured as the point in three-dimension space.

A summary of "realized" and "nonrealized" potential is a full "potential" of MSP-system:

$$\Phi = \Phi_R + \Phi_D \tag{1}$$

D6 - Efficiency of MSP-System (R): The rate of exploitation of accumulated adaptive potential. Efficiency is equal to realized potential per entire potential ratio. This value describes at macroscopic level the efficiency of adaptive process in MSP-system:

$$R = \frac{\Phi_R}{\Phi} \tag{2}$$

Lamarck's laws of evolution can be formulated by means of feedback loops: the increment of "realized potential" (of adaptive abilities which are used) via adaptive activity of the system and the decrease of "nonrealized potential" (of adaptive abilities which are not used) as consequence of general principle of growth of entropy. Figure 1 illustrates the action of these laws. Mathematically this process can be described as follows:

E1 - Equation for "Realized Potential" of MSP-System[2]:

$$\dot{\Phi}_R = a \cdot \Phi_R \tag{3}$$

Adaptive abilities which are applied in adaptive activities of the system develop and strengthen.

E2 - Equation for "Non-Realized Potential" of MSP-System:

$$\dot{\Phi}_D = -d \cdot \Phi_D \tag{4}$$

Figure 1. The structure of MSP-system (complex adaptive system at macroscopic level)

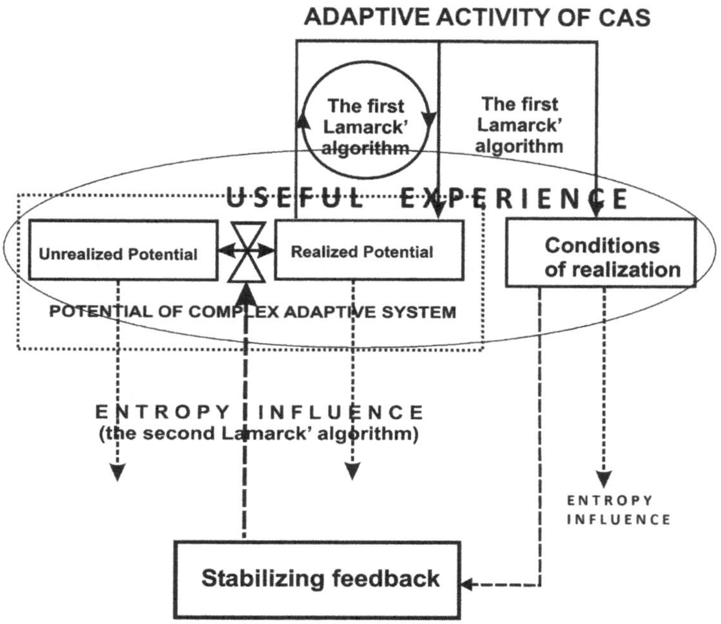

The adaptive abilities that are not applied in adaptive activities of the system are degenerate.

Equation (E2) can be rewritten in other form:

$$\frac{d\left(\Phi - \Phi_R\right)}{dt} = -d \cdot \left(\Phi - \Phi_R\right) \tag{5}$$

The equation for "potential" follows from (3)-(4):

E3 - Equation for "Potential" of MSP-System:

$$\dot{\Phi} + d \cdot \Phi = \left(a + d\right) \cdot \Phi_R = \left(a + d\right) \cdot R \cdot \Phi \tag{6}$$

Analogic principle is in the basis of the equation for "conditions of realization". The "conditions" grow via adaptive activity of the system. The "conditions" decrease as consequence of general principle of growth of entropy. Volume of adaptive activity depends on "realized potential" of the system since adaptive activity and realization of potential are synonyms. Mathematically this process can be described as follows:

E4 - Equation for "Conditions of Realization" in MSP-System:

$$\dot{U} + \Lambda \cdot U = \nu \cdot \Phi_R = \nu \cdot R \cdot \Phi \tag{7}$$

According to MSP the triad of equations (3), (6) and (7) describes macroscopic adaptive process in the real complex adaptive systems. Parameters $\left(a; d; \nu; \Lambda\right)$ characterize adaptive properties of the system.

These equations determine long-term dynamics of the system. If $t \rightarrow \infty$ we have:

$$\frac{U}{\Phi} \rightarrow \frac{\nu}{a + \Lambda} \text{ and } R \rightarrow 1 \tag{8}$$

The ratio $z \equiv \dfrac{U}{\Phi}$ describes abundance of "conditions" necessary for realization of adaptive abilities in activity of the system.

D7 - "Density of Conditions": Quantity of "conditions" per unit of "potential":

$$z \equiv \frac{U}{\Phi} \tag{9}$$

Long-term dynamics of the system can be described by means of the following variables: $z \equiv \dfrac{U}{\Phi}$ and $R = \dfrac{\Phi_R}{\Phi}$. The point $\left(z_0 \equiv \dfrac{\nu}{a + \Lambda}; R = 1\right)$ in the plane $\left(z; R\right)$ is the attractor (long-term equilibrium) of the system. Equations for variables R and z follow from equations (3), (6) and (7).

E5 - Equation for "Efficiency":

$$\dot{R} = \left(a + d\right) \cdot R \cdot \left(1 - R\right) \tag{10}$$

E6 - Equation for "Density of Conditions":

$$\dot{z} = \left(\nu - \left(a + d\right)z\right) \cdot R + \left(d - \Lambda\right)z \tag{11}$$

The ordinary differential equation for function $R\left(z\right)$ follows from equations (10)-(11).

E7 - Equation for Function $R\left(z\right)$:

$$R'_z \cdot \left[\left(\nu - \left(a + d\right) \cdot z\right) \cdot R + \left(d - \Lambda\right) \cdot z\right] - \left(a + d\right) \cdot R \cdot \left(1 - R\right) = 0^3. \tag{12}$$

Analytical solution of equations (E1)-(E7) can be found for the simplest case of constant parameters:
Solution of equation (E1):

$$\Phi_R\left(t\right) = \Phi_R\left(0\right) \cdot e^{at} \tag{13}$$

Solution of equation (E2):

$$\Phi_D\left(t\right) = \Phi_D\left(0\right) e^{-d \cdot t} \tag{14}$$

Solution of equation (E3):

$$\Phi\left(t\right) = \Phi_R\left(0\right) \cdot e^{a \cdot t} + \left(\Phi\left(0\right) - \Phi_R\left(0\right)\right) \cdot e^{-d \cdot t} \tag{15}$$

Solution of equation (E4):

$$U\left(t\right) = \frac{\nu \cdot \Phi_R\left(0\right)}{a + \Lambda} \cdot e^{a \cdot t} + \left(U\left(0\right) - \frac{\nu \cdot \Phi_R\left(0\right)}{a + \Lambda}\right) \cdot e^{-\Lambda \cdot t} \tag{16}$$

Solution of equation (E5):

$$R(t) = \frac{1}{1 + b \cdot e^{-(a+d) \cdot t}}; \; b \equiv \frac{1 - R(0)}{R(0)} \qquad (17)$$

Solution of equation (E6):

$$Z(t) = \frac{Z_0 + e^{-(a+d)t}\left((1+b)Z(0) - Z_0\right)}{1 + b \cdot e^{-(a+d)t}}; \; z_0 \equiv \frac{\nu}{a + \Lambda}. \qquad (18)$$

Solution of equation (E7):
Upper evolutionary branch:

$$z_U(R): \quad z = z_0 \cdot R - C_U \cdot R^{-\chi} \cdot (1 - R)^{1+\chi}; \qquad (19)$$

subject to $z < z_0 \cdot R$;
Lower evolutionary branch:

$$z_L(R): \quad z = z_0 \cdot R + C_L \cdot R^{-\chi} \cdot (1 - R)^{1+\chi}; \qquad (20)$$

subject to $z > z_0 \cdot R$;

$$C_U > 0; \; C_L > 0;$$

$$z_0 \equiv \frac{\nu}{a + \Lambda}; \; \chi \equiv \frac{\Lambda - d}{a + d}; \; -1 < \chi < \frac{\Lambda}{a}. \qquad (21)$$

This is non-trivial solution of equation (E7). We don't consider trivial solution of this equation $Z = Z_0 \cdot R$ which is particular case of solution (19)-(20) when the constants in equations (19)-(20) equal zero, $C_U = C_L = 0$. Non-trivial solution is possible if only initial conditions for efficiency and density of conditions satisfy the equality $Z(0) = Z_0 \cdot R(0)$. Any small deviation from this condition transforms trivial solution into solution of kind (19) or (20)[4].

The trajectory of MSP-system consists of two evolutionary branches – Figure 2. Temporary equilibrium states of a MSP-System correspond to points on the path (19)-(20) in the plane $(z; R)$. Each pair $(z; R)$ corresponds to a definite ray running through the point of origin in the space $\left(\Phi;U;\Phi_{R}\right)$. Geometric form of evolutionary branches depends on MSP-parameters – Figures 3-5.

Equations (E1)-(E7) describe the change of temporary equilibrium state of MSP-system.

D8 - Temporary Equilibrium State of MSP-System: Can be mathematically depictured either as the point in the space $\left(\Phi;U;\Phi_{R}\right)$ or as the point on the plane $\left(z;R\right)$.

Trajectory of MSP-system depends in the general case on specification of MSP-parameters $\left(a;d;\nu;\Lambda\right)$ and initial values $\left(z\left(0\right);R\left(0\right)\right)$ or $(\Phi(0);U(0);\Phi_{R}(0))$.

D9 - MSP-Parameters of MSP-System:

1. Parameter a is the rate of growth of "realized potential" of the system.
2. Parameter d is the rate of decrease of "non-realized potential" of the system (influence of entropy).
3. Parameter ν is the rate of increment of "conditions of realization" as consequence of adaptive activity of the system.
4. Parameter Λ is the rate of decrease of "conditions of realization" of the system (influence of entropy).

Figure 2. Evolutionary branches and evolutionary cycle of MSP-system

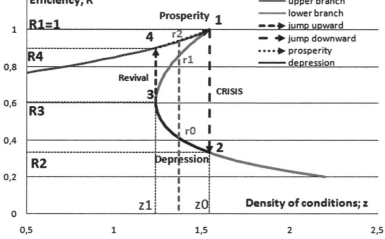

Figure 3. Evolutionary branches for $\chi > 0$

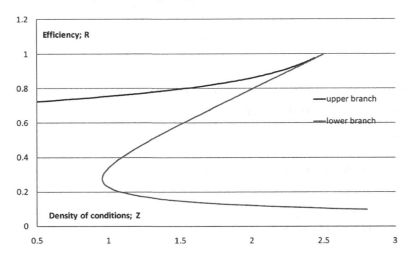

Figure 4. Evolutionary branches: left picture for $\chi < 0$

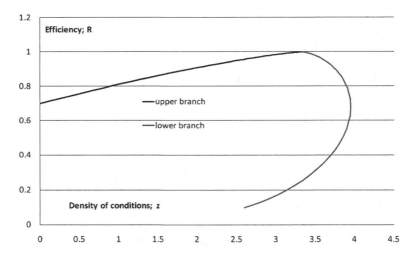

Figure 5. Evolutionary branches for $\chi = 0$

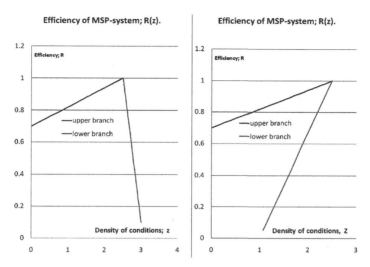

MSP-parameters can be either the constants or the functions of some MSP-variables. Figure 2 illustrate that MSP-system evolve in direction to the point of long-term (global) equilibrium.

D10 - Global (Long-Term) Equilibrium of MSP-System: The centre of attraction (attractor) of MSP-system in the plane $(z; R)$. This is the state with maximal efficiency and the definite "density of conditions" $\left(z_0 \equiv \dfrac{\nu}{a + \Lambda}; R = 1 \right)$.

MSP-system evolves along either upper (19) or lower (20) evolutionary branch (if parameters of MSP-system are constants). The position of evolutionary branches in the plane $(z; R)$ depends on initial values $R(0)$ and $z(0)$. MSP introduces the notion of "preferable evolutionary branches".

D11 - Preferable Evolutionary Branches: In the plane $(z; R)$ satisfy two conditions: 1) these curves coincide with either "upper" (19) or "lower" (20) branch at a certain choice of the constants $C^{(-)}$ and $C^{(+)}$; 2) points of these curves are "temporary equilibrium states" of MSP-system. What happens to the System if we take the existence of random perturbations of MSP-system into consideration? Under the influence of such perturbations (internal or external perturbing factors), MSP-System deviates from "preferable evolutionary branch". MSP postulates the existence of stabilizing feedback which ensures

Figure 6. Dynamics of MSP-system

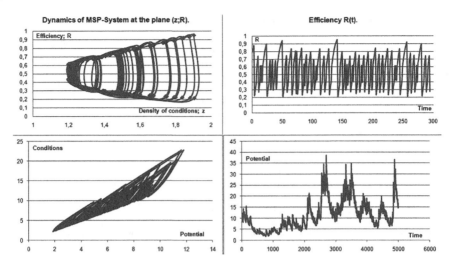

the stability of temporal equilibrium states of MSP-system: deviation from temporal equilibrium state → effect of stabilising feedback loop → return to original temporal equilibrium state. This is a short-run adjustment of CAS. This is rapid process. MSP-system maintains its temporal equilibrium state due to this adjustment. Short-run adjustment acts in many real complex adaptive systems for example such as living systems (homeostatic balance), economic systems (economic balance between the demand and supply). The existence of short-term adjustment in the real complex adaptive systems mathematically can be formulated as the existence of "preferable evolutionary branches". The points of "preferable evolutionary branches" describe mathematically the temporal equilibrium states of MSP-system. MSP-system returns into its temporal equilibrium state after any external effects onto the system.

The "potential", Φ, and the "conditions of realisation", U, may not be changed quickly in response to sudden external influences onto MSP-system. These are inertial values. Consequently, the "density of conditions" $z = \dfrac{U}{\Phi}$ is not controlled by MSP-system. The "realized potential" Φ_R is the only variable which MSP-system can control. The MSP-System may react operatively to external perturbations by means of reducing or increasing the efficiency $R = \dfrac{\Phi_R}{\Phi}$, thus shifting its current state upwards or downwards along the axis R in the plane $(z; R)$. It is this process which stabilizes the temporal equilibrium state of an MSP-System (Figure 1).

Figure 7. Self-organized criticality in MSP-system

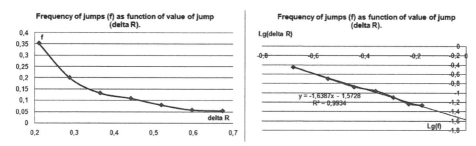

The choice of mathematical form of the short-term adjustment in general is not universal. The simplest mathematical equation describing this process is anti-gradient law:

E8 - Equation of Short-Term Adjustment of MSP-System:

$$\frac{dR}{dt} = -\frac{\partial W\left(R;z\right)}{\partial R} \tag{22}$$

D12 - Stabilizing Function $W\left(R;z\right)$ **:** Describes the properties of stability of temporal equilibrium states of MSP-system. The temporary equilibrium states $\left(z;R_E\left(z\right)\right)$ correspond to the stationary points of function $W\left(R;z\right)$ provided that variable z is constant:

$$\frac{\partial W\left(R;z\right)}{\partial R} = 0 . \tag{23}$$

Points of minimum of the stabilizing function correspond to stable temporal equilibrium states of an MSP-System. Points of maximum (and inclination) correspond to unstable temporal equilibrium states. Dynamics of MSP-system in the plane $\left(z;R\right)$ is the result of superposition of long-term evolution, i. e. the motion along the upper (or lower) preferable evolutionary branch (19)-(20) and of short-term adjustment (23). Random perturbations deviate MSP-system from its temporal equilibrium state on the upper (or lower) preferable evolutionary branch but stabilizing feedback returns MSP-system into its temporal equilibrium state. The choice of mathematical form of the stabilising mechanism is not universal. The simplest approximation of a stabilizing function is four-degree polynomial:

$$W_R'\left(R, z\right) = C \cdot \left(R - r_0\right) \cdot \left(R - r_1\right) \cdot \left(R - r_2\right) \tag{24}$$

Points $\left(z; r_{0;1;2}\right)$ are located on the evolutionary branches (Figure 2):

$$z = z_U\left(r_2\right); \; z = z_L\left(r_{0;1}\right) \tag{25}$$

$$W\left(R; z; \chi\right) = \left[\frac{R^4}{4} - A\left(r_0; r_1; r_2\right) \cdot \frac{R^3}{3} + B\left(r_0; r_1; r_2\right) \cdot \frac{R^2}{2} - r_0 \cdot r_1 \cdot r_2 \cdot R\right] \cdot C_1 + C_2$$

$$A\left(r_0; r_1; r_2\right) = r_0 + r_1 + r_2; \; B\left(r_0; r_1; r_2\right) = r_0 \cdot r_1 + r_1 \cdot r_2 + r_0 \cdot r_2; \tag{26}$$

C_1 and $C_2 > 0$ are some constants.

Stabilizing function and preferable evolutionary branches ("upper branch" – blue color and "lower branch" – red color) are depictured in Figure 8[5]. The points of minimum of stabilizing function $W\left(R; z\right)$ are disposed on the upper evolutionary branch and on the lower part of the lower evolutionary branch. These are points of stable temporal equilibrium of MSP-System. The points of maximum for the function $W\left(R; z\right)$ are disposed on the upper part of the lower evolutionary branch. These are points of unstable temporal equilibrium states of MSP-System.

Points of preferable evolutionary branches (temporal equilibrium states) are situated in potential well $W\left(R; z\right)$. While MSP-system is approaching the points 1 or 3 (Figure 2), the depth of the potential well decrease (Figure 8). However, this means that the stability of temporal equilibrium state of the MSP-System is falling. Points 1 and 3 are the bifurcation points of stabilizing function $W\left(R; z\right)$ (z is bifurcation parameter) at which the minimum point of the function $W\left(R; z\right)$ transfers into a point of inflection. At points 1 and 3 (Figure 2) the MSP-System, following small perturbation, will move from the upper (from the lower) branch to the lower (to the upper) branch. *There are two critical points at which the temporal equilibrium state of the MSP-System becomes unstable. In these points the System makes a leap from one evolutionary branch to another. Dynamics of an MSP-System subject to $\chi > 0$ is a sequence of discontinuous cycles. Each evolutionary cycle, 1 →*

Figure 8. Stabilizing function $W(R;z)$ *and "evolutionary branches" of MSP-system*
(*Figure 7 in Pushnoi and Bonser (2008). Reprinted by permission of the publisher IGI-Global*)

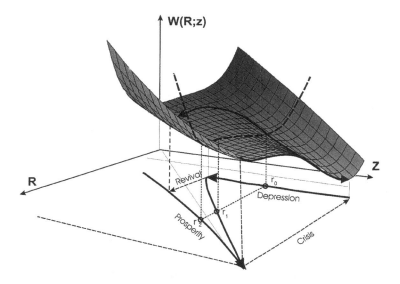

$2 \rightarrow 3 \rightarrow 4...$, consists of two catastrophic jumps and two stages of the gradual motion of the MSP-System along either lower or upper evolutionary branches. For proper characterization of these four phases of the cycle, it is convenient to use the names borrowed from the business cycle theory: 1) jump downwards - "crisis", 2) jump upwards - "revival", 3) the stage of the gradual development along the lower evolutionary branch - "depression" and 4) stage of the gradual development along the upper evolutionary branch – "prosperity". (Pushnoi and Bonser, 2008, p. 56).

Figures 2 and 6[6] illustrate the typical picture of evolutionary cycle of MSP-system. The size of jumps from upper (lower) to lower (upper) evolutionary branch (the change in efficiency of MSP-system $\Delta R \equiv \left| R_{upper} - R_{lower} \right|$) is the stochastic quantity with inverse power law distribution (Figure 7). MSP-system demonstrates inverse-power law for stochastic quantity ΔR when the size of random perturbations exceeds some threshold. There are four special points at the plane $(z;R)$: point 1, $(z_0; R_1 = 1)$; point 2, $(z_0; R_2)$; point 3, $(z_1; R_3)$ and point 4, $(z_1; R_4)$ (Figure 2). The section $1 \rightarrow 2$ is the jump downwards ("crisis"); the section $3 \rightarrow 4$ is the jump upwards ("crisis"). Values $z_0; z_1; R_1; R_2; R_3; R_4$ can be found from the following equations.

- Point 1 of "evolutionary cycle" is the point of the global (long-term) but unstable equilibrium of MSP-system

$$z_0 = \frac{\nu}{a + \Lambda} \tag{27}$$

$$R_1 = 1 \tag{28}$$

- Point 2 of "evolutionary cycle" is the finishing point of the stage "crisis". Value R_2 is the smaller root of the equation:

$$z_0 = z_0 R_2 + C_L \cdot R_2^{-\chi} \cdot \left(1 - R_2\right)^{1+\chi} \tag{29}$$

- Point 3 of "evolutionary cycle" is the starting point of the stage "revival".

Values z_1 and R_3 in the point 3 satisfy the system of equations:

$$\begin{cases} z_1 = z_0 \cdot \dfrac{R_3\left(1 + \chi\right)}{R_3 + \chi} \\ z_1 = z_0 R_3 + C_L \cdot R_3^{-\chi} \cdot \left(1 - R_3\right)^{1+\chi} \end{cases} \tag{30}$$

The first equation follows from the condition $\dfrac{dz_L}{dR} = 0$. The second equation determines the "lower evolutionary branch".

- Point 4 of "evolutionary cycle" is the finishing point of the stage "revival". Value R_4 is the root of equation:

$$z_1 = z_0 R_4 - C_U \cdot R_4^{-\chi} \cdot \left(1 - R_4\right)^{1+\chi} \tag{31}$$

Many multi-agent models demonstrate a typical picture of four-phase discontinuous cycles of the stochastic duration, for example, Powers' (2016) model of evolution of human societies (Figure 3); Cenek & Dahl' (2016) model of adaptive agents (Figures 3-6); Trueba' et al. (2016) model of "canonical embodied evolution" (Figures 3-4); Shorten & Nitschke' (2016) model of evolution of Boolean networks (Figure 1); Setzler & Izquiero' (2016) model of minimally cognitive agents (Figure 1), Rothkegel & Lehnertz' (2014) model of small-world networks, Aymanns' et al. (2016) model of leverage cycle in financial system and others.

Episodic jumps in efficiency of MSP-system represent the processes of reconfiguration of complex adaptive system at macroscopic level. The size of the change in efficiency of MSP-system $\Delta R \equiv \left| R_{\text{upper}} - R_{\text{lower}} \right|$ during the jump from one evolutionary branch onto another branch is the random value with power law distribution (Figure 7). MSP-system demonstrates inverse-power law for stochastic quantity ΔR when the size of random perturbations exceed some threshold. It indicates the existence of self-organized criticality (SOC-phenomenon) within MSP-system.

A rigorous definition of self-organized critical behaviour is elusive. A working definition is that a system is in a state of self-organized criticality if a measure of the system fluctuates about a state of marginal stability. In self-organized criticality, the 'input' to a complex system is constant, whereas the 'output' is a series of events or 'avalanches' that follow a power-law (fractal) frequency–size distribution. (Turcotte, 1999; p. 1380)

Random perturbations of MSP-system trigger the jumps of MSP-system from one "preferable evolutionary branch" onto another. Figure 7 demonstrates SOC-phenomenon in MSP-system. As mean value of random perturbations of MSP-system grows the power law for the distribution ΔR is visualized more definitely. MSP-system demonstrates the phenomenon of so-called "self-organized insta- bility". Sole et al. (2002) introduced this term for the description of the general universal peculiarity of evolution of complex ecosystems.

MSP-modelling of complex adaptive systems is based upon very simple and obvious algorithms of adaptation that are acting at macroscopic level: (1) stabilization of temporary equilibrium state, (2) the increment of the "adaptive potential" and of the "conditions of realization" via the channel of adaptive activity, (3) the decrease of adaptive abilities that are not used in adaptive activity of the system (the decrease of "nonrealized potential" as consequence of influence of entropy). These general simple principles give very complex dynamics with catastrophic jumps in efficiency of the system and discontinuous cycles consisting of four stages.

Evolutionary cycles of MSP-system are similar to economic cycles. It is very probable that the economy evolves as the complex adaptive system in accordance with general MSP principles. First, the temporal equilibrium in the economic system is maintained via market mechanisms of demand-supply-price or investment-savings interdependence. Second, the economy tends to use all available resources i. e. realize the "economic potential". Sudden economic crises often are similar to catastrophe, especially, in the financial markets where quotations of securities can suddenly collapse during one day or even one hour. Alternation of phases of "prosperity" and "depression" is obvious fact of the economic development.

REFERENCES

Arthur, W. B., Durlanf, S. N., & Lane, D. A. (Eds.). (1997). The Economy as an evolving complex system. *Proceedings of the Santa Fe Institute*, *27*, 1–14.

Aymanns, C., Caccioli, F., Farmer, J. D., & Tan, V. W. C. (2016). Taming the Basel leverage cycle. *Journal of Financial Stability*, *27*, 263–277. doi:10.1016/j.jfs.2016.02.004

Cenek, M., & Dahl, S. (2016). Towards emergent design: analysis, fitness and heterogeneity of agent based models using geometry of behavioral spaces framework. In C. Gershenson, T. Froes, J. M. Siqueiros, W. Aguilar, E. J. Isquierdo, & H. Sayama (Eds.), *Proceedings of the ALife 2016, the Fifteenth International Conference on the Synthesis and Simulation of Living Systems,* (pp. 46–53). Cancun, Mexico: Latin America. doi:10.7551/978-0-262-33936-0-ch013

Dmitriev, V. K. (1974). *Economic essays on value, competition and utility, 1898-1902. Translation introduced by D. M. Nuti*. Cambridge, UK: Cambridge University Press.

Epstein, J. M. (2002). Modeling civil violence: an agent-based computational approach. *Proceedings of the National Academy of Sciences of the U.S.* Washington, DC: National Academy of Sciences. doi:10.1073/pnas.092080199

Erlingsson, E. J., Cincotti, S., Stefansson, H., Sturlusson, J. T., Teglio, A., & Raberto, M. (2013). *Housing market bubbles and business cycles in agent-based credit economy*. Economics Discussion Papers, No. 2013-32. Kiel Institute for the World Economy. Retrieved from http://www.economics-ejournal.org/economics/discussionpapers/2013-32

Gell-Mann, M. (1994). *The quark and the jaguar: adventures in the simple and complex*. New York: W.H. Freeman.

Holland, J. (1995). *Hidden order: how adaptation builds complexity*. Reading, MA: Addison – Wesley.

Holland, J. H. (1992). *Adaptation in natural and artificial systems: an introductory analysis with applications to biology, control, and artificial intelligence*. Cambridge, MA: MIT Press.

Hommes, C. H. (2002). Modeling the stylized facts in finance through simple non-linear adaptive systems. *Proceedings of the National Academy of Sciences of the U.S.* Washington, DC: National Academy of Sciences. doi:10.1073/pnas.082080399

Kamke, E. (1971). *The handbook of ordinary differential equations* (4th ed.). Moscow: Nauka.

Kauffman, S. (1993). *The origins of order: Self organization and selection in evolution*. Oxford University Press.

Kephart, J. O. (2002). Software agents and the route to the information economy. *Proceedings of the National Academy of Sciences of the U.S.* Washington, DC: National Academy of Sciences. doi:10.1073/pnas.082080499

Lamarck, J. B. (1809). Philosophie zoologique. Paris: Macmillan.

Marx, K. (1867). Das Kapital: Kritik der politischen Oekonomie. Hamburg: Verlag von Otto Meissner.

Marx, K. (1885). Das Kapital: Kritik der politischen Oekonomie; herausgegeben von Friedrich Engels. Hamburg: Verlag von Otto Meissner.

Marx, K. (1894). Das Kapital: Kritik der politischen Oekonomie; herausgegeben von Friedrich Engels. Hamburg: Verlag von Otto Meissner.

McMillan, E. (Ed.). (2004). *Complexity, Organizations and Change*. London: Routledge. doi:10.4324/9780203507124

Milner, T., & Rosenstreich, D. (2013). A review of consumer decision-making models and development of a new model for financial services. *Journal of Financial Services Marketing, 18*(2), 106–120. doi:10.1057/fsm.2013.7

Neumann, J. V., & Morgenstern, O. (1944). *Theory of games and economic behavior*. Princeton University Press.

Perez, P. (2008). Foreword. In A. Yang & J. Shan (Eds.), *Intelligent Complex Adaptive Systems* (pp. vi–vii). Hershey, PA: IGI-Publishing.

Powers, S. T. (2016). The institutional approach for modelling the evolution of human societies. In *Proceedings of the ALife 2016, the Fifteenth International Conference on the Synthesis and Simulation of Living Systems* (pp. 30-37). Academic Press.

Pushnoi, G. S. (2003). Dynamics of a system as a process of realization of its "potential". *Proceedings of*, (July), 20–24.

Pushnoi, G. S. (2010). *Crisis as Reconfiguration of the Economic Complex Adaptive System.* AAAI Fall CAS Simposium.

Pushnoi, G. S. (2014). Method of system's potential as holistic approach for CAS-modelling. In M. Khosrow-Pour (Ed.), *Encyclopedia of Information Science and and Technology* (3rd ed.; pp. 7180–7191). Hershey, PA: IGI-Publishing.

Pushnoi, G. S., & Bonser, G. L. (2008). Method of systems potential as "top-bottom" technique of the complex adaptive systems modelling. In A. Yang & Y. Shan (Eds.), *Intelligent Complex Adaptive Systems* (pp. 26–73). Hershey, PA: IGI-Publishing. doi:10.4018/978-1-59904-717-1.ch002

Rothkegel, A., & Lehnertz, K. (2014). Irregular macroscopic dynamics due to chimera states in small-world networks of pulse-coupled oscillators. *New Journal of Physics*, 16.

Setzler, M., & Izquiero, E. (2016). Evolvability of minimally cognitive agents. In C. Gershenson, T. Froes, J. M. Siqueiros, W. Aguilar, E. J. Isquierdo, & H. Sayama (Eds.), *Proceedings of the ALife 2016, the Fifteenth International Conference on the Synthesis and Simulation of Living Systems,* (pp. 284–286). Cancun, Mexico: Latin America.

Shorten, D., & Nitschke, G. (2016). The relationship between evolvability and robustness in the evolution of Boolean networks. In C. Gershenson, T. Froes, J. M. Siqueiros, W. Aguilar, E. J. Isquierdo, & H. Sayama (Eds.), *Proceedings of the ALife 2016, the Fifteenth International Conference on the Synthesis and Simulation of Living Systems,* (pp. 276–283). Cancun, Mexico: Latin America. doi:10.7551/978-0-262-33936-0-ch048

Sole, R. V., Alonso, D., & McKane, A. (2002, May29). Self-organized instability in complex ecosystems. *Philosophical Transactions of the Royal Society of London. Series B, Biological Sciences*, 357(1421), 667–671. doi:10.1098/rstb.2001.0992 PMID:12079528

Trueba, P., Prieto, A., Bellas, F., & Duro, R. J. (2016). How complexity pervades specialization in canonical embodied evolution. In C. Gershenson, T. Froes, J. M. Siqueiros, W. Aguilar, E. J. Isquierdo, & H. Sayama (Eds.), *Proceedings of the ALife 2016, the Fifteenth International Conference on the Synthesis and Simulation of Living Systems,* (pp. 123–130). Cancun, Mexico: Latin America. doi:10.7551/978-0-262-33936-0-ch026

Turcotte, D. L. (1999). Self-organized criticality. *Reports on Progress in Physics,* 62(10), 1377–1429. doi:10.1088/0034-4885/62/10/201

Wallis, S. (2008). From reductive to robust. In A. Yang & J. Shan (Eds.), *Intelligent Complex Adaptive Systems* (pp. 1–25). doi:10.4018/978-1-59904-717-1.ch001

Walras, L. (1874a). Principe d'une théorie mathématique de l'échange. *Journal des économistes.*

Walras, L. (1874b). Éléments d'économie politique pure, ou théorie de la richesse sociale [Elements of Pure Economics, or the theory of social wealth]. Academic Press.

Westerhoff, F., & Franke, R. (2012). *Agent-based models for economic policy design: two illustrative examples.* Bamberg University. Working paper No. 88.

ENDNOTES

[1] Designations D1;D2 and so on enumerate the definitions of the basic MSP-notions; designations E1; E2 and so on enumerate the basic MSP-equations.

[2] Sign "dot" above a variable means time derivative and sign "touch" means derivative with respect to variable.

[3] This is Jacobi's ordinary differential equation. See for example equation 1.250 in Kamke (1971).

[4] Trivial solution plays role in dynamics of MSP-systems with variable parameters which are considered in the Chapter 5.

[5] The following values of parameters were used for creation of stabilizing function depictured in Figure 8: $a = 0.03; d = 0.02; \Lambda = 0.07; \nu = 0.3; C_U = 2.0; C_L = 1.8; C_1 = 20.0; C_2 = 80.0$. Software "Mathematica 8.1: was used.

[6] The following values of parameters were taken for the modeling of MSP-system represented in Figures 6 and 7: $a = 0.05; d = 0.001; \Lambda = 0.0571; \nu = 0.2142; C_U = 0.1; C_L = 0.438$. This choice gives: $z_0 = 2; z_1 = 1.2; R_3 = 0.44$.

Chapter 1
MSP–Model of the Economic Complex Adaptive System (ECAS):
Economy as a Complex Adaptive System

According to MSP the development of Complex Adaptive System at macroscopic level is regulated by means of two feedback loops. Stabilizing feedback maintains the stability of macroscopic temporal equilibrium state. The second feedback (reinforcing feedback process – Figure 1) describes the accumulation of "useful experience" ("potential" and "conditions of realization") in MSP-system. This feedback generates the slow gradual change of temporal equilibrium state in direction to long-term equilibrium.

The "temporal equilibrium" in the economy is sustained by means of demand-supply and investment-saving adjustments. Walras (1874a, 1874b) and Marshall (1920) proposed description of short-term adjustment in terms:

DOI: 10.4018/978-1-5225-2170-9.ch001

"excess demand" and "excess demand price". "General Equilibrium Analysis" (GE) arose as the attempt to formalize these ideas: Debreu (1951), Arrow (1951), Arrow & Debreu (1954). Keynes (1935) argued that "investment" and "saving" are the key notions for the analysis of equilibrium in economy.

DEMAND-SUPPLY (WALRASIAN) ADJUSTMENT

This is stabilizing mechanism based on demand and supply interrelation: excess demand for the goods triggers the growth of price. Walras's (1874) theory of general equilibrium in the modern formulation is based on three statements:

1. Walras's law (aggregate demand equals to aggregate supply) is fulfiled;
2. Excess demand $E_n(\vec{p})$ is homogeneous function of degree zero (excess demand does not depend on the choice of price scale);
3. Utility of goods consumed by any agent subject to budget constraint is maximal in equilibrium state.

Samuelson (1941) proposed equations describing the change of prices in response to excess demand for the goods.

$$\dot{p}_n = H_n\left[D_n(\vec{p}) - S_n(\vec{p})\right] = H_n\left[E_n(\vec{p})\right]; \quad n = 1;...;N \tag{1}$$

$$E_n(\vec{p}) = D_n(\vec{p}) - S_n(\vec{p}) \tag{2}$$

A sign-preserving continuous function $H_n\left[E_n(\vec{p})\right]$ depends on excess demand $E_n(\vec{p})$ for the n-th commodity. Equations (1) can be analyzed by means of comparative statics methods. Vector of equilibrium prices is the solution of the following system of equations:

$$E_n\left(p_1^*; p_2^*;...; p_n^*;...p_N^*\right) = 0 \tag{3}$$

After Walras's system of general equilibrium was formulated rigorously the question about the existence and uniqueness of equilibrium arose. Wald

(1951) proved that equality between the number of equations and the number of unknown variables in Walras's system guarantees neither existence nor uniqueness of solution.

Arrow & Debreu (1954) used Brouwer's fixed point theorem in order to explore the problem of existence of equilibrium states for this system. Hicks (1939) formulated the stability problem for equilibrium state (perfect and imperfect stability). The problem of uniqueness and stability of equilibrium was discussed in many works (Samuelson (1941; 1944); Metzler (1945); Arrow & Hurwicz (1958); Arrow, Block & Hurwicz (1959); McKenzie (1960); Morishima (1964); Dierker (1972); Varian (1975); Fisher (1975) and others). Samuelson (1944) proved that Hicksian conditions of stability generally do not guarantee in the general case the dynamical stability of equilibrium. Mosak (1944); Metzler (1945) and Morishima (1964) used the 'gross substitution' hypothesis as the necessary assumption that guarantees the existence of unique and stable equilibrium. It was proved also that the unique stable equilibrium exists if the economy has 'dominant negative diagonal' in Jacobi' matrix $\left\| \partial_i E_k \right\|$ of 'excess demand' functions. These 'conditions of global stability' imposed onto the properties of Jacobi' matrix are not always suitable for the actual economy. Rader (1972) indicated that the 'gross substitutability' hypothesis contradicts to real situation at the markets of production factors. Arrow & Hurwicz (1958) noted that unstable equilibrium points can exist generally in economy free from these restrictive special 'conditions'. Scarf (1960) considered some examples where the global equilibrium is unstable. Debreu (1970) proposed algorithm for the analysis of economy having multiple equilibrium points. The analysis of the problem of uniqueness and stability of general equilibrium is not finished.

According to MSP the global equilibrium in the economic complex adaptive system is always unstable. The economic system evolves toward the unstable global equilibrium state (the property of so-called "self-organized instability" in complex adaptive systems). This general idea about the global instability of the economic CAS can be concretized by means of economic describing of instability in terms of properties of "excess demand functions" and price-demand-supply adjustment.

The temporal macroscopic equilibrium state of the economic system is the state with zero "excess demand" for each commodity. The progress in conditions of production (adoption of innovations) and growth of output gradually change the temporal equilibrium state of the economic system. Equation (1) describes short-term adjustment in the economic system. It is the stabilizing feedback acting within the economic CAS. Equations (2)-(3) determine the equilibrium states of the economic system. "Excess demand" functions depend not only on price-vector but also on the changes in demand-functions influenced by qualitative changes of both goods and consumers (new goods → new needs of consumers → the qualitative change of demand functions). According to MSP principles the long-term development of the economic system is directed toward the point of unstable equilibrium. The bifurcation of dynamical system (1)-(3) is possible. The number of equilibrium states (solutions of the system) can change with progress of the economy. The stable equilibrium can become unstable if economic parameters change. Any small shock (the perturbation of a System) can trigger sudden jump of the economic system into a new stable equilibrium state. Consequently 'price-demand-supply adjustment' can contain implicitly the possibility of catastrophic jumps (crisis) in the economic system.

Marshall's short-term adjustment describes the change in excess demand influenced by the difference between 'demand-price' and 'offer-price'.

'DEMAND-OFFER-PRICE' (MARSHALLIAN) ADJUSTMENT

$$\dot{q}_n = G_n \left[p_n^{(D)} (\vec{q}) - p_n^{(S)} (\vec{q}) \right] = G_n \left[E_n^{-1} (\vec{q}) \right] \tag{4}$$

Sign-preserving function $G\left(E_n^{-1}\right)$ depends on excess demand price.

The unification of both Walrasian and Marshallian adjustments into cross-dual adjustment process can be formalized as two-dimensional dynamical system. Consider for example Lorenz's (1993) version:

$$\begin{cases} \dot{p} = f\left[x(p) - y\right] \\ \dot{y} = k\left[y^{(d)}(p) - y\right] \end{cases} \tag{5}$$

The Linear Approximation is:

$$\begin{cases} \dot{p} = \alpha \cdot \left[x(p) - y\right] \\ \dot{y} = \beta \cdot \left[y^{(d)}(p) - y\right] \end{cases} \tag{6}$$

Value $y^{(d)}(p)$ is 'desired output' and $x(p)$ is aggregate demand. Goodwin (1953; 1970) and Morishima (1959) analyzed the 'cross-dual adjustment process' as the possible mechanism describing both Walrasian and Marshallian adjustment. Flaschel (1991; 1992) and Flaschel & Semmler (1987) explored some economical aspects of stabilizing process in the 'cross-dual' system. Equilibrium state of 'cross-dual' system is locally asymptotically stable if the demand-function is negatively sloped. Sonnenschein (1972) and Debreu (1974) have demonstrated the cases when this necessary condition of stability is not fulfilled. The aggregate demand function $x(p)$ can be positively sloped in a certain region of the $(y; p)$ plane. This fundamental result means that equilibrium of economic system can become unstable. Mas-Colell (1986) considered 'cross-dual system' with S-shaped demand-function. If the fixed point $y^{(d)}(p^*) = x(p^*) = y^*$ is located in the region where the demand function has the positive slope this fixed point will be unstable and at least one closed orbit in the $(y; p)$ domain exists according to Poincare-Bendixson theorem. Consequently 'cross-dual' system can demonstrate the cyclic dynamics. Moreover the cycles consisting of two stages of gradual change and two sharp jumps (so-called 'relaxation' cycles') are possible if the speed of price adjustment in the system (37) is much larger than the speed of output adjustment. Radner (1967) assumed that discontinuity may play the important role in the economic theory. Models displaying 'relaxation oscillations' were considered in Chiarella' (1990a; 1990b) and Franke & Lux' (1992) works. The general overview of the possible nonlinear phenomena in the economic system is contained in Lorenz (1993).

Balasko (1989) noted that the determination of equilibrium condition in the general equilibrium analysis: "excess demand" equals to zero ($Z(p; w) = 0$ where w - vector of parameters) contains implicitly the possibility of catastrophic jumps from old into a new equilibrium state.

Singularity is just another word for a multiple root of equation $Z(p; w) = 0$ where the unknown is the vector p. One easily sees ... that multiple roots, and especially double roots, correspond to borderline cases associated with changes in the number of solutions, the standard picture being that solutions appear and disappear in pairs of these double roots. Clearly enough, this may entail discontinuous behavior of the equilibrium solution... Catastrophe theory has often been unduly identified to this discontinuity property... For an economy where the trade vector remains small to some extent, equilib-

rium is unique and depends smoothly on the parameters defining the economy. On the other hand, when this trade vector is large, the economy is likely to have multiple equilibria so that, 'catastrophic' changes of the equilibrium prices and allocations are susceptible of being observed. (Balasko, 1989; p. 68)

Kehoe (1987) argued that GE (general equilibrium) concept does not exclude the possibility of catastrophes in long-term dynamics of the economic system:

We must pay attention to the historical forces that have brought about the original equilibrium position and to the transitional process involved in the adjustment from one equilibrium position to another... If then we start with a historically given equilibrium that is locally stable with respect to so.e adjustment process, we can run into problems in the face of mathematical catastrophes. (Kehoe, 1987; p. 82)

Araujo & Maldonado (1999) noted the possibility of different scenarios of long-term economic dynamics including cycles and stochastic equilibrium. They argued that GE model does not contain the criterion for the choice one equilibrium from multiple available equilibrium states within this economic approach.

When there exists multiplicity of equilibria in intertemporal equilibrium models, the Arrow-Debreu model is insufficient to explain theoretically which of them will prevail... The actual dynamics can converge to steady states, cycles or stochastic equilibria... (Araujo & Maldonado, 1999; p. 58)

Grandmont (1998) demonstrated how expectations can generate the local instability within the economic system situated in neighborhood of steady state. His 'principle of *uncertainty*'

...relates the sensitivity of expectations in the economy with the ability of the learning rule for extrapolating trends out of small past deviations from equilibrium. (Grandmont, 1998; p. 71)
If ... agents are uncertain about the local dynamics of the system (and thus, they are ready to extrapolate a wide range of regularities out of past deviations) then the actual dynamics is local unstable. (Grandmont, 1998; p. 71)

Let's summarize the most essential findings of GE analysis.

1. Stabilizing feedback via Walrasian-Marshallian adjustment ensure 'temporal equilibrium' in the competitive economy. Two schemes describe this stabilizing process:
    a. **Walrasian Stabilizing Feedback:** Deviation of prices from its equilibrium level → the change in excess demand → the decrease in deviation of price.
    b. **Marshallian Stabilizing Feedback:** Deviation of excess demand from zero → the change in demand price→ the decrease in deviation of excess demand.
2. **Reinforcing Feedback Process:** This mechanism within GE framework is presented as the change in 'temporal equilibrium' due to progress of the economy and accumulation of capacity. Increase in output, adoption of new techniques, the change in expectations of economic agents, the growth of welfare function and many other factors drift the current equilibrium. As consequence the stability of equilibrium can change.

Beckmann & Ryder (1969) and Mas-Colell (1986) were used S-shaped marginal cost and demand functions for simulation of long-term drifts in equilibrium state of economic system. Grandmont (1998) explored the increase of instability of temporal equilibrium because of influence of expectations near equilibrium state. Many investigators in GE approach (Kehoe, 1987; Balasko, 1989) argued that catastrophic jumps in long-term development of economy are possible. Balasko (1989) explains such jumps as the consequence of the change in number of solutions i.e. as the result of bifurcation of the dynamical system describing 'demand-supply adjustment'. The coincidence of two different roots of the system (1) - (3) into one double root (bifurcation) results in the stable equilibrium state becomes unstable. Jumps into a new equilibrium state will display the picture of 'relaxation cycles'. Very complex intermittent dynamics can emerge. Periods of 'stasis' (gradual changes in the current equilibrium) and episodic rapid sudden changes of equilibrium state can form complex picture of discontinuous cycles. Consequently according to GE approach the economic system can demonstrate so-called 'punctuated equilibrium' phenomenon through the sequence of discontinuous cycles.

INVESTMENT-SAVING STABILIZING MECHANISM (KEYNESIAN ADJUSTMENT)

Keynes (1935) proposed the macroscopic description of self-regulation in economy by means of "investment and saving functions". According to 'Keynesian model' ex ante investment and saving determine the dynamics of national income.

$$\dot{Y} = F\left[I\left(Y;K;...\right) - S\left(Y;K;...\right)\right] \qquad (7)$$

Sign preserving function $F[*]$ depends on ex ante 'excess investment':

$$E\left(Y;K;...\right) = I\left(Y;K;...\right) - S\left(Y;K;...\right) \qquad (8)$$

Linearization of equation (7) gives:

$$\dot{Y} = \alpha \cdot E\left(Y;K;...\right), \; \alpha \gg 0. \qquad (9)$$

Equilibrium points $\left(Y^*;K^*;...\right)$ satisfy the equation:

$$E\left(Y^*;K^*;...\right) = 0 \qquad (10)$$

$$Y^* = Y^*\left(K^*;...\right) \qquad (11)$$

Investment $I\left(Y;K;...\right)$ and saving $S\left(Y;K;...\right)$ functions depend on many economic variables including national income and stock of capital. It is necessary to add the equations for these variables in order to close this dynamic system. Kalecki (1937; 1939) considered 'the business cycle problem' on the basis of Keynesian analysis. Kaldor' (1940), Chang & Smyth' (1971) and Varian' (1979) models contain the additional variable – the capital stock - as bifurcation parameter of Keynesian dynamic system. Ackley (1961) and Torre (1977) added the equation for the interest rate. Varian' (1981) and George' (1981) introduced two additional variables - the capital and wealth. Boldrin' (1984; 1988) used the capital and interest rate as additional variables of dynamic system. Since the speed of income adjustment α is much larger than the change in additional variables (capital, interest rate and others) these additional variables play the role of parameters (slow variables) in adjustment equation (9).

Above listed models use some realistic (reasonable) assumptions for configurations of investment and saving functions. As a rule the sigmoid shape for one (or both) functions is used. Sigmoid shape reflects the long-term changes in the marginal propensity to invest (or save). Kaldor (1940) described these long-run regularities as follows:

The marginal propensity to invest

... will be small for low levels of activity because when there is a great deal of surplus capacity, an increase in activity will not induce entrepreneurs to undertake additional construction: the rise in profit will not stimulate investment. But it will also be small for unusually high levels of activity because rising costs and increasing difficulty of borrowing will dissuade entrepreneurs from expanding still faster – at a time when they already have large commitments. (Kaldor, 1940; p. 81)

The sigmoid shape of investment and saving functions reflects the long term dynamics of economic agents' expectations. The economic progress leads to the shift of these functions relative to each other. Both sigmoid form of investment (saving) functions and their shift increase instability of current equilibrium in course of long-term development of economy.

The increase of instability of temporal equilibrium in course of complex systems evolution is well known as phenomenon of '*self-organized instability*'. Indeed this property of complex systems is the basis of its intermittent dynamics known as 'punctuated equilibrium'. All above mentioned models can display the picture of discontinuous cycles. Each cycle consists of two stages of gradual change and two catastrophic jumps just as in MSP-model of complex adaptive system. Catastrophes emerge as the consequence of bifurcations of dynamical system (9). The number of solutions (10) can change and depends on values of additional variables $\left(K^*;...\right)$ playing the role of bifurcation parameters. If the number of roots of equation (10) change it is enough to make dynamic system (9) bifurcate. Stable states can become unstable triggering for catastrophic jumps into a new stable state.

The long-range attractor of the economic system is unstable equilibrium within these models. Right after economy attains unstable long-term equilibrium state, transitional process into a new stable equilibrium (catastrophic jump) begins. These jumps create cyclical pattern in the economic dynamics – Kaldor-type business cycle. "Self-organized instability" (SOI) is universal property of complex evolving systems and in particular of the economic system too:

One view of systems driven out of equilibrium is that they should tend to a uniform "minimally" stable state generated by some type of optimization process. In traffic flow such a state would correspond to a uniform flow of cars with all cars moving at maximal velocity possible. But these optimized states often are catastrophically unstable, exhibiting breakdown events or avalanches, such as traffic jams. In tokomaks, this means that the ideal state of the plasma with the highest possible energy density is locally stable, but globally unstable with respect to explosive breakdown events. (Paczuski & Bak, 1999; p. 3)

Two peculiarities – local stability and global instability – determine interconnection of a short-term and a long-term dynamics in complex evolving systems. Two forces regulate dynamics of such systems. The first force is regulating (stabilizing) feedback tending to return the system into its temporal equilibrium state. The second force is reinforcing feedback process ensuring the search of global equilibrium which is long-term attractor for the system. Superposition of these adaptive mechanisms is the basis of dynamics of the economic system. Since long-term equilibrium state is unstable these systems will demonstrate intermittent dynamics – "punctuated equilibrium' phenomenon. The long periods of "stasis" will be interrupted by events of sharp jumps of the system into a new equilibrium state.

Above listed economic models contain implicitly of both stabilizing and reinforcing feedbacks. Stabilizing feedback eliminates deviations of the economic system from its temporal equilibrium state. Reinforcing feedback ensures the convergence toward long-term equilibrium. Discontinuous cycles arise as consequence of these feedbacks interplay. A system tends to approach to unstable equilibrium but in neighborhood of one it catapults into a new and stable equilibrium state.

Since the actual business oscillations demonstrate much more complex dynamics than regular relaxation cycles these economic models is rather only an illustration of operation of fundamental economic laws than their exact formulation. Varian (1979) writes:

The "business cycle" proposition is clearly the result intuited by Kaldor thirty years ago. However the existence of a regular, periodic business cycle

causes certain theoretical and empirical difficulties. Recent theoretical work involving rational expectations (Lucas (1975)) and empirical work on business cycles (McCullough (1975); Savin (1977)) have argued that (1) regular cycles seem to be incompatible with rational economic behavior, and (2) there is a little statistical significant evidence for a business cycle anyway. However, there does seem to be some evidence for a kind of "cyclic behavior" in the economy. It is commonplace to hear descriptions of how exogenous shocks may send the economy spiraling, into a recession, from which it sooner or later recovers. Leijonhufvud (1973) has suggested that economies operate as if there is the kind of "corridor of stability": that is there is the local stability of equilibrium, but global instability. Small shocks are dampened out, but large shocks may be amplified.
The catastrophe model… offers the way of rationalizing these features… The resulting equilibrium is easily seen to be locally stable. However it is globally unstable. (Varian, 1979; p. 8).

Pure mathematical relaxation oscillations with regular duration are far from real business oscillations. The increase of instability of temporal equilibrium ('self-organized instability phenomenon') appear itself as the sensitivity to exogenous shocks. The larger instability is the higher ensitivity to external influences is. Therefore the system which is close to unstable state will amplify the exogenous shocks. The larger instability is the higher probability of jumps into a new stable state (amplification of exogenous shock) is. Exogenous shocks are working as perturbations which trigger (with some probability) the jumps of a system into a new equilibrium state. These irregular sudden jumps influenced by exogenous shocks form the picture of irregular stochastic relaxation cycles.

INFLUENCE OF STOCHASTIC SHOCKS

According to MSP approach the exogenous shocks deviate the economic CAS from its temporary equilibrium state. The "stabilizing feedback" returns a system into equilibrium state but even very small shock can trigger catastrophic jumps into a new equilibrium state if a system is disposed near points of unstable equilibrium: point 1 at the "upper evolutionary branch" and point 3 at the "lower evolutionary branch" (Figure 2). Therefore the dynamics of a System driven by stochastic shocks demonstrates either small oscillations relative to state of stable equilibrium or sudden jumps from one equilibrium state to another.

The first attempts to explain business cycle as aggregate outcome of stochastic exogenous shocks were in 1930-s (Frish (1933) and Slutzky (1937)). Linear models with superimposed stochastic shocks are called Frish-type models. Later numerous models describing the business oscillations as shocks-driven processes were proposed. Samuelson (1947) and Zarnowitz (1985) considered the conditions under which shocks can generate persistent oscillations in rate of growth. Krelle (1959) proposed solid theoretical background for stochastic business cycles analysis. The stochastic shocks can arise from either objective or subjective causes. The shocks originating in real, monetary, political, and natural events are objective. Changes in 'expectations' of economic agents create the subjective stochastic shocks. Many models describing how 'expectations' are forming were proposed: hypothesis of 'adaptive expectations' (Cagan (1956); Nerlove (1958)); concept of 'rational expectations' (Muth (1961)) and others. Introduction of 'expectations' into the economic theory opened a new possibilities for the economic analysis. "Expectations" are the basis of many multi-agents economic models.

In 1980-s the Real Business Cycle (RBC) theory came into being. Kydland & Prescott (1982) and Long & Plosser (1983) demonstrated that rational agents of the economic system are capable to response onto the real (non-monetary) stochastic shocks through the cyclical pattern in macroscopic dynamics. King, Plosser & Rebelo (1988) proposed so-called canonic RBC model unifying neoclassical growth model with some additional principles (utility maximization subject to resources constraints). Hairault (1995) in overview devoted to RBC Approach describes the essence of this economic approach as follows:

RBC theory considers economic fluctuations as the result of the optimal response of economic agents to stochastic shocks on global productivity. (Hairault, 1995; p. 24)

CAPACITY UTILIZATION

Macroeconomists often consider the economic system as a 'goal-seeking' macro-agent. The macro-models of this sort differ by specification of 'goal-seeking' procedure. Researchers postulate that usually some maximization (optimization) mechanism regulates the activity of the economic system as a whole. According to this type of theories the economy as a whole seeks to maximize macro-variable ('utility', 'welfare', 'capacity') subject to some restrictions superimposed onto the structural and dynamical properties of the economy. This global property of the economic system can be interpreted as the increase of MSP-efficiency in the economic CAS.

MSP-principles can be the basis of new macroscopic MSP-model of the economic system. The basic difficulty in formulation of MSP-model is the economic interpretation of very abstract terms such as "potential" and "conditions of realization".

FORMULATION OF MSP-ECAS-MODEL: BASIC NOTIONS AND EQUATIONS

The economy as the Complex Adaptive System (CAS) consists of many interacting adaptive agents: firms, entrepreneurs and individuals. The Economy as a Complex Adaptive System (ECAS) evolves on the basis of general principles formulated in MSP-approach of CAS-modeling. MSP-variables: "potential", "realized potential" and "conditions of realization" can be interpreted as some economic indicators. "Potential of the Economic CAS" and "conditions for realization" are two constituents of the "useful experience" accumulated (installed) within the Economic System.

Productive activity of economic agents (firms, entrepreneurs etc.) in the economy is proportional to "realized economic potential". The more the activity of economic agents is the higher the realized economic potential is. Consequently the notion "output" Y in economics is the quantitative measure of employed (realized) economic potential.

"Potential of the Economic CAS" is the "economic potential" (or "productive capacity") of the Economic System. The "economic potential" depends on available resources and know-how incorporated in technologies, organizations, management rules, and human capital. LDCR (2006) gives the following definition for "productive capacity":

Productive capacities are defined in this Report as the productive resources, entrepreneurial capabilities and production linkages which together determine the capacity of a country to produce goods and services and enable it to grow and develop. For tradable goods and services, what matters is the capacity to produce in an internationally competitive manner. Productive capacities develop within a country through three closely interrelated processes: capital accumulation, technological progress and structural change. Capital accumulation is the process of maintaining and increasing stocks of natural, human and physical capital through investment. Achieving technological progress is the process of introducing new goods and services, new or improved methods, equipment or skills to produce goods and services, and new and improved forms of organizing production through innovation. Structural change is the change in the inter- and intrasectoral composition of production, the pattern of inter- and intrasectoral linkages and the pattern of linkages amongst enterprises. Such change often occurs through investment and innovation, and the emerging production structure in turn influences the potential for further investment and innovation. (UNCTAD (2006); p. II)

"Potential of the Economic CAS" can be economically measured by means of "maximum output" Y_m i. e. the output of the Economic System subject to full utilization of all available production resources, its optimal allocation and optimal cost-minimizing factor prices. The basic production factors of the market economy are technologies and "know-how" embodied into plants and human capital, as well as the "labor", the "capital", and the "land". Gabish & Lorenz (1989; p.28) define the "potential output" as "GNP which can be produced by full-employment of all factors of production".

Robert Solow (1957) established that the significant share of increment in nonfarm GNP depends on so-called "technological factor" A, i.e. "technologies" in a broad sense (quality of physical and human capital). This factor describes the influence of technical progress on productivity of the "capital" and "labor". Peculiarities of the growth of "technological factor" reflect Schumpeterian (1939) cyclic dynamics of the Economic System (so-called "life cycles of innovations").

Schumpeter has stressed the role of innovation by pointing to the special interdependence between economic development and innovation development observed in the process of qualitative and quantitative application of innovations in business practice. (Pachura, 2012; p. 129)

According to Schumpeter' the basic cause of the business cycle are in periodic qualitative renewal of economy. Each crisis initiates the active search and adoption of new radical innovations. Diffusion of radical profitable innovations across the economy leads to increase of the productivity of labor. This is long process. In the beginning, only some entrepreneurs-pioneers might consider taking a risk with installing new technology. They do it because they have a reasonable hope that this innovation will be profitable. After some time the most of economic agents install this profitable innovation. This is avalanche-like process of diffusion of innovation across the economy. Finally when the modernization of economy is finished the growth ends. System is exhausted its sources of growth. Profit is diminishing and the new crisis stimulates the search of new profitable innovations.

Such an explanation of the business cycle complies with statistical researches. Impulses (or clusters) of innovations were discovered independently by many scientists; Mensch (1979); Hochgraf (1983); van Duijn (1983); Kleinknecht (1984). Qualitative improvement of the economy after each crisis is well-established fact. Technologies, rules of management and forms of organizations change qualitatively after each crisis. This process can be interpreted as reconfiguration of the Economic CAS. According to Eis (1969) and Nelson (1959) the peaks of merges and acquisitions of firms take place during the crisis and depression of the business cycle.

MSP-notion "efficiency of ECAS" close to economic concept "capacity utilization rate" in economics. The economic notion "capacity utilization" describes the actual per "maximal (or potential!) output" ratio. This index is used as indicator of business activity in the Economic System.

MSP-notion "potential of ECAS" close to economic concept "capacity". The economic indicator "capacity" (i. e. the "maximum output" or "potential output") depends on available resources, technologies, business organization and rules of management in the society. The economic notion "factual output" characterizes the realized capacity (the realized economic potential) of the economic system. The economic notion "capacity utilization rate" describes the efficiency of the economic system. There are many economic approaches to the problem of measuring of "potential output" and "capacity utilization rate". "Factual output" per "maximal (or potential) output" ratio can be evaluated in different ways.

The degree of utilization of each production factor can be described as the ratio of its current value to maximal value. For example, the employed labor force index characterizes the degree of utilization of labor.

The third MSP-notion - "Conditions for realization of economic potential" - is much more difficult to define precisely. Intuitively this notion must depend first of all on available stock of capital, investment conditions, the economic legislation, and so-called routines i. e. traditional regulative rules of agents' interactions in the country. This MSP-term must correspond to economic variable which describes the conditions of exploitation of available factors of production. "Conditions of realization of the economic potential" in the Economic CAS depend on economic factors which influence on the utilization rate of available factors of production. The capital is the main driving force for productive utilization of the labor, land, plant, and knowledge in the modern economy. The definite amount of capital must be advanced in order to combine (and to transform) the potential forces of the labor, machines, land, and technologies into the real production. Consequently the store of capital determines the ability of economy to exploit the available resources in actual production.

Fernando de Soto (2000) argued that indeed the capital stock (as tool for exploitation of resources) is the necessary condition for productive application of available economic resources in market economy. Therefore the "stock of capital" K can be used as approximate evaluation for value of "conditions of realization" in the Economic CAS.

Both the "potential" of a system and the "conditions for realization" within the system are created via productive activity of the economic agents. In a broad sense the growth of the Economic System is the result of growth of complexity of the system. Complexity of the economic CAS depends on embodied knowledge installed within the economic system. New technologies of production, new methods of distribution, new forms of organization and of management - all together increase the complexity of the economic system. The growth of complexity creates the new possibilities for the growth of the "economic potential". On the other hand the growth of complexity influences onto the stability of the economic system. The fall of stability of economic system is a sort of "payment" for prosperity and welfare. As complexity of the economic system grows the system spontaneously evolves toward unstable equilibrium state $(Z_0; R = 1)$. In vicinity of this point even small random perturbations of the system can trigger the dramatic process of system's reconfiguration.

So, MSP-model of the Economic Complex Adaptive System (ECAS) can be formulated as the dynamic system respective to three economic variables: 1) "output" in a broad sense, 2) capital and 3) maximal "output".

Gross Output (GO), Gross Domestic Product (GDP) or Gross National Product (GNP) can be used as indicators of the "realized economic potential" ("output" in a broad sense). The "economic potential" in this case is defined as the Maximal Gross Output (MGO), Maximal Gross Domestic Product (MGDP) and Maximal Gross National Product (MGNP) respectively. We use bellow GDP (or GNP) – as indicators of "realized economic potential".

1. Maximum (maximal) "output", Y_{m}, is quantitative measure for the "economic potential":

$$\Phi \rightarrow Y_{\mathrm{max}}; \tag{12}$$

2. The actual output, Y, is quantitative measure for the "exploited (realized) economic potential":

$$\Phi_R \to Y ; \tag{13}$$

3. Actual per maximal output ratio is efficiency of the Economic CAS ("capacity utilization rate"):

$$R = \frac{Y}{Y_{max}} ; \tag{14}$$

4. The capital stock, K, is quantitative measure of "conditions of realization" of "economic potential" in the Economic CAS:

$$U \to K . \tag{15}$$

"Maximal output" is used here as a synonym of economic notion "capacity" of economy.

The "capital" can be divided into two big parts: (1) physical capital (fixed capital plus circulating capital in production of goods and services), (2) financial capital (securities and money). The physical capital plays the main role in production whereas the financial capital is only a secondary condition of production. We use in MSP-model fixed capital as measure for "conditions of realization" in the economic system. This is of course only approximate evaluation for "conditions of realization". Economic interpretation of basic MSP-variables can be concretized via inclusion of other economic indicators which influence onto the "economic potential" and the "conditions of realization of the economic potential".

The basic equations of MSP-model (E1)-(E4) (Introduction) can be rewritten in terms of economic variables as follows:

E1 - Equation for Output: Reinforcing feedback process, equation (E1) from the Introduction gives the equation for the actual output[1]:

$$\frac{\dot{Y}}{Y} = a ; \tag{16}$$

17

E2 - Equation for the Capital: Equation for accumulation of 'conditions', the equation (E4) from the Introduction in Economic CAS gives the equation for accumulation of fixed capital:

$$\dot{K} + \Lambda \cdot K = \nu \cdot Y \; ; \tag{17}$$

E3 - Equation for the Maximal Output: Finally, equation (2) from the Introduction for the 'economic potential' describes the long-term adjustment of actual output in direction toward the maximal output:

$$\frac{d}{dt}\left[Y_{\max} - Y\right] = -d \cdot \left[Y_{\max} - Y\right]. \tag{18}$$

Evolutionary parameters a, Λ, ν, d describe the properties of the Economic CAS.

a = The rate of growth of output;
Λ = The depreciation rate;
ν = The rate of gross investment;
d = Adjustment coefficient.

E4 - Equation for "Capacity Utilization Rate" R : Follows from equations (16) and (18):

$$\dot{R} = \left(a + d\right) \cdot R \cdot \left(1 - R\right) \tag{19}$$

The solution of this equation subject to constant parameters is logistic function.

Equations (16)-(18) are the basic equations of MSP-model of the Economic CAS. These equations in the case of constant evolutionary parameters describe long-term dynamics of economic system along either "upper" or "lower" evolutionary branch.

"Density of conditions" Z depends on "productivity of capital", P and "capacity utilization rate", R :

$$Z = \frac{U}{\Phi} = \frac{K}{Y_m} = \frac{R}{P} \tag{20}$$

$$P = \frac{Y}{K} \tag{21}$$

In the point of long-term equilibrium ($R = 1$; $Y = Y_m$) "density of conditions" equals to "capital coefficient":

$$Z = Z_0 = \frac{K}{Y_m} = \frac{\nu}{a + \Lambda} \tag{22}$$

E5 - Equation for Productivity of Capital: The productivity of the capital satisfies to logistic equation (follows from (16)-(17)):

$$\dot{P} = \nu \cdot P \cdot \left(P_0 - P \right) \tag{23}$$

$$P_0 = \frac{1}{Z_0} = \frac{a + \Lambda}{\nu} \tag{24}$$

The "stabilizing function" of the economic MSP-system can be introduced into MSP-model of ECAS via "investment-function" and "saving-function". Stabilizing feedback describes short-term adjustment of the Economic System:

$$\frac{dR}{dt} = -\frac{\partial W\left(R; Z\right)}{\partial R} \tag{25}$$

Value Y_m don't change during short-term adjustment. Therefore the equation (25) can be rewritten in the economic terms as follows:

E6 - Equation for Short-Term Adjustment (Stabilizing Feedback):

$$\dot{Y} = -Y_m^2 \cdot \frac{\partial W\left(Y; K\right)}{\partial Y} \tag{26}$$

Keynesian short-term adjustment (9) in the Economic CAS can be modeled as follows:

$$\dot{Y} = -\alpha \cdot \left[S(Y;K) - I(Y;K) \right]; \ \alpha > 0 \tag{27}$$

$I(Y;K)$ - is the investment function; and $S(Y;K)$ - is the savings function. Strictly speaking it is necessary to distinguish the "national income" - Y in the equation (27) and "Gross Domestic Product" (GDP) - Y in the equation (26). "GDP" equals "national income" plus "capital consumption allowance" (for depreciation of fixed capital) plus indirect taxes. We neglect in MSP-model "indirect taxes" (this is small quantity in comparison with GDP). Capital consumption allowance ($= \Lambda \cdot K$) depends on fixed capital K and depreciation rate Λ. But neither fixed capital nor depreciation rate don't change in short-term adjustment (27). Therefore derivatives $\dot{Y}$ in the equations (26) and (27) are equal.

The equation for "stabilizing function" follows from equalizing of left parts in the equations (26)-(27):

$$\frac{\partial W(Y;K)}{\partial Y} = \frac{\alpha}{Y_m^2} \cdot \left[S(Y;K) - I(Y;K) \right] \tag{28}$$

E7 - Equation for "Stabilizing Function": Using the equation (28) it is possible to construct the stabilizing function on the basis of investment-function and savings-function.

$$W(Y;K) = \int \frac{\alpha}{Y_m^2} \cdot \left[S(Y;K) - I(Y;K) \right] dY \tag{29}$$

Kaldor (1940) assumed that schedules of investment function and savings function have S-shape geometry. Figures 1-3 illustrate interrelation between stabilizing function and functions of investment and savings[2] for four stages of evolutionary cycle ("prosperity and depression" – Figure 1; "revival" – Figure 2; "crisis" – Figure 3). Formula (29) connects economical notions "investment function" and "savings function" with MSP-notion the "stabilizing function".

Figure 1. Investment function $I(Y;K)$, *saving function* $S(Y;K)$ *and stabilizing function* $W(Y;K)$ *constructed on the base of these functions. Prosperity and depression stages of evolutionary cycle.*

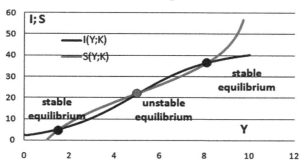

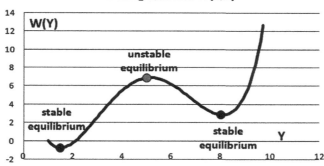

Figure 2. Investment function $I(Y;K)$, *saving function* $S(Y;K)$ *and stabilizing function* $W(Y;K)$ *constructed on the base of these functions. Revival stage of evolutionary cycle.*

Investment and saving functions.

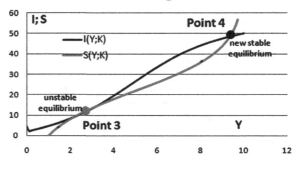

**Stabilizing function W(Y;K)
(revival)**

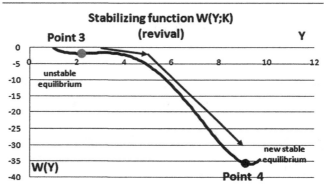

Figure 3. Investment function $I(Y;K)$, saving function $S(Y;K)$ and stabilizing function $W(Y;K)$ constructed on the base of these functions (equation (28)). Crisis stage of evolutionary cycle.

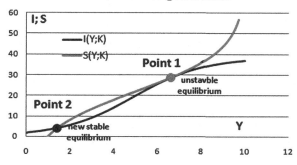

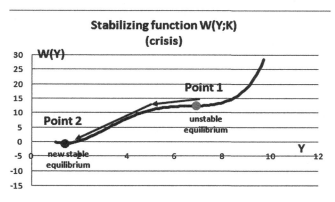

REFERENCES

Ackley, G. (1961). *Macroeconomic theory*. New York: Macmillan.

Araujo, A. P., & Maldonado, W. L. (1999). Learning in intertemporal equilibrium models and the sunspot case. In F. Petri & F. Hahn (Eds.), *General Equilibrium*. London, New York: Routledge.

Arrow, K. J. (1951). An extension of the basic theorems of classical welfare economics. In J. Nyman (Ed.), *Proceedings of the Second Berkley Symposium on Mathematical Statistics and Probability* (pp. 507-532). University of California Press.

Arrow, K. J., Block, H. D., & Hurwicz, L. (1959). On the stability of the competitive equilibrium, II. *Econometrica, 27*(1), 82–109. doi:10.2307/1907779

Arrow, K. J., & Debreu, G. (1954). Existence of an equilibrium for a competitive economy. *Econometrica, 22*(3), 265–290. doi:10.2307/1907353

Arrow, K. J., & Hurwicz, L. (1958). On the stability of the competition equilibrium, I. *Econometrica, 26*(4), 522–552. doi:10.2307/1907515

Balasko, Y. (1989). Catastrophe theory. In J. Eatwell et al. (Eds.), *The new palgrave: general equilibrium* (pp. 68–69). New York: Norton. doi:10.1007/978-1-349-19802-3_5

Beckmann, M. J., & Ryder, H. E. (1969). Simultaneous price and quantity adjustment in a single market. *Econometrica, 37*(3), 470–484. doi:10.2307/1912794

Boldrin, M. (1984). *Applying bifurcation theory: some simple results on Keynesian business cycles, DP 8403*. University of Venice.

Boldrin, M. (1988). Persistent oscillations and chaos in economic models: notes for a survey. In P. W. Anderson et al. (Eds.), *The Economy as an evolving complex system* (pp. 49–75). Redwood City: Addison – Wesley.

Cagan, P. (1956). The Monetary dynamics of hyperinflation. In M. Friedman (Ed.), *Studies in the quantity theory of money* (pp. 25–117). Chicago: The University of Chicago Press.

Chang, W. W., & Smyth, D. J. (1971). The existence and persistence of cycles in a nonlinear model: Kaldors 1940 model reexamined. *The Review of Economic Studies, 38*(1), 37–44. doi:10.2307/2296620

Chiarella, C. (1990a). *The elements of a nonlinear theory of economic dynamics*. Berlin: Springer – Verlag. doi:10.1007/978-3-642-46707-3

Chiarella, C. (1990b). Monetary and fiscal policy under nonlinear exchange rate dynamics. In G. Feichtinger (Ed.), *Dynamic economic models and optimal control* (pp. 527–546). Amsterdam: North – Holland.

De Soto, F. (2000). *The mystery of capital*. New York: Basic Books.

Debreu, G. (1951). The coefficient of resource utilization. *Econometrica, 19*(3), 273–292. doi:10.2307/1906814

Debreu, G. (1970). Economics with a finite set of equilibria. *Econometrica, 38*(3), 387–392. doi:10.2307/1909545

Debreu, G. (1974). Excess demand functions. *Journal of Mathematical Economics, 1*(1), 15–23. doi:10.1016/0304-4068(74)90032-9

Dierker, E. (1972). Two remarks on the number of equilibria of an economy. *Econometrica, 40*(5), 951–953. doi:10.2307/1912091

Eis, C. (1969). The 19191930 merger movement in American Industry. *The Journal of Law & Economics, 12*(2), 267–296. doi:10.1086/466669

Fisher, F. M. (1975). *The stability of general equilibrium: results and problems*. MIT Working paper, No. 153.

Flaschel, P. (1991). Stability – independent of economic structure? A prototype analysis. *Structural Change and Economic Dynamics, 2*(1), 9–35. doi:10.1016/0954-349X(91)90003-B

Flaschel, P. (1992). *Macrodynamics – income distribution, effective demand and cyclical growth*. Frankfurt: Peter Lang Verlag.

Flaschel, P., & Semmler, W. (1987). Classical and neoclassical competitive adjustment processes. *The Manchester School, 55*(1), 13–37. doi:10.1111/j.1467-9957.1987.tb01287.x

Franke, R., & Lux, T. (1992). *Adaptive expectations and perfect foresight in a nonlinear Metzler model of the inventory cycle*. Bielefeld University, mimeo.

Frish, R. (1933). Propagation problems and impulse problems in dynamic economics. In *Economic Essays in Honor of Gustav Cassel* (pp. 171–206). London: Allen & Unwin.

Gabish, G., & Lorenz, H. W. (1989). *Business cycle theory. A survey of methods and concepts*. Berlin: Springer-Verlag. doi:10.1007/978-3-642-74715-1

George, D. (1981). Equilibrium and catastrophes in economics. *Scottish Journal of Political Economy*, 28(1), 43–61. doi:10.1111/j.1467-9485.1981. tb00073.x

Goodwin, R. M. (1953). *Static and dynamic general equilibrium models*. London: Macmillan.

Goodwin, R. M. (1970). *Elementary economics from the higher standpoint*. Cambridge University Press.

Grandmont, J.-M. (1998). Expectations formation and stability of large socioeconomic systems. *Econometrica*, 66(4), 741–781. doi:10.2307/2999573

Hairault, J.-O. (1995). The RBC approach. In P. Y. Henin (Ed.), Advances in Business Cycle Research. With Applications to the French and US Economies (pp. 21-54). Springer.

Hicks, J. R. (1946). Value and capital: an inquiry into some fundamental principles of economic theory (2nd ed.). Oxford, UK: Clarendon Press.

Hochgraf, N. (1983), The future technological environment. *Proceedings of 11ᵗʰ World Petroleum Congress* (pp. 1-10). London: John Willey & Sons.

Kaldor, N. (1940). A model of the trade cycle. *The Economic Journal*, 50(197), 78–92. doi:10.2307/2225740

Kalecki, M. (1937). A Theory of the business cycle. *The Review of Economic Studies*, 4(2), 77–97. doi:10.2307/2967606

Kalecki, M. (1939). A Theory of the business cycle. In *Essays in the Theory of Economic Fluctuations*. London: Allen-Unwin.

Kehoe, T. J. (1987). Comparative statics. In J. Eatwell (Ed.), *The new Palgrave*. New York, London: General Equilibrium. doi:10.1057/978-1-349-95121-5_322-1

Keynes, J. M. (1935). *The general theory of employment, interest and money*. Macmillan Cambridge University Press.

King, R., Plosser, C., & Rebelo, S. (1988). Production, growth and business cycles I. *Journal of Monetary Economics*, 21(2/3), 196–232.

Kleinknecht, A. (1987). *Innovation patterns in crisis and prosperity. Schumpeter's long cycle reconsidered.* London: the Macmillan Press Ltd.

Krelle, W. (1959). Grundlagen einher stochastichen Konjunkturtheorie. *Zeitschrift fur die Gesamte Staatswissenschaft, 115,* 472–494.

Kydland, F., & Prescott, E. (1982). Time to build and aggregate fluctuations. *Econometrica, 50*(6), 1345–1370. doi:10.2307/1913386

Leijonhufvud, A. (1973). Effective demand failures. *The Swedish Journal of Economics, 75*(1), 27–48. doi:10.2307/3439273

Long, J. Jr, & Plosser, C. (1983). Real business cycle. *Journal of Political Economy, 91*(1), 39–69. doi:10.1086/261128

Lorenz, H. W. (1993). *Nonlinear dynamical economics and chaotic motion.* Berlin: Springer-Verlag. doi:10.1007/978-3-642-78324-1

Lucas, R. Jr. (1975). An equilibrium model of the business cycle. *Journal of Political Economy, 83*(6), 1113–1144. doi:10.1086/260386

Marshall, A. (1920). *Principles of economics (8th ed.).* London: Macmillan.

Mas-Colell, A. (1986). Notes on price and quantity tatonnement dynamics. In H. Sonnenschein (Ed.), *Models of Economic Dynamics* (pp. 49–68). Berlin: Springer. doi:10.1007/978-3-642-51645-0_5

McCullough, J. (1975). The Monte Carlo cycle in business activity. *Economic Inquiry, 13*(3), 303–321. doi:10.1111/j.1465-7295.1975.tb00251.x

McKenzie, L. W. (1960). Stability of equilibrium and the value of positive excess demand. *Econometrica, 28*(3), 606–617. doi:10.2307/1910134

Mensch, G. (1979). *Stalemate in technology.* Cambridge, MA: Ballinger.

Metzler, L. (1945). Stability of multiple markets: The Hicks conditions. *Econometrica, 13*(4), 272–292. doi:10.2307/1906922

Morishima, M. (1960). A reconsideration of the Walras-Cassel-Leontieff Model of general equilibrium. In *Mathematical Models in the Social Sciences. 1959: Proceedings of the first Stanford symposium* (pp. 63–76). Stanford, CA: Stanford University Press.

Morishima, M. (1964). *Equilibrium, stability and growth.* Oxford, UK: Clarendon Press.

Mosak, J. L. (1944). *General equilibrium. Theory in international trade.* Bloomington, IN: Principia Press.

Muth, J. F. (1961). Rational expectations and the theory of price movements. In R. E. Lucas & T. J. Sargent (Eds.), Rational Expectations and Econometric Practice (pp. 3-22). Minneapolis, MN: The University of Minnesota Press. doi:10.2307/1909635

Nelson, R. (1959). *Merger movements in American industry 1895-1956.* Princeton, NJ: Princeton University Press.

Nerlove, M. (1958). Adaptive expectations and cobweb phenomena. *The Quarterly Journal of Economics, 72*(2), 227–240. doi:10.2307/1880597

Pachura, A. (2012). Innovation theory – an epistemological aspects. *Polish Journal of Management Studies, 5*, 128–135.

Paczuski, M. & Bak, P. (1999). Self-Organization of Complex Systems. *Proceedings of 12th Chris Engelbrecht Summer School.*

Rader, T. (1972). General equilibrium theory with complementary factors. *Journal of Economic Theory, 4*(3), 372–380. doi:10.1016/0022-0531(72)90128-7

Radner, R. (1967). Equilibre des marches a terme at an comptant en cas d'incertitude. *Cahiers d'Econometrie.* Paris. *CNRS, 4*, 35–52.

Samuelson, P. A. (1941). The stability of equilibrium: Comparative statics and dynamics. *Econometrica, 9*(April), 97–120. doi:10.2307/1906872

Samuelson, P. A. (1944). The Relation between Hicksian stability and true dynamical stability. *Econometrica, 12*(3/4), 256–257. doi:10.2307/1905436

Samuelson P. A. (1947). Foundations of Economic Analysis. *Harvard Economic Studies,* 80.

Savin, N. (1977). A Test of the Monte Carlo hypothesis [Comment]. *Economic Inquiry, 15*(4), 613–617. doi:10.1111/j.1465-7295.1977.tb01124.x

Scarf, H. (1960). Some examples of global instability of the competitive equilibrium. *International Economic Review, 1*(3), 157–172. doi:10.2307/2556215

Schumpeter, J. A. (1939). *Business cycles.* New York: McGraw-Hill Book Company.

Slutzky, E. (1937). The summation of random causes as the source of cyclic processes. *Econometrica*, *5*(2), 105–146. doi:10.2307/1907241

Solow, R. M. (1957). Technical change and production function. *The Review of Economics and Statistics*, *39*(3), 312–320. doi:10.2307/1926047

Sonnenschein, H. (1972). Market excess demand functions. *Econometrica*, *40*(3), 549–563. doi:10.2307/1913184

Torre, V. (1977). Existence of limit cycles and control in complete Keynesian systems by theory of bifurcations. *Econometrica*, *45*(6), 1457–1466. doi:10.2307/1912311

UNCTAD secretariat. (2006). *The least developed country report 2006*. UNCTAD 2006, Geneva, Switzerland.

Van Duijn, J. (1983). *The long wave in economic life*. London: Allen and Unwin.

Varian, H. R. (1975). A Third remark on the number of equilibria of an economy. *Econometrica*, *43*(5/6), 985–986. doi:10.2307/1911341

Varian, H. R. (1979). Catastrophe theory and the business cycle. *Economic Inquiry*, *17*(1), 14–28. doi:10.1111/j.1465-7295.1979.tb00293.x

Varian, H. R. (1981). Dynamical systems with application to economics. In K.J. Arrow & M.D. Intriligator (Eds.), Handbook of Mathematical Economics (pp. 93-110). Amsterdam: North Holland.

Wald, A. (1951). On some systems of equations of mathematical economics. *Econometrica*, *19*.

Walras, L. (1874a). Principe d'une théorie mathématique de l'échange. *Journal des économistes*.

Walras, L. (1874b). Éléments d'économie politique pure, ou théorie de la richesse sociale [Elements of Pure Economics, or the theory of social wealth]. Academic Press.

Zarnowitz, V. (1985). Recent work on business cycles in historical perspective: A review of theories and evidence. *Journal of Economic Literature*, *23*(2), 523–580.

ENDNOTES

[1]   The main equations of MSP-model of ECAS are designated as E-1; E-2;…

[2]   Stabilizing function was constructed by means of numerical integration.

Chapter 2
Main Properties of MSP–ECAS–Model:
Application to the European Economy

EVOLUTIONARY BRANCHES, LONG-TERM EQUILIBRIUM AND TEMPORAL EQUILIBRIUM STATES OF ECAS

MSP-modeling opens new possibilities for deeper understanding of the Economic System. MSP-model of ECAS reveals existing implicitly non-trivial economic interrelations between economic indicators. We consider below two cases: 1) MSP-model with constant parameters (Chapter 2 and 3) MSP-model with changing parameters (Chapter 4). Surely MSP-model with constant parameters simplifies of course the economic reality but this model gives important qualitative description of the economy as the complex system which evolves cyclically through a sequence of discontinuous cycles with different durations.

DOI: 10.4018/978-1-5225-2170-9.ch002

MSP-model with constant parameters introduces into economics new fundamental notion – "evolutionary branch" - locus of temporal equilibrium states of the Economic System in the plane $(Z; R)$. The fact of existence of such special curves is surprising. We can rewrite equations (19)-(20) from the Introduction for "evolutionary branches" via "productivity of capital" P and "capacity utilization rate" $R = \dfrac{Y_m}{Y}$.

"Upper Evolutionary Branch" for economic system:

$$P = \frac{P_0}{1 - C_U \cdot P_0 \cdot \left(\dfrac{Y_m}{Y} - 1\right)^{1+\chi}} \; ; \; P > P_0 \tag{1}$$

"Lower Evolutionary Branch" for economic system:

$$P = \frac{P_0}{1 + C_L \cdot P_0 \cdot \left(\dfrac{Y_m}{Y} - 1\right)^{1+\chi}} \; ; \; P < P_0 \tag{2}$$

Symbol P_0 designates productivity of capital in the point of long-term equilibrium (Point 1 in Figure 2). The following interrelations are fulfilled:

$$P_0 = \frac{1}{Z_0} = \frac{a + \Lambda}{\nu} \text{ or } Z_0 = \frac{1}{P_0} = \frac{\nu}{a + \Lambda} \tag{3}$$

Efficiency of economic system depends on productivity of capital (equations (1)-(2)):

"Upper Evolutionary Branch" of economic system:

$$R \equiv \frac{Y}{Y_m} = \frac{1}{1 + \left(\dfrac{P - P_0}{C_U \cdot PP_0}\right)^{\frac{1}{1+\chi}}} \; ; \tag{4}$$

"Lower Evolutionary Branch" of economic system:

$$R \equiv \frac{Y}{Y_m} = \frac{1}{1 + \left(\dfrac{P_0 - P}{C_L \cdot PP_0}\right)^{\frac{1}{1+\chi}}} \; ; \tag{5}$$

Productivity of capital equals tangent of angle of inclination α of radius-vector in the plane $(Z; R)$:

$$P \equiv \frac{Y}{K} = \frac{R}{Z} = Tan(\alpha) \tag{6}$$

Parameter $\chi \equiv \dfrac{\Lambda - d}{a + d}$ influences onto the geometric shape of "evolutionary branches". According to formula (30) from the Introduction this parameter equals to ratio of length of two line segments along Z-axis.

$$\chi = \frac{Z_0 - Z_1}{Z_1 - Z_0 R_3} \tag{7}$$

There are two types of the economic systems:

Type 1: The systems with $\chi > 0$ (or $\Lambda > d$). These systems evolve via sequence of evolutionary cycles.

Type 2: The systems with $\chi \le 0$ (or $\Lambda > d$). These systems evolve non-cyclically.

We shall limit our consideration by only cyclic type of development because the majority of developed economies evolve cyclically. Condition $\Lambda > d$ means that spontaneous degradation (due to entropy) of "conditions of realization" of economic potential proceeds quicker than degradation of "economic potential". Possibly, it is the law of life. The life experience proves that "conditions" is easier to destroy than "potential" embodied in technologies, human knowledge, social and economic institutions and so on.

Function $R(P)$ is depictured at Figure 1[1]. Productivity of capital decreases as Economic System moves along "upper evolutionary branch" toward long-term equilibrium state. Formulas (1)-(2) determine interrelation between economic indicators: output, maximal output and productivity of capital. Formulas (4)-(5) determine interrelation between "efficiency" of ECAS and

Figure 1. Efficiency of the economic system as function of "productivity of capital"

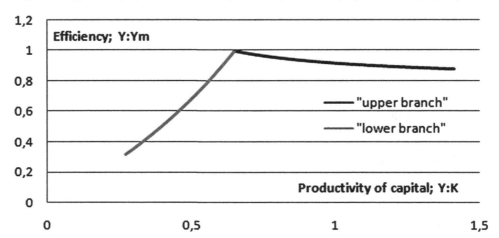

productivity of capital. "Capacity utilization rate" (CUR) is eligible (although only approximate) indicator of "efficiency" of ECAS. Productivity of capital can be computed on the basis of data about "fixed assets" (FA) and "gross domestic product" (GDP). Stylized facts for indicators FA and GDP in U.S. Economy are in database of U.S. BEA[2]. Data about CUR are in FRED[3] database. Cyclic dynamics of indicator CUR is depictured in Figure 2-3. Evolutionary cycles of the U.S. economic system are depictured in Figure 4. The dynamics of the U.S. economy consists of cycles. Trajectories in the coordinate plane, "density of conditions" and "efficiency of ECAS", are directed clockwise. Capacity Utilization Rate (CUR) was used as indicator of "efficiency" of ECAS. Capacity Utilization Rate (CUR) per "productivity of capital" ratio was used as indicator of "density of conditions". This is of course only approximate raw evaluation of "efficiency" of the U.S. economy and "density of conditions" in the U.S. economic system. Moreover the real "evolutionary cycles" differ from theoretical pure MSP-cycles of ECAS with constant evolutionary parameters. "Evolutionary branches" of real ECAS can drift and change the geometrical form because the evolutionary parameters can vary. Each crisis as a rule changes (sometimes considerably) evolutionary parameters of ECAS. Point 1 of long-term equilibrium in the plane $\left(Z_0; R = 1\right)$ (Figure 2) shifts and disposition of "evolutionary branches" changes after the crisis. Moreover, the economic parameters are slightly trembling quantities that oscillate around mean values. For example "rate of growth" is not constant in real ECAS. Therefore the theoretical "evolutionary branches" for the economic system with constant evolutionary parameters

Figure 2. Capacity utilization rate for the U.S. economy (monthly)

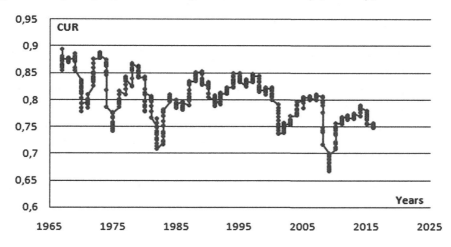

Figure 3. Capacity utilization rate for the U.S. economy (quarter data)

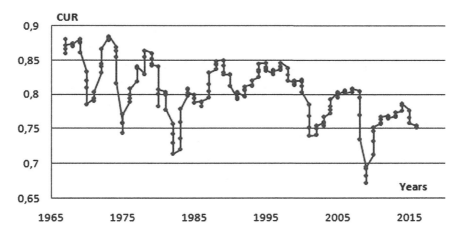

differ from the real "evolutionary branches" for the real economic system with variable evolutionary parameters.

Real dynamics of the economic system is outcome of all above mentioned influencing factors:

Influencing Factor 1: Stochastic shocks that deviate the system from temporary equilibrium state at preferable evolutionary branch,

Influencing Factor 2: The changes in disposition of preferable evolutionary branches due to the changes of evolutionary parameters and

Influencing Factor 3: The changes in disposition of long-term equilibrium point in the plane "density of conditions" – "efficiency" of ECAS.

Pure mathematically correct "evolutionary branches" rarely occur in real economy. Figure 5 illustrates the typical behavior of real economic system. We see that although evolutionary cycles obviously exist the shape of their trajectories differs from pure theoretical "evolutionary branches". Figure 6 demonstrates the case of "complex dynamics" when all three above listed "influencing factors" play important role in the economic dynamics.

Disposition of long-term equilibrium $\left(Z_0; R = 1\right)$ in the plane $\left(Z; R\right)$ depends on evolutionary parameters by means of the equation (24) from Chapter 1. The rate of growth in the point of long-term equilibrium equals:

$$a = \nu P_0 - \Lambda = \frac{\nu}{Z_0} - \Lambda = \frac{\nu Y_m}{K} - \Lambda \tag{8}$$

Rate of growth a increases if the "productivity of capital", P_0 and "investment rate" ν grow. The increase of "depreciation rate", Λ reduces the rate of growth. Formula (8) explains why rate of growth in "developing countries" often higher than in "developed countries". "Rate of growth" for "developing" and "developed" countries are listed in Table 1. Data for "rate of growth" were taken from Database of Central Intelligence Agency (CIA).

There are two basic causes of variations in "rate of growth" between countries: (1) variations in "investment rate", ν and (2) variations in "productivity of capital", $Y_m : K$. "Rate of investment" in "developing countries" higher in average than in "developed countries" (Table 1). Moreover, "den-

Figure 4. Evolutionary cycles in the U.S. economy; Capacity Utilization Rate (CUR) is used as indicator of "efficiency" of the economic system.
Source: U.S. BEA; Tables 1.1.5 and 1.1 and FRED database.

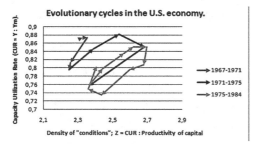
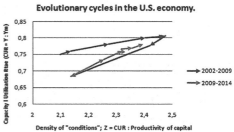

Figure 5. "Efficiency" of the U.S. economy vs. "productivity of capital"
Source: U.S. BEA; Tables 1.1.5 and 1.1 and FRED database.

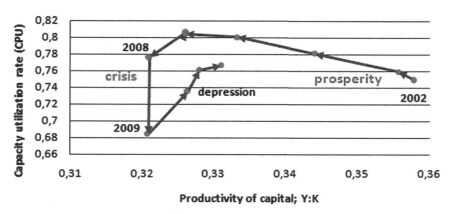

Figure 6. "Efficiency" of the U.S. economy (CUR-index) vs. "density of conditions"
Source: U.S. BEA; Tables 1.1.5 and 1.1 and FRED database.

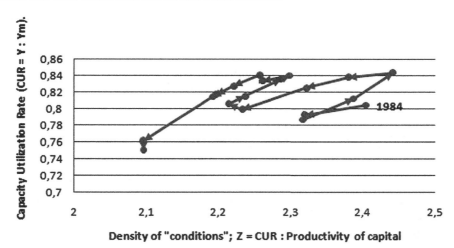

Table 1. Rate of growth in "developed" and "developing" countries

Evolutionary Parameters of economies of "developing" and "developed" countries. Source: database of CIA and World Bank.									
Developing countries					Developed countries				
Country	Rate of growth for 2015 (%); Source: CIA	Investment rate for 2014 (%); Source: World Bank	Productivity of capital; P0 = Ym : K	Density of conditions; Z0 = 1 : P0	Country	Rate of growth for 2015 (%); Source: CIA	Investment rate for 2014 (%); Source: World Bank	Productivity of capital; P0 = Ym : K	Density of conditions; Z0 = 1 : P0
1 Ethiopia	10.2	38	0.453	2.209	1 Ireland	7.8	20	0.740	1.351
2 Bhutan	7.7	58	0.253	3.946	2 Luxembourg	4.5	19	0.605	1.652
3 Laos	7	30	0.467	2.143	3 Sweden	4.1	24	0.463	2.162
4 Tanzania	7	31	0.452	2.214	4 Iceland	4	17	0.647	1.545
5 Cambodia	6.9	22	0.632	1.583	5 Slovakia	3.6	21	0.505	1.981
6 Rwanda	6.9	26	0.535	1.871	6 New Zealand	3.4	23	0.452	2.212
7 Vietnam	6.7	27	0.507	1.971	7 Spain	3.2	20	0.510	1.961
8 Senegal	6.5	26	0.519	1.926	8 Slovenia	2.9	20	0.495	2.020
9 Bangladesh	6.4	29	0.462	2.164	9 Israel	2.6	20	0.480	2.083
10 Mozambique	6.3	46	0.289	3.459	10 Australia	2.5	27	0.352	2.842
11 Panama	5.8	47	0.272	3.672	11 Hong Kong	2.4	24	0.392	2.553
12 Kenya	5.4	22	0.564	1.774	12 United States	2.4	20	0.470	2.128
13 Benin	5.2	25	0.488	2.049	13 United Kingdom	2.2	17	0.541	1.848
14 Malaysia	5	25	0.480	2.083	14 Netherlands	1.9	18	0.494	2.022
15 Uganda	5	27	0.444	2.250	15 Norway	1.6	28	0.307	3.256
16 Morocco	4.5	32	0.359	2.783	16 Germany	1.5	19	0.447	2.235
17 Nicaragua	4.5	27	0.426	2.348	17 Belgium	1.4	23	0.365	2.738
18 Namibia	4.5	33	0.348	2.870	18 Canada	1.2	24	0.342	2.927
19 Egypt	4.2	14	0.800	1.250	19 Denmark	1.2	20	0.410	2.439
20 Pakistan	4.2	15	0.747	1.339	20 France	1.1	23	0.352	2.840
21 Montenegro	4.1	20	0.555	1.802	21 Switzerland	0.9	23	0.343	2.911
22 Sudan	3.5	18	0.583	1.714	22 Austria	0.9	23	0.343	2.911
23 Ghana	3.5	27	0.389	2.571	23 Italy	0.8	16	0.488	2.051
24 Mauritius	3.4	23	0.452	2.212	24 Japan	0.5	22	0.341	2.933
Average:	5.90	29.52	0.48	2.27	Average:	2.44	21.29	0.45	2.32

sity of conditions" $Z_0 = K : Y_m$ in "developing countries" lower in average than in "developed countries". Therefore (the equation (8)) the "rate of growth" in "developing countries" higher than in "developed countries".

EVOLUTIONARY CYCLES OF ECAS

Economists divide economic oscillations into several groups: (1) Kitchin cycle (inventory cycle) of 3-5 years; (2) Juglar (investment cycle) of 7-11 years; (3) Kuznets cycle of 15-25 years (technological cycles) and (4) Kondratieff long waves of 45-60 years (cycles of radical innovations or technological revolutions). There is no final consent between economists concerning the reasons of these cycles. All sectors and technological chains of economic system are interconnected. Therefore upswing (or downswing) spreads over huge number of sectors and industries of economy irrespective to the initial cause of cycle. Each type of cycle indicates represents some special case in the process of qualitative change of the economic system. Economic cycles indicate that process of qualitative updating happens either in all economic system or in some its sectors and industries.

Mitchell (1928) estimated the duration of the different phases of a business cycle as follows:

... the phases of recession and revival are relatively brief. Put together, they account for only one-quarter of the duration of business cycles on the average. On the remaining three quarters, the prosperous phase occupies a somewhat longer time, than the phase of depression. But the ratio of months of prosperity to months of depression varies widely from country to country, and within any country it varies widely from cycle to cycle. (p.420)

Mitchell (1951) gave detailed quantitative description of different phases of "typical" business cycle on the basis of analysis of major volume of statistical information. Mitchell refers in this book to research of Willard L. Thorp, "Business Annals", 1926. Table 28 on page 408 contains figures based on Thorp' results. Relative duration of different phases of business cycles (as a percent of duration of a cycle) calculated on the basis of investigation of cycles in seventeen countries during 1890-1925 is equal: 39.3% - for prosperity phase, 23.9% - for both recession and revival phases and, 36.8% - for depression phase. This result (duration of "prosperity" in average larger than duration of "depression") is consistent with general properties of "evolutionary cycles". Average duration of stages "depression" and "prosperity" of "evolutionary cycle" of the economic system with constant evolutionary parameters depends on mean value of stochastic perturbations of the system. Ideally if stochastic shocks are absent the theoretical duration of "prosperity" equals infinity while duration of "depression" can be computed via the following equation:

$$T_{2\to3} = \frac{1}{a+d} \cdot Ln \left| \frac{\frac{1}{r_2} - 1}{\frac{1}{r_3} - 1} \right| \tag{9}$$

This equation follows from logistic law for "efficiency" (equation (17) from the Introduction). Values r_2 and r_3 are minimal and maximal efficiency of the economic system during "depression" stage of "evolutionary cycle". This equation gives infinite duration of "prosperity stage" of "evolutionary cycle" (the process $4\to1$ in Figure 2 of the Introduction) because maximal "efficiency" in this case equals unit ($r_1 = 1$) and the denominator under a logarithm in the equation (9) aspires to a zero if the economic system approaches to the point 1 (Figure 2 from the Introduction) along "upper evolutionary branch". Consequently the duration of "prosperity" is infinite in pure theoretical evolutionary cycle with infinitely small stochastic shocks. If stochastic shocks are absent then MSP-system don't display the picture of discontinuous cycles. In this case the system approaches infinitely long to the equilibrium point along either "upper" or "lower" evolutionary branch. Stochastic shocks (perturbations of system) reduce duration of "prosperity" and "depression" but if these shocks are small the phase of prosperity will remain being longer than a depression phase.

There are three types of evolutionary cycles: (1) "expansion cycles" (Figure 7), (2) "contraction cycles" (Figure 8) and (3) "stagnation cycles" (Figure 9). According to MSP-approach the "potential" and "conditions of realization" characterize the level of development of complex adaptive system. The "potential" and "conditions of realization" grow in the long run if the system evolves via sequence of "expansion cycles" and vice versa the "potential" and "conditions of realization" decrease in the long run if the system evolves via sequence of "contraction cycles". Third case ("stagnation cycles") describes the situation with almost constant "potential" and "conditions of

Figure 7. "Expansion cycles" in the plane $\left(\Phi;U\right)$. *The following evolutionary parameters were used:* $a = 0.00897$; $d = 0.03$; $\Lambda = 0.07$; $\nu = 0.158$; $C_U = 10$; $C_L = 2$; $\delta = 0.01$.

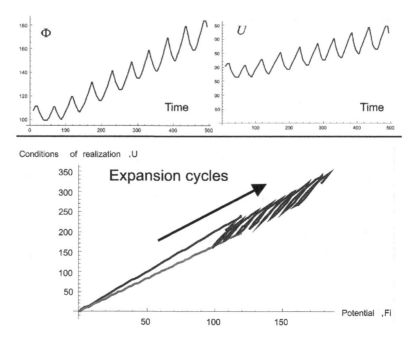

Figure 8. "Contraction cycles" in the plane $\left(\Phi;U\right)$. *The following evolutionary parameters were used:* $a = 0.006$; $d = 0.032$; $\Lambda = 0.07$; $\nu = 0.152$; $C_U = 10$; $C_L = 2$; $\delta = 0.01$

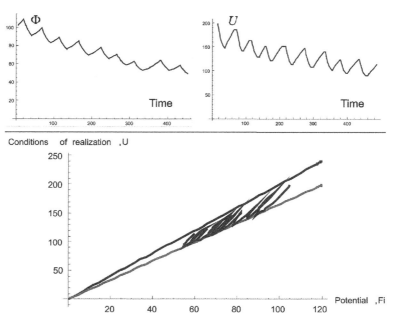

realization". Straight lines in the plane $\left(\Phi;U\right)$ (Figures 7-9) are lines of minimal Z_1 and maximal Z_0 "density of conditions". Evolutionary trajectory of MSP-system is located between these lines. Each jump downwards of "evolutionary cycle" ("crisis" stage of cycle) diminishes the growth rate of "potential" and "conditions of realization" and vice versa each jump upwards of "evolutionary cycle" ("revival" stage of cycle) increases the rate of growth of these variables. The following formulas for the rate of growth follow from equations (E3; E4 and E6 from the Introduction):

$$\frac{\dot{\Phi}}{\Phi} = \left(a + d\right) \cdot \left(R - \frac{d}{a + d}\right) \tag{10}$$

$$\frac{\dot{U}}{U} = \frac{\nu}{Z} \cdot \left(R - \frac{\Lambda}{\nu} \cdot Z\right) \tag{11}$$

Figure 9. "Stagnation cycles" in the plane $\left(\Phi;U\right)$. *The following evolutionary parameters were used:* $a = 0.0074$; $d = 0.0313$; $\Lambda = 0.07$; $\nu = 0.1548$; $C_U = 10$; $C_L = 2$; $\delta = 0.01$

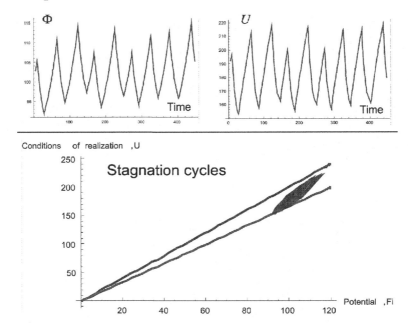

$$\frac{\dot{Z}}{Z} = \left(a + d\right) \cdot \left[\left(1 + \chi\right)\frac{Z_0}{Z} - 1\right] \cdot \left(R - \frac{\chi}{\left(1 + \chi\right)\frac{Z_0}{Z} - 1}\right) \quad (12)$$

Standard MSP-designations were used: $Z_0 = \dfrac{\nu}{a + \Lambda}$; $\chi = \dfrac{\Lambda - d}{a + d}$.

Equations $\dot{\Phi} = 0$; $\dot{U} = 0$; $\dot{Z} = 0$ determine three curves in the plane $\left(Z;R\right)$:

1. Curve of constant "potential" ($\dot{\Phi} = 0$) is a straight line:

$$R = \frac{d}{a + d} \quad (13)$$

2. Curve of constant "conditions of realization" ($\dot{U} = 0$) is a straight line:

$$R = \frac{\Lambda}{\nu} \cdot Z \tag{14}$$

3.   Curve of constant "density of conditions" ($\dot{Z} = 0$) is a hyperbole:

$$R = \frac{\chi}{\left(1 + \chi\right)\dfrac{Z_0}{Z} - 1} \tag{15}$$

Asymptotes of the hyperbole (15): $R = -\chi$ and $Z = \left(1 + \chi\right)Z_0$. Regions of plane $\left(Z; R\right)$ above (below) of these curves correspond to the growth (the decrease) of variable. Pushnoi (2003) introduced notion "version of development" for triad of signs of derivatives $\left\{\dot{\Phi}\left(t\right); \dot{U}\left(t\right); \dot{Z}\left(t\right)\right\}$. If sign of derivative $\dot{\Phi}\left(t\right)$ is positive (negative) function $\Phi\left(t\right)$ increases (↑) (decreases (↓)). Arrows mean growth (↑) or decrease (↓) of a variable. Each "version of development" is described mathematically as a triad of type $\left\{\Phi \uparrow; U \uparrow; Z \downarrow\right\}$. It means that "potential" and "conditions of realization" grow and "density of conditions" decreases. There are six "versions of development":

1.   **"Strong Prosperity":** $\left\{\Phi \uparrow; U \uparrow; Z \uparrow\right\}$,
2.   **"Weak Prosperity":** $\left\{\Phi \uparrow; U \uparrow; Z \downarrow\right\}$,
3.   **"Strong Depression":** $\left\{\Phi \downarrow; U \downarrow; Z \downarrow\right\}$,
4.   **"Weak Depression":** $\left\{\Phi \downarrow; U \downarrow; Z \uparrow\right\}$,
5.   **"Transition Period - I":** $\left\{\Phi \uparrow; U \downarrow; Z \downarrow\right\}$,
6.   **"Transition Period-II":** $\left\{\Phi \downarrow; U \uparrow; Z \uparrow\right\}$.

Figure 10 illustrates splitting of plane $\left(Z; R\right)$ onto six "regions" with definite monotonicity properties of functions $\left\{\Phi\left(t\right); U\left(t\right); Z\left(t\right)\right\}$. Each region of plane $\left(Z; R\right)$ in Figure 10 corresponds to definite "version of development". "Upper evolutionary branch" (states of "prosperity") in Figure 10 corresponds to the version of "strong prosperity" whereas "lower evolutionary branch" corresponds to the version of "strong depression". Relative positioning of evolutionary branches and curves $\dot{\Phi} = 0; \dot{U} = 0; \dot{Z} = 0$ are depictured in

Figure 10. "Versions of development" in the plane $(Z;R)$. *The following evolution-ary parameters were used:* $a = 0.019$; $d = 0.0255$; $\Lambda = 0.07$; $\nu = 0.178$; $C_U = 10$; $C_L = 0.5$

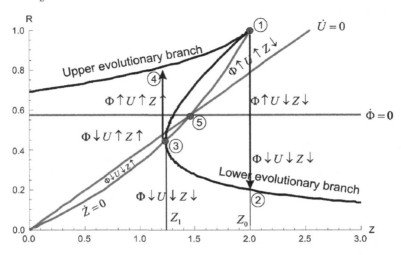

Figures 11-13. Point 5 in these Figures is the point of intersection of curves $\dot{\Phi} = 0; \dot{U} = 0; \dot{Z} = 0$. Point 3 is the point of "lower evolutionary branch" with coordinate Z_1. This is the point of unstable equilibrium on the lower part of "lower evolutionary branch".

Three cases of relative positioning of evolutionary branches and curves $\dot{\Phi} = 0; \dot{U} = 0; \dot{Z} = 0$ are possible:

Case 1 (Figure 11): Point 5 is located above point 3 in the plane $(Z;R)$.

The sequence of "versions of development" in this case is following: "upper evolutionary branch" - "Transition Period-II" and "Strong Pros-perity"; "lower evolutionary branch" - "Strong Depression".

Case 2 (Figure 12): Point 5 is located below point 3 in the plane $(Z;R)$.

The sequence of "versions of development" in this case is following: "upper evolutionary branch" - "Strong Prosperity"; "lower evolutionary branch" - "Strong Depression", "Transition Period - I", "Weak Prosper-ity".

Case 3 (Figure 13): Points 5 and 3 coincide. The sequence of "versions of development" in this case is following: "upper evolutionary branch" - "Strong Prosperity"; "lower evolutionary branch" - "Strong Depression".

Figure 11. Relative positioning of evolutionary branches and curves $\dot{\Phi} = 0; \dot{U} = 0; \dot{Z} = 0$ *(point 5 is above point 3)*

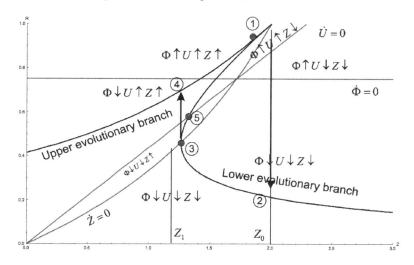

Figure 12. Relative positioning of evolutionary branches and curves $\dot{\Phi} = 0; \dot{U} = 0; \dot{Z} = 0$ *(point 5 is below point 3)*

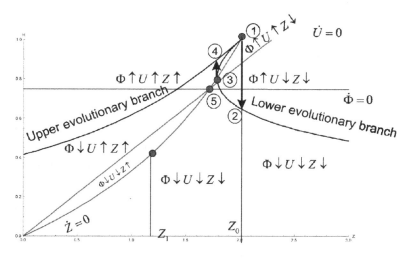

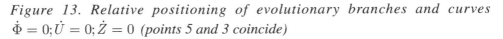

Figure 13. Relative positioning of evolutionary branches and curves $\dot{\Phi} = 0; \dot{U} = 0; \dot{Z} = 0$ *(points 5 and 3 coincide)*

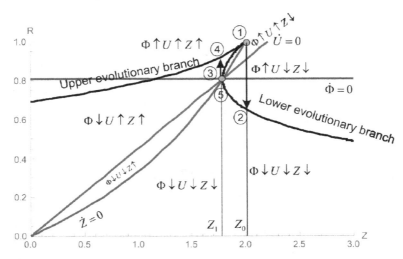

Version of development "Weak Depression" is possible for pure "evolutionary cycles" only in the case-1 during "revival stage" of cycle (Figure 11).

Economic interpretation of "evolutionary cycles" ("potential" is "maximal output"; $\Phi \rightarrow Y_m$ and "conditions of realization" is "capital stock"; $U \rightarrow K$) can be used for the analysis of the economic development of the real economic systems. The actual dynamics of economic indicators of course is much more complex than the simple picture of four-stage discontinuous cycles. Nevertheless just evolutionary cycles in their simple form are the basis of the strongest and sudden changes in economic dynamics. Four stages of the "business cycle" ("prosperity" – "crisis" - "depression" – "revival") are actually the stages of "evolutionary cycle" of the economic complex adaptive system. Economy evolves as complex adaptive system and general regularities of these systems are working in the economic system also. Deviations of actual economic dynamics from simple sequence of irregular quadric-phase evolutionary cycles can be explained (and described) via terms of MSP-model of the economic CAS. The basic causes which deform simple picture are the following: 1) the influence of external factors, 2) the changes of evolutionary parameters and 3) the change of location of "preferable evolutionary branches" (for example the shift of "evolutionary branches").

The next chapter contains description of MSP-model of ECAS with constant evolutionary parameters. We specify (concretize) model due to choice of production function $Y = Y(K; L; ...)$. This step opens new possibilities for applications of the model in economics.

SPECIFICATION OF MSP-MODEL OF ECAS[4]

The choice of production function is ambiguous. There are many possibilities for the choice of mathematical expression of production function: Cobb-Douglas function, Leontief' production function, CES production function and so on. Quantity of production factors (independent variables of production function) also variate. We consider the simplest case – classical Cobb-Douglas production function:

$$Y(t) = Y\left(K_e(t), L_e(t), A(t)\right) = A(t) \cdot K_e(t)^{\beta} \cdot L_e(t)^{\alpha} \tag{16}$$

Symbol "e" designates that production function depends on employed capital and labor. The physical capital stock K is functioning in both ways, as constituent of economic potential and as the main condition for realization of economic potential in production. Labor L is the second determinant factor of economic potential. The third factor, A total factor productivity, describes aggregate influence of technologies, institutions and human capital onto "economic potential". "Economic potential" and "realized potential" can be quantitatively estimated by means of "economic capacity" (maximal output, Y_m) and actual output, Y. Expansion and contraction of production follows oscillations of demand. This is relatively rapid process. The change of total factor productivity A (adoption of innovations, installation of know-how and so on) is much slower process. Therefore the short-run expansion (or contraction) of production (short-term adjustment) proceeds at almost constant factor A. In "steady state" the growth of production factors (capital and labor) in λ times provides for the growth of output also in λ times if the total factor productivity (TFP) doesn't change. It means that Cobb-Douglas function displays constant returns to scale:

$$\alpha + \beta = 1 \tag{17}$$

In this case the equations are:

$$Y\left(t\right) = A\left(t\right) \cdot K_e\left(t\right)^{\beta} \cdot L_e\left(t\right)^{1-\beta} \qquad (18)$$

$$\lambda \cdot Y\left(t\right) = A\left(t\right) \cdot \left(\lambda \cdot K_e\left(t\right)\right)^{\beta} \cdot \left(\lambda \cdot L_e\left(t\right)\right)^{1-\beta} \qquad (19)$$

Let's use the following designations:

$$k = \frac{K_e}{L_e} = \text{The capital intensity,} \qquad (20)$$

$$y = \frac{Y}{L_e} = \text{The productivity of labor,} \qquad (21)$$

$$f_L \equiv \frac{L_e}{L} = \text{The rate of utilization of labor,} \qquad (22)$$

$$f_K \equiv \frac{K_e}{K} = \text{The rate of utilization of capital,} \qquad (23)$$

$$k_0 = \left(\frac{\beta}{1-\beta}\right) \cdot \frac{w}{r} = \text{Optimal capital intensity.} \qquad (24)$$

Rates of utilization of capital and labor are equal if capital intensity is constant. Real wage w paid for labor and rental price of capital r in (24) determine optimal capital intensity, k_0 with maximum output under condition of fixed expenditure (when output is maximal while expenditures are fixed)[5]:

$$Y \to \max ; \text{ subject to } w \cdot L_e + r \cdot K_e = Const \qquad (25)$$

Main Properties of MSP-ECAS-Model

Let $L; K$ are maximal available stocks of labor and capital for production with optimal capital intensity. The factual output depends on employed capital K_e and on employed labor L_e and the total factor productivity A (Solow, 1957). We have in our model:

$$Y = A \cdot K_e^{\beta} \cdot L_e^{1-\beta} = A \cdot L_e \cdot k^{\beta} \tag{26}$$

$$y = A \cdot k^{\beta} \tag{27}$$

$$P = \frac{y}{k} = \frac{A}{k^{1-\beta}} = \frac{A \cdot k^{\beta}}{k} \tag{28}$$

"Maximal output" Y_m in this model can be determined as output subject to optimal capital intensity and full utilization of production factors.

$$Y_m = A_m \cdot K^{\beta} L^{1-\beta} = A_m \cdot L \cdot k_m^{\beta} \tag{29}$$

$$y_m \equiv \frac{Y_m}{L} = A_m \cdot k_m^{\beta} \; ; \; k_m \equiv \frac{K}{L} \tag{30}$$

$$P_0 = \frac{y_m}{k_m} = \frac{A_m}{k_m^{1-\beta}} = \frac{A_m k_m^{\beta}}{k_m} \tag{31}$$

$$k_m = k_0 \tag{32}$$

The substitution of production function (29) into the general formulas of MSP-model give us new non-trivial regularities which exist between economic indicators such as "productivity of capital", "productivity of labor", "capital intensity" and "capacity utilization rate". The following equation for "efficiency of the Economic CAS" can be deduced using from the equations (22), (26)-(32):

$$R = \frac{Y}{Y_m} = f_L \cdot \frac{A}{A_m} \cdot \left(\frac{k}{k_0}\right)^{\beta} = f_L \cdot \frac{P \cdot k}{P_0 \cdot k_0} = \frac{f_L \cdot y}{y_m} \qquad (33)$$

Productivity of labor y follows from the equation (33) which can be re-written as:

$$R = f_L \cdot \frac{y}{P_0 \cdot k_0}$$

$$y = R \cdot \frac{P_0 \cdot k_0}{f_L} \qquad (34)$$

Let's substitute MSP-equations (4)-(5) for "efficiency of economic CAS" into the equation (34). It gives us two equations which connect "productivity of labor" and "productivity of capital".

$$y(P) = \frac{P_0 \cdot k_0}{f_L \cdot \left[1 + \left(\dfrac{P - P_0}{C_U \cdot PP_0}\right)^{\frac{1}{1+\chi}}\right]} \text{ for "upper evolutionary branch"}, \qquad (35)$$

$$y(P) = \frac{P_0 \cdot k_0}{f_L \cdot \left[1 + \left(\dfrac{P_0 - P}{C_L \cdot PP_0}\right)^{\frac{1}{1+\chi}}\right]} \text{ for "lower evolutionary branch"}, \qquad (36)$$

$$k_0 = \left(\frac{A_m}{P_0}\right)^{\frac{1}{1-\beta}} \qquad (37)$$

Capital intensity equals:

$$k(P) = \frac{y(P)}{P} \qquad (38)$$

STATISTICAL REGULARITIES IN STYLIZED FACTS: APPLICATION OF MSP-MODEL TO THE EUROPEAN ECONOMIC SYSTEM

We obtained functional dependence $y(P)$ (equations (35)-(36)) between productivity of labor and productivity of capital if optimal productivity of capital P_0 and capital intensity k_0 are fixed. The existence of functional dependence (35)-(36) is non-trivial surprising fact which follows from MSP-model of ECAS. Equations (35)-(36) and (38) determine parametrically the function $y(k)$. Graphs of functions $y(P)$ ("productivity of labor" versus "productivity of capital") and $y(k)$ ("productivity of labor" versus "capital intensity") are depictured in Figures 14 and 15. The different curves in the planes $(P; y)$ (Figure 14) and $(k; y)$ (Figure 15) correspond to different constants $C_U; C_L$. Parameters P_0 and k_0 for these schedules are fixed. This assumption is not fulfilled in the long run because parameter k_0 changes with time. Technological progress can be described as the growth of maximal total factor productivity A_m. For example, we can model technological progress in mathematical form of exponential growth i.e.:

$$A_m(t) = A_m(0) \cdot Exp\{n \cdot t\}; \; n > 0 \qquad (39)$$

If optimal productivity of capital P_0 and parameter β don't change with time optimal capital intensity k_0 grows with time according to the equation (37). This growth shifts upwards with time the curves $y(P)$ depictured in Figure 14. Parameter β is almost constant during the long run. Productivity of capital changes insignificantly in long-run. For example the productivity of employed capital in the U.S. nonfarm industry before 1930 was almost the constant (≈ 0.3) – Figure 16.

Figure 14. Productivity of labor ($y = \dfrac{Y}{L}$) as function of productivity of capital (

$P = \dfrac{Y}{K}$)(equations (35)-(37)). The following parameters were used: $a = d = 0.02$;

$P_0 = 0.32$; $\nu = 0.2$; $\beta = 0.3$; $A_m = 20$ $fL = 1$. Curves in this Figure differ by
value of constants: $C_U = C_L$ = {0.01; 0.05; 0.1; 0.2; 0.3; 0.5; 0.6; 0.8; 1}.*

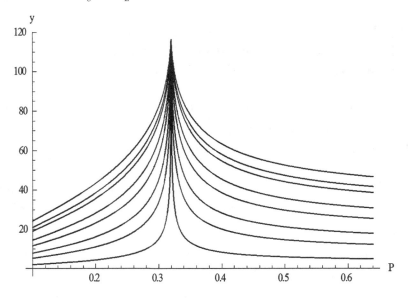

Cusp peak is the typical geometric form for the function $y(P)$ with fixed
parameters P_0 and k_0 . This dependence is not that obvious because parameters P_0 and k_0 are not constant and change in course of time. However, if
we consider large numbers of points depicturing productivity of capital and
productivity of labor for different years and (or) in different countries, we
can find that all these points are located inside of the area with a frontier of
geometric form of cusp. Giussani (2004) depictured stylized facts about
"productivity of capital" and "productivity of labor" in 118 countries during
period 1963-2000 as points in the plane (P, y) . Envelope curve for these
empirical points (Giussani, 2005; Figure 4) is very similar to theoretical curve
$y(P)$ with geometric form of cusp. Envelope curve for empirical points
(k, y) (Giussani, 2005; Figure 3) is very similar to theoretical curve $y(k)$.

Figure 15. Productivity of labor ($y = \dfrac{Y}{L}$) as function of capital intensity ($k = \dfrac{K}{L}$) (formulas (35)-(38)). The following parameters were used: $a = d = 0.02$; $P_0 = 0.32$; $\nu = 0.2$; $\beta = 0.3$; $A_m = 20$ fL $= 1$. Curves in this Figure differ by value of constants: $C_U = C_L = \{0.01; 0.05; 0.1; 0.2; 0.3; 0.5; 0.6; 0.8; 1\}$.

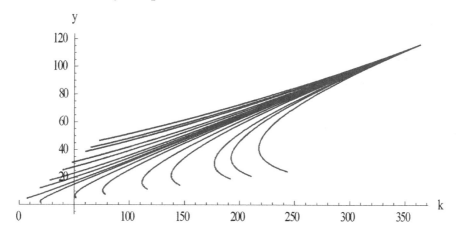

Figure 16. Productivity of employed capital in U.S. nonfarm industry during 1909-1945 years
Source: Sollow (1957).

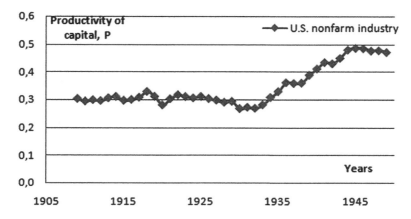

Figures 17 and 18 illustrate the existence of these statistical regularities for 68 countries during 1950-2014 years. We used Penn World Tables, version 9.0. Labor input was calculated as the product of average annual hours worked by persons engaged and number of persons engaged (in millions), the product of PWT-concepts "emp" and "avh". The output, Y is the real GDP at constant 2011 national prices (in mil. 2011US$), PWT-concept "rgdpna". The capital stock, K is the capital stock at constant 2011 national prices (in mil. 2011US$), PWT-concept "rkna". Visual comparison of Figure 14 and 17 and Figures 15 and 18 confirm the existence of statistical regularities which can be theoretically explained on the basis of MSP-model of ECAS.

According to MSP-model of ECAS the conditions for realization of economic potential basically depend in on the quantity of capital stock in the country. However the conditions of realization of economic potential of a country often depend on the influence of external factors also. Therefore, strictly speaking, MSP-model of ECAS describes only self-sufficient (almost closed) economic systems. Macroscopic dynamics of economic systems of this type is regulated mainly by inner factors. European Union (EU) is the example of almost closed and self-sufficient economic system. European

Figure 17. Productivity of labor ($y = \dfrac{Y}{L}$) vs. productivity of capital ($P = \dfrac{Y}{K}$) for 68 countries; 1950-2014
Source: Penn Tables 9.0.

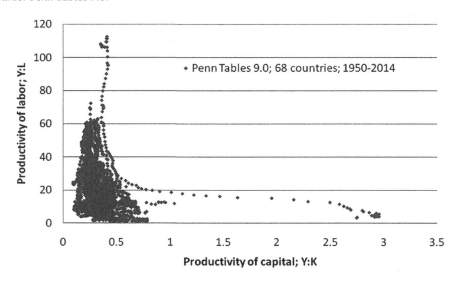

Figure 18. Productivity of labor vs. capital intensity for 68 countries; 1950-2014
Source: Penn Tables 9.0.

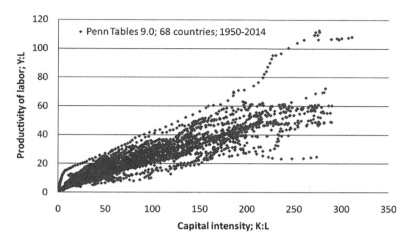

Union as a holistic economic system was created at the end of 1950s. The Treaty establishing the European Economic Community (The Treaty of Rome), was signed on 25 March 1957 by Belgium, France, Italy, Luxembourg, the Netherlands and West Germany. This Treaty came into force on 1 January 1958. Therefore stylized facts about economic development of European countries before 1960 year can't be interpreted as data about European economic system as a whole. It is necessary to divide economic history of Europe on two qualitatively different periods, before and after 1960.

We consider below the economic stylized facts for 18 countries of Europe: Austria, Belgium, Switzerland, Cyprus, Germany, Denmark, Spain, Finland, France, United Kingdom, Ireland, Iceland, Italy, Luxembourg, Netherlands, Norway, Portugal, and Sweden (1950-2014). These are the countries of European Union before 1990. We consider only the largest countries of Europe which mainly determine dynamics of all European economic system. We used Penn World Tables (PWT), version 9.0. In Penn Tables data for Greece are given only for beginning of the year 1951. Therefore we excluded Greece from our list[6].

Documentation of the different PWT-concepts is given in the paper Feenstra et al. (2015). We used the following PWT-concepts as economic variables of MSP-model:

1. **The Output,** Y : Real GDP at constant 2011 national prices (in mil. 2011US\$), PWT-concept "rgdpna";
2. **The Capital Stock,** K : Capital stock at constant 2011 national prices (in mil. 2011US\$), PWT-concept "rkna";
3. **Labor Input,** Le : The product of average annual hours worked by persons engaged and number of persons engaged (in millions), the product of PWT-concepts "emp" and "avh".
4. **Investment Rate:** Share of gross capital formation at current PPPs, PWT-concept "csh_i";
5. **Depreciation Rate:** Average depreciation rate of the capital stock, PWT-concept "delta";
6. **Share of Labor in GDP:** Share of labour compensation in GDP at current national prices; PWT-concept "labsh".

We also used data about unemployment: database of World Bank (after 1990) and database Knoema (1956-1990). Labor force of each country was calculated via unemployment rate and number of persons engaged. GDP, capital stock, labor force, and labor input of European economy were calculated as summation over these countries. The investment rate and the share of labor in GDP were calculated as weighted arithmetic means where the weight of separate country equals its share in total GDP. The depreciation rate was calculated as a sum of depreciation over 18 countries per the total capital ratio. The employment rate, f_L, in European economy was calculated as total number of persons engaged per the total labor force ratio.

Table 2 contains data for the economic system consisting of 18 European countries. Productivity of labor, $y = \dfrac{Y}{L}$, productivity of capital, $P = \dfrac{Y}{K}$, and capital intensity, $k = \dfrac{K}{L}$ are presented in columns (6)-(8) of this Table. We used Solow' (1957) algorithm for calculation of "Solow' residual", total factor productivity, TFP (column (9) of the Table 2). Least-square procedure for Cobb-Douglas production function (18) determines parameter β. This parameter equals $\beta \approx 0.347$ (column (10). Normalized TFP is calculated by means of the equation (27): $A_{norm} = \dfrac{y}{k^{\beta}}$ (column (11)).

The factual dependence of productivity of labor versus productivity of capital, $y(P)$, is depictured in Figure 19 by solid line. According to MSP-model of ECAS the theoretical dependence $y_{theor.}(P)$ can be described by

Table 2. Stylized facts for European economy, 1950-2014

Years	Real GDP; Y (in mil. 2011US$)	Capital Stock; K (in mil. 2011US$)	Labor; L (millions of man-hours)	Share of labor compensation in GDP.	Productivity of labor	Productivity of capital	Capital intensity	A	β	A norm.
	rgdpna	rkna	emp*avh	labish	$y = Y : L$	$P = Y : K$	$k = K : L$	Solow' residual	Least Square Procedure	$\dfrac{y}{k^\beta}$
(1)	(2)	(3)	(4)	(5)	(6)	(7)	(8)	(9)	(10)	(11)
1950	2297581.1	7845911.2	287840.7	0.6723	7.982	0.293	27.258	1.0000	0.347	2.535
1951	2451783.1	8128897.2	290813.0	0.6708	8.431	0.302	27.952	1.0479	0.347	2.654
1952	2545556.0	8424810.5	292073.1	0.6738	8.715	0.302	28.845	1.0722	0.347	2.714
1953	2676344.1	8748102.1	294069.5	0.6705	9.101	0.306	29.748	1.1087	0.347	2.804
1954	2830984.5	9131375.5	297623.8	0.6706	9.512	0.310	30.681	1.1473	0.347	2.900
1955	3010646.5	9609805.3	301292.0	0.6692	9.992	0.313	31.895	1.1903	0.347	3.005
1956	3151034.9	10102923.4	302695.9	0.6683	10.410	0.312	33.376	1.2218	0.347	3.082
1957	3276062.7	10612324.6	303564.7	0.6680	10.792	0.309	34.959	1.2474	0.347	3.144
1958	3357376.0	11093316.0	302346.3	0.6675	11.104	0.303	36.691	1.2630	0.347	3.181
1959	3517657.0	11621159.8	302919.5	0.6645	11.613	0.303	38.364	1.3016	0.347	3.276
1960	3778666.7	12289940.1	304999.3	0.6636	12.389	0.307	40.295	1.3667	0.347	3.436
1961	3989834.5	13001415.3	304800.3	0.6627	13.090	0.307	42.656	1.4171	0.347	3.559
1962	4188458.3	13730488.5	303217.4	0.6655	13.813	0.305	45.283	1.4659	0.347	3.679
1963	4383273.3	14453501.6	301953.8	0.6646	14.516	0.303	47.867	1.5126	0.347	3.792
1964	4634265.4	15297175.1	304269.3	0.6630	15.231	0.303	50.275	1.5615	0.347	3.912
1965	4843082.3	16152098.0	301785.0	0.6616	16.048	0.300	53.522	1.6113	0.347	4.033
1966	5024764.9	17029459.1	300085.8	0.6609	16.744	0.295	56.749	1.6483	0.347	4.123
1967	5194946.3	17896356.5	296127.2	0.6600	17.543	0.290	60.435	1.6906	0.347	4.227
1968	5489298.0	18847830.7	294589.8	0.6591	18.634	0.291	63.980	1.7620	0.347	4.402
1969	5801961.5	19908176.1	294092.6	0.6563	19.728	0.291	67.694	1.8307	0.347	4.570
1970	6139867.5	21122676.2	293218.7	0.6556	20.940	0.291	72.037	1.9027	0.347	4.747
1971	6362631.2	22349438.1	290134.4	0.6549	21.930	0.285	77.031	1.9472	0.347	4.857
1972	6655456.6	23603464.9	287617.8	0.6558	23.140	0.282	82.065	2.0108	0.347	5.014
1973	7051004.5	24926148.6	289117.0	0.6537	24.388	0.283	86.215	2.0842	0.347	5.194
1974	7221031.3	26164868.0	286566.4	0.6525	25.198	0.276	91.305	2.1109	0.347	5.261
1975	7143438.6	27252025.5	279978.1	0.6565	25.514	0.262	97.336	2.0889	0.347	5.210
1976	7460874.5	28338818.1	280970.5	0.6563	26.554	0.263	100.860	2.1480	0.347	5.356
1977	7675758.2	29431748.3	279066.7	0.6555	27.505	0.261	105.465	2.1913	0.347	5.463
1978	7909538.7	30540247.8	276916.2	0.6565	28.563	0.259	110.287	2.2410	0.347	5.585
1979	8210695.3	31681732.7	276968.1	0.6544	29.645	0.259	114.388	2.2973	0.347	5.724
1980	8348670.4	32794401.6	276337.9	0.6539	30.212	0.255	118.675	2.3115	0.347	5.759
1981	8383282.2	33762530.1	271352.5	0.6523	30.894	0.248	124.423	2.3249	0.347	5.794
1982	8457803.3	34662248.5	267358.3	0.6520	31.635	0.244	129.647	2.3467	0.347	5.848
1983	8614571.2	35537922.0	265627.8	0.6494	32.431	0.242	133.788	2.3797	0.347	5.931
1984	8832612.9	36429466.3	264893.0	0.6417	33.344	0.242	137.525	2.4234	0.347	6.039
1985	9069950.6	37348033.5	264651.5	0.6398	34.271	0.243	141.122	2.4681	0.347	6.152
1986	9316130.7	38328198.8	265786.7	0.6362	35.051	0.243	144.207	2.5048	0.347	6.245
1987	9595746.3	39405687.1	269046.5	0.6352	35.666	0.244	146.464	2.5344	0.347	6.320
1988	10004157.3	40664156.7	273615.8	0.6305	36.563	0.246	148.618	2.5846	0.347	6.447
1989	10376280.2	42044720.4	275500.6	0.6290	37.663	0.247	152.612	2.6367	0.347	6.580
1990	10697515.0	43379613.2	276547.8	0.6336	38.682	0.247	156.861	2.6808	0.347	6.694
1991	10905532.7	44620125.0	272293.3	0.6365	40.051	0.244	163.868	2.7318	0.347	6.826
1992	11041647.3	45790557.7	268283.9	0.6377	41.157	0.241	170.679	2.7659	0.347	6.916
1993	11022152.9	46747191.1	262454.7	0.6327	41.996	0.236	178.115	2.7787	0.347	6.954
1994	11327612.1	47766334.6	262554.2	0.6230	43.144	0.237	181.929	2.8328	0.347	7.091
1995	11611108.8	48905847.3	264435.3	0.6154	43.909	0.237	184.944	2.8653	0.347	7.176
1996	11828486.0	50073358.8	266027.0	0.6142	44.463	0.236	188.227	2.8819	0.347	7.223
1997	12154926.7	51259630.1	267604.3	0.6093	45.421	0.237	191.550	2.9244	0.347	7.333
1998	12517791.0	52592823.0	272410.7	0.6069	45.952	0.238	193.064	2.9495	0.347	7.399
1999	12890021.8	54019731.1	276766.2	0.6124	46.574	0.239	195.182	2.9767	0.347	7.471
2000	13387637.4	55510013.5	279754.4	0.6095	47.855	0.241	198.424	3.0394	0.347	7.632
2001	13675032.3	56947131.2	281900.7	0.6098	48.510	0.240	202.011	3.0596	0.347	7.689
2002	13828920.3	58295025.1	281309.5	0.6094	49.159	0.237	207.227	3.0697	0.347	7.723
2003	13961687.0	59620736.6	281400.7	0.6078	49.615	0.234	211.871	3.0713	0.347	7.735
2004	14285835.9	60997229.9	284082.9	0.5995	50.288	0.234	214.716	3.0967	0.347	7.804
2005	14564586.2	62463115.9	286465.4	0.5959	50.842	0.233	218.048	3.1117	0.347	7.848
2006	15016726.6	64064665.9	290816.1	0.5921	51.637	0.234	220.293	3.1473	0.347	7.942
2007	15450965.8	65755137.7	296256.3	0.5870	52.154	0.235	221.954	3.1692	0.347	8.001
2008	15501888.4	67302908.8	297693.5	0.5910	52.073	0.230	226.081	3.1399	0.347	7.938
2009	14831837.4	68311224.9	288710.4	0.6085	51.373	0.217	236.608	3.0379	0.347	7.708
2010	15158254.3	69298755.4	288958.0	0.5996	52.458	0.219	239.823	3.0859	0.347	7.834
2011	15431013.2	70314726.0	290316.2	0.5973	53.152	0.219	242.200	3.1145	0.347	7.911
2012	15374045.7	71193475.7	287933.3	0.5990	53.394	0.216	247.257	3.1025	0.347	7.890
2013	15401526.6	71964256.0	286028.8	0.5997	53.846	0.214	251.598	3.1069	0.347	7.909
2014	15598647.8	72802264.2	288868.1	0.6000	53.999	0.214	252.026	3.1136	0.347	7.927

Source: Penn Tables, version 9.0.

Figure 19. Productivity of labor versus productivity of capital; European economy, 1950-2014; solid line corresponds to factual data, dashed line show theoretical values (Table 3, columns (11)-(12))
Source: Penn Tables 9.0.

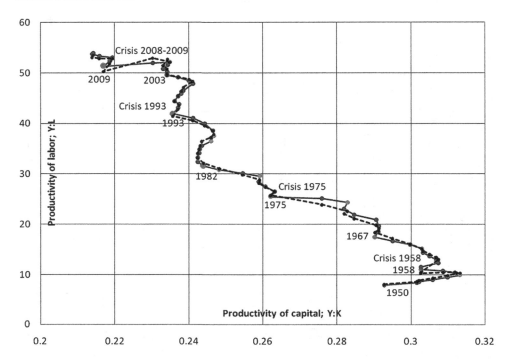

means of equations (35)-(37). However these equations contain two unknown variable parameters: long-term productivity of capital, P_0 and maximal total factor productivity, TFP, A_m.

We can estimate parameter P_0 using equation of the model: $P_0 = \dfrac{a + \Lambda}{\nu}$. Annual estimates of parameter P_0 can be calculated on the basis of annual data about rate of growth, depreciation rate and investment rate. These values are presented in the Table 3 (columns (2)-(5)). Figure 20 shows the change of estimate P_0 with time. We see that long-term productivity of capital in average decreases with time. Estimates for parameter P_0 oscillate around trend due to the high volatility of the rate of growth. Figure 21 shows the dynamics of the rate of growth with time. Schedule at this Figure have peaks and troughs. Oscillations in the current rate of growth drift estimate for the

Main Properties of MSP-ECAS-Model

Table 3. Long-term productivity of capital, maximal total factor productivity and productivity of labor (factual and theoretical) for European economy; 1950-2014. Values in columns (2)-(4) are calculated on the basis of data from the Table 2. "True" long term productivity of capital was calculated via equation (41). Factual values for maximal total factor productivity, TFP max (column (9)) were calculated via equations (42)-(43). Theoretical values of TFP max (column (10)) were calculated via equation (45). Theoretical values of productivity of labor (column (12)) were calculated via equations (46)-(47).

Year	Rate of growth	Depreciaton rate; Λ	Investment rate; ν	Estimate for long-term productivity of capital	"True" long-term productivity of the capital	Unemployment rate; %	Utilization of labor force	TFP max	TFP max	y, factual	y theor.
	a	Weighted mean for 18 countries	Weighted mean for 18 countries	$\dfrac{a+\Lambda}{\nu}$	P0 = quadratic trend with multipliers k1; k2; k3	Knoema Database and Database of World Bank	100% - (7)	Am, factual.	Am, theor.; linear thrend		
(1)	(2)	(3)	(4)	(5)	(6)	(7)	(8)	(9)	(10)	(11)	(12)
1950		0.0396	0.2304	0.4314	0.3536	n/a	97.000%	3.551	3.6000	7.982	8.150
1951	0.0671	0.0408	0.2501	0.4314	0.3536	n/a	97.000%	3.532	3.6000	8.431	8.680
1952	0.0382	0.0415	0.2513	0.3175	0.3504	n/a	97.000%	3.550	3.6000	8.715	8.905
1953	0.0514	0.0423	0.2500	0.3745	0.3472	n/a	97.000%	3.533	3.6000	9.101	9.365
1954	0.0578	0.0431	0.2631	0.3834	0.3442	n/a	97.000%	3.510	3.6000	9.512	9.887
1955	0.0635	0.0441	0.2849	0.3776	0.3411	n/a	97.000%	3.510	3.6000	9.992	10.389
1956	0.0466	0.0449	0.2907	0.3150	0.3381	3.271%	96.729%	3.566	3.6000	10.410	10.564
1957	0.0397	0.0456	0.2963	0.2880	0.3351	2.912%	97.088%	3.661	3.6000	10.792	10.519
1958	0.0248	0.0461	0.2906	0.2439	0.3321	2.916%	97.084%	3.790	3.6000	11.104	10.265
1959	0.0477	0.0463	0.3011	0.3123	0.3292	2.626%	97.374%	3.846	3.6000	11.613	10.495
1960	0.0742	0.0467	0.3243	0.3728	0.3264	2.019%	97.981%	3.858	4.0003	12.389	13.094
1961	0.0559	0.0471	0.3148	0.3272	0.3235	1.758%	98.242%	3.950	4.0305	13.090	13.498
1962	0.0498	0.0472	0.3053	0.3177	0.3208	1.696%	98.304%	4.065	4.1254	13.813	14.130
1963	0.0465	0.0470	0.3025	0.3091	0.3180	1.716%	98.284%	4.168	4.2177	14.516	14.782
1964	0.0573	0.0469	0.3198	0.3257	0.3153	1.514%	98.386%	4.236	4.2342	15.231	15.224
1965	0.0451	0.0471	0.3167	0.2911	0.3126	1.725%	98.275%	4.384	4.3954	16.048	16.114
1966	0.0375	0.0472	0.3110	0.2725	0.3100	1.809%	98.191%	4.558	4.6432	16.744	17.229
1967	0.0339	0.0473	0.2986	0.2719	0.3074	2.383%	97.617%	4.739	4.8913	17.543	18.416
1968	0.0567	0.0470	0.2992	0.3465	0.3048	2.428%	97.572%	4.812	4.8414	18.634	18.808
1969	0.0570	0.0470	0.3095	0.3360	0.3023	2.120%	97.880%	4.909	4.8314	19.728	19.250
1970	0.0582	0.0468	0.3275	0.3207	0.2998	2.049%	97.951%	5.039	4.8708	20.940	19.877
1971	0.0363	0.0467	0.3115	0.2665	0.2974	2.306%	97.694%	5.301	5.1813	21.930	21.174
1972	0.0460	0.0465	0.2995	0.3087	0.2950	2.718%	97.282%	5.479	5.3223	23.140	22.133
1973	0.0594	0.0456	0.3068	0.3423	0.2926	2.532%	97.468%	5.541	5.2753	24.388	22.619
1974	0.0241	0.0447	0.3054	0.2254	0.2903	2.755%	97.245%	5.828	5.6329	25.198	23.918
1975	-0.0107	0.0447	0.2712	0.1250	0.2880	4.035%	95.965%	6.308	6.3516	25.514	25.785
1976	0.0444	0.0446	0.2823	0.3154	0.2857	4.611%	95.389%	6.297	6.2920	26.554	26.520
1977	0.0288	0.0447	0.2743	0.2679	0.2835	4.912%	95.088%	6.440	6.4204	27.505	27.376
1978	0.0305	0.0443	0.2694	0.2773	0.2813	5.140%	94.860%	6.571	6.5143	28.563	28.185
1979	0.0381	0.0435	0.2787	0.2926	0.2792	5.190%	94.810%	6.615	6.5052	29.645	28.894
1980	0.0168	0.0426	0.2820	0.2107	0.2771	5.657%	94.343%	6.797	6.7431	30.212	29.844
1981	0.0041	0.0425	0.2587	0.1803	0.2750	7.222%	92.778%	7.038	7.0685	30.894	31.099
1982	0.0089	0.0427	0.2602	0.1983	0.2730	8.513%	91.487%	7.205	7.2913	31.635	32.216
1983	0.0185	0.0428	0.2560	0.2396	0.2710	9.417%	90.583%	7.258	7.3743	32.431	33.230
1984	0.0253	0.0428	0.2593	0.2625	0.2690	9.834%	90.166%	7.260	7.3716	33.394	34.131
1985	0.0269	0.0432	0.2589	0.2707	0.2671	9.880%	90.120%	7.260	7.3513	34.271	34.935
1986	0.0271	0.0433	0.2626	0.2681	0.2653	9.647%	90.353%	7.259	7.3402	35.051	35.651
1987	0.0300	0.0433	0.2678	0.2738	0.2634	9.620%	90.380%	7.209	7.3169	35.666	36.489
1988	0.0426	0.0433	0.2812	0.3054	0.2616	9.060%	90.940%	7.096	7.1869	36.563	37.282
1989	0.0372	0.0436	0.2871	0.2813	0.2599	8.300%	91.700%	7.114	7.1468	37.663	37.929
1990	0.0310	0.0430	0.2792	0.2650	0.2582	7.723%	92.277%	7.166	7.1566	38.682	38.602
1991	0.0194	0.0431	0.2780	0.2250	0.2565	8.294%	91.706%	7.327	7.2704	40.051	39.575
1992	0.0125	0.0429	0.2760	0.2005	0.2548	9.286%	90.714%	7.508	7.4403	41.157	40.589
1993	-0.0018	0.0427	0.2618	0.1562	0.2532	10.576%	89.424%	7.787	7.7178	41.996	41.428
1994	0.0277	0.0426	0.2641	0.2662	0.2517	11.144%	88.856%	7.685	7.6471	43.144	42.816
1995	0.0250	0.0425	0.2701	0.2499	0.2501	10.665%	89.335%	7.669	7.6330	43.909	43.592
1996	0.0187	0.0423	0.2571	0.2374	0.2486	10.799%	89.201%	7.698	7.6949	44.463	44.436
1997	0.0276	0.0422	0.2460	0.2837	0.2472	10.623%	89.377%	7.638	7.6482	45.421	45.515
1998	0.0299	0.0422	0.2422	0.2977	0.2458	9.867%	90.133%	7.560	7.6021	45.952	46.344
1999	0.0297	0.0424	0.2381	0.3030	0.2444	9.097%	90.903%	7.511	7.5708	46.574	47.143
2000	0.0386	0.0428	0.2358	0.3450	0.2431	8.125%	91.875%	7.386	7.4381	47.855	48.369
2001	0.0215	0.0427	0.2265	0.2833	0.2418	7.174%	92.826%	7.470	7.4920	48.510	48.732
2002	0.0113	0.0423	0.2155	0.2484	0.2405	7.585%	92.415%	7.634	7.6431	49.159	49.254
2003	0.0096	0.0416	0.2208	0.2317	0.2393	7.808%	92.192%	7.806	7.8012	49.615	49.567
2004	0.0232	0.0409	0.2337	0.2742	0.2381	8.086%	91.914%	7.749	7.7996	50.288	50.789
2005	0.0195	0.0403	0.2445	0.2447	0.2370	8.033%	91.967%	7.789	7.8532	50.842	51.490
2006	0.0310	0.0400	0.2565	0.2768	0.2358	7.616%	92.384%	7.681	7.7895	51.637	52.758
2007	0.0289	0.0397	0.2675	0.2566	0.2348	6.876%	93.124%	7.759	7.7596	52.154	52.158
2008	0.0033	0.0396	0.2649	0.1620	0.2337	6.948%	93.052%	7.911	8.0006	52.073	52.979
2009	-0.0432	0.0396	0.2344	-0.0156	0.2328	8.904%	91.096%	8.804	8.6856	51.373	50.319
2010	0.0220	0.0395	0.2429	0.2533	0.2318	9.331%	90.669%	8.661	8.6018	52.458	51.906
2011	0.0180	0.0394	0.2512	0.2286	0.2309	9.170%	90.830%	8.593	8.5645	53.152	52.885
2012	-0.0037	0.0394	0.2407	0.1483	0.2300	10.061%	89.939%	8.803	8.7465	53.394	52.869
2013	0.0018	0.0392	0.2306	0.1778	0.2292	10.429%	89.571%	8.929	8.8467	53.846	53.090
2014	0.0128	0.0389	0.2303	0.2245	0.2284	9.817%	90.183%	8.885	8.8340	53.999	53.530

Figure 20. Annual estimate of long-term productivity of capital, $P_0 = \dfrac{a + \Lambda}{\nu}$

(Table 3, column (5)); Europe, 1950-2014
Source: Penn Tables, version 9.0.

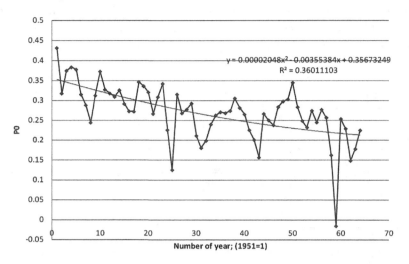

Figure 21. Rate of growth in European economy; 1951-2014
Source: Penn Tables, version 9.0.

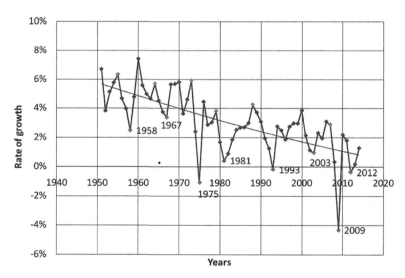

parameter P_0 upwards and downwards. Therefore only average means can be used as approximate estimate for a true value of parameter P_0.

We consider quadratic trend for annual estimates P_0 using least square procedure for calculation of the parameters of this trend. This trend is depictured by the solid curve at Figure 20. The values of P_0 on this trend give us approximate estimates for a true (unknown) long-term productivity of capital. We see that these estimates decrease slowly with time. It is very probable that behavior of true values P_0 is identical to behavior of this trend although exact values for each year can slightly differ. Quadratic trend $P_0\left(n\right)$ (n-the number of year) for the years 1951-2014 has the following parameters:

$$P_{0;TREND}\left(n\right) = 2.048 \cdot 10^{-5} \cdot n^2 - 0.00355384 \cdot n + 0.35673249 \tag{40}$$

Let's suppose that the "true" long-term productivity of capital, $P_{0;TRUE}$ insignificantly differs from values of the trend (40). Mathematically it means that coefficients in the "true" quadratic trend, $P_{0;TRUE}\left(n\right)$, differ by a multipliers $k_{1;2;3} \approx 1$.

$$P_{0;TRUE}\left(n\right) = k_1 \cdot 2.048 \cdot 10^{-5} \cdot n^2 - k_2 \cdot 0.00355384 \cdot n + k_3 \cdot 0.35673249 \tag{41}$$

The "true values" $P_{0;TRUE}$ depend of the constants $k_1; k_2; k_3$. Column (6) of Table 3 contains these values calculated for the constants $k_1 = 0.9339; k_2 = 0.9090; k_3 = 1.0001$.

The second problem which consists in determination of the maximal total factor productivity TFPM, parameter, A_m, is. We don't know how this parameter changes with time. We know only that Solow' residual, A, grows, and, as a rule, the inequality $A \leq A_m$ is fulfilled.

The parameter TFPM depends on organization of production, technologies, infrastructure, legislation, management, human capital and many other factors which help to save resources (capital and labor) due to improvements of conditions for business. The productivity of capital, P, depends on these factors too. Therefore the parameter TFPM and the productivity of capital apparently are interconnected. Some dependence (or strong correlation) between these values must exist. We will seek some regularity between the TFPM and the productivity of capital.

Figure 22. Maximal total factor productivity TFPM, A_m vs. productivity of capital, P for the best fit parameters of linear approximation of dependence The European economy; 1951-2014. $A_m(P)$ The European economy; 1951-2014

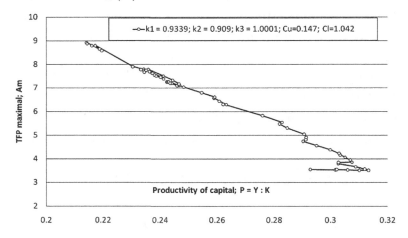

Let's try to find a dependence using equations (35)-(37) for calculation of the TFPM. We can calculate TFPM, A_m via equations (35)-(37):

For the "lower evolutionary branch":

$$A_{m;fact} = P_{0;TRUE}^{\beta} \cdot \left[y \cdot f_L \cdot \left(1 + \left(\frac{P_{0;TRUE} - P}{C_L P P_{0;TRUE}} \right)^{\left(\frac{1}{1+\chi} \right)} \right) \right]^{1-\beta} ; \tag{42}$$

For the "upper evolutionary branch":

$$A_{m;fact} = P_{0;TRUE}^{\beta} \cdot \left[y \cdot f_L \cdot \left(1 + \left(\frac{P - P_{0;TRUE}}{C_U P P_{0;TRUE}} \right)^{\left(\frac{1}{1+\chi} \right)} \right) \right]^{1-\beta} . \tag{43}$$

Parameter $P_{0;TRUE}$ in these equations satisfies the equation (41).

We can observe the curves $A_{m;fact}(P)$ for the different values of parameters $C_L; C_U; \chi; k_1; k_2; k_3$. We can tune these parameters in such a way which transform the dependence $A_{m;fact}(P)$ into the almost straight line in the plane

$\left(P;A_m\right)$ (Figures 23 and 24). It is unexpected and, we think, important finding. We discuss later the cause of this regularity. Graph $A_{m;fact}\left(P\right)$ can be transformed into almost straight line in the plane $\left(P;A_m\right)$ by means of the choice of the following values of parameters:

Period 1960-2014:

$$k_1 = 0.9339; \ k_2 = 0.9090; \ k_3 = 1.0001; \ \chi = 0; \ C_U = 0.147; \ C_L = 1.042. \tag{44}$$

Figure 20 shows that all points of curve $A_{m;fact}\left(P\right)$ during the period 1960-2014 well lay down on a straight line:

Period 1960-2014:

$$A_{m;theor}\left(P\right) = -51.86424112 \cdot P + 19.94647086 \tag{45}$$

Parameters of this trend were found by means of the least square procedure. These parameters depends on the choice of six parameters $k_1; k_2; k_3; C_L; C_U; \chi$. Figure 23 illustrates the change of curve $A_{m;fact}\left(P\right)$ as parameters change. Parameters (44) are the best fit parameters for the linear model of the depen-

Figure 23. Transformation of dependence $A_m\left(P\right)$ into the linear trend. European economy; 1960-2014

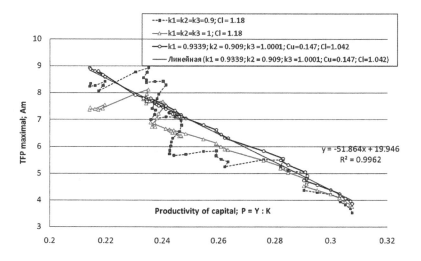

dence $A_{m;fact}\left(P\right)$. Coefficient of determination ($R^2 = 0.9962$) indicates that linear model for the dependence $A_{m;fact}\left(P\right)$ is fulfilled very well.

The period of 1950-1959 qualitatively differs from the period of 1960-2014 (Figure 22). The TFPM $A_{m;fact}\left(P\right)$ in this period is almost constant and the curve $A_{m;fact}\left(P\right)$ in the plane $\left(P;A_m\right)$ is almost horizontal. Therefore we can approximate the dependence $A_{m;fact}\left(P\right)$ by some constant value $A_{m;fact} \approx 3.6$ during the period of 1950-1959. The qualitative difference between dependencies $A_{m;fact}\left(P\right)$ for the period of 1950-1959 and the period of 1960-2014 reflects the qualitative difference of the European economic systems before and after the Treaty of Rome.

Table 3 contains factual values $A_{m;fact}\left(P\right)$ calculated for best fit parameters by means of equations (42)-(43) (column (9)) and theoretical values $A_{m;theor.}\left(P\right)$ calculated for the linear trend (45). Black dashed line at Figure 19 corresponds to the theoretical dependence predicted by MSP-model of ECAS (equations (35)-(37)). We can rewrite these equations as follows:

For the "lower evolutionary branch":

Figure 24. Transformation of dependence $A_m\left(P\right)$ into the linear trend, European economy; 2001-2014

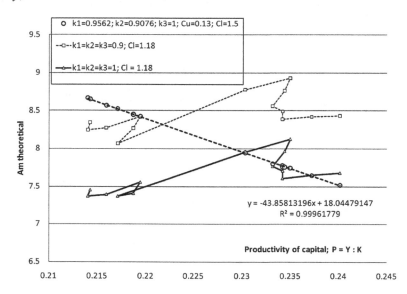

$$y_{theor.}\left(P\right) = \frac{A_m^{\frac{1}{1-\beta}}}{P_0^{\frac{\beta}{1-\beta}} \cdot f_L \cdot \left[1 + \left(\frac{P_0 - P}{C_L \cdot PP_0}\right)^{\frac{1}{1+\chi}}\right]} \tag{46}$$

For the "upper evolutionary branch":

$$y_{theor.}\left(P\right) = \frac{A_m^{\frac{1}{1-\beta}}}{P_0^{\frac{\beta}{1-\beta}} \cdot f_L \cdot \left[1 + \left(\frac{P - P_0}{C_U \cdot PP_0}\right)^{\frac{1}{1+\chi}}\right]} \tag{47}$$

We can substitute into this equations of MSP-model values $P_0 = P_{0;TRUE}$ and $A_m = A_{m;theor.}$. The dashed line at the Figure 19 describes theoretical productivity of labor $y_{theor.}\left(P\right)$ calculated by means of the equations (46)-(47). Columns (11)-(12) of Table 3 contain values for theoretical and factual pro-

Figure 25. Efficiency of European economic system versus density of conditions; 1950-2014

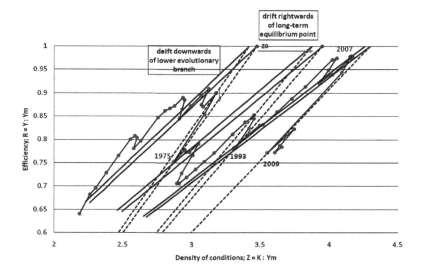

ductivity of labor. We can see that theoretical dependence $y_{theor.}(P)$ is confirmed very well.

It should be noted that theoretical equations (46)-(47) depend on 6 parameters: (1) three parameters $k_1; k_2; k_3$ of quadratic trend $P_{0;TRUE}(n)$, and (2) three parameters of evolutionary branches, $C_L; C_U; \chi$. Two parameters of the linear model $A_{m;theor}(P)$ are determined by the least square procedure. In general case we have 6-parametric theoretical model consisting of four equations (41), (45), (46)-(47) for calculation of productivity of labor via productivity of capital.

Calculations of efficiency and density of conditions of economic system show that parameters (44) correspond to the location of the European economic system on the lower evolutionary branch during the entire period 1950-2014 except for one year only, 2007 when the economic system moves along the upper evolutionary branch. Therefore the parameter C_U almost does not influence on the quality of the model. The parameter χ equals zero. Consequently we can construct linear approximation with the high coefficient of determination for the dependence $A_{m;theor}(P)$ varying only 4 parameters: $C_L; k_1; k_2; k_3$. This linear model is confirmed very well by factual data during the entire period of 1960-2014 (55 years) (Figures 22 and 23).

Parameters of the best linear approximation of data $(P; A_{m;fact})$ depend on the choice of period. Figure 24 illustrates the dependence $A_{m;fact}(P)$ for period 2001-2014 (15 years). We have in this case the following best fit parameters:

Period 2001-2014:

$$k_1 = 0.9562; k_2 = 0.9076; k_3 = 1.0; \chi = 0; C_L = 1.5; C_U = 0.13.$$

In this case we have the following theoretical dependence:

$$A_{m;theor}(P) = -43.85813196 \cdot P + 18.04479147$$

Coefficient of determination equals $R^2 = 0.9996$.

Although we can't explain theoretically the existence of a linear dependence between the TFPM and the productivity of capital it is obvious that this dependence really exists. The decrease in productivity of capital is accompanied by the increase of the maximal total factor productivity. Mensch (1979), Hochgraf, (1983), Van Duijn (1983), and Kleinknecht (1984; 1987) found that intensive seek and installation of innovations take place after each crisis. It means that the maximal total factor productivity, A_m, increases after the crises. From the other hand, each crisis leads to the fall in productivity of the capital. Therefore we have here two simultaneous processes: the fall in productivity of the capital, P and the growth of maximal total factor productivity, A_m after the crises and partially due to the crises. Mathematically it means that there is a dependence $A_m(P)$ which can be described by a decreasing function. Our analysis shows that this is a linear decreasing function.

We can use the equations (4)-(5) of the MSP-model for calculation of efficiency, R, and density of conditions, $Z = \dfrac{R}{P}$ in the European economic system during 1950-2014 (Table 4). Figure 25 illustrates dynamics of this system in the plane $(Z;R)$. Black dashed lines show the locations of the evolutionary branches in various years. Dynamics of the European economic system during the period of 1950-2014 can be theoretically explained as a motion along the lower evolutionary branch with decreasing long-term productivity of capital. The point of long-term equilibrium $(Z_0;R=1)$ during this period was drifting rightwards in the plane $(Z;R)$. Therefore the growth of efficiency was slowed down by the drift of the lower evolutionary branch. The long-term drift rightwards of long term equilibrium point is accompanied by the drift downwards of the evolutionary branch. The deceleration of growth in density of conditions creates the situation of "crisis" because the growth of efficiency due to the motion of the system along the evolutionary branch became less than the fall in the efficiency due to the drift downwards of the evolutionary branch. Figure 25 shows that the crisis begins when the efficiency stops growing along with the density of conditions.

According to this understanding of the European economic dynamics the crises of 1975, 1993 and of other years, except for the crisis 2008-2009, have happened due to deceleration in the rate of increase of the density of conditions against the background of long-term decrease of long-term productivity of capital. These were rather moderate crises which cardinally differed from for example the indeed severe crisis of 1929-1933 when the economic system catapulted from the upper into the lower evolutionary branch. We found only one year, 2007, when the European economic system has appeared on the

Table 4. Efficiency and density of conditions of European economic system

Year	Density of conditions	Efficiency	Year	Density of conditions	Efficiency
1950	2.185	0.640	1983	2.910	0.705
1951	2.259	0.681	1984	2.965	0.719
1952	2.303	0.696	1985	3.029	0.736
1953	2.380	0.728	1986	3.092	0.752
1954	2.468	0.765	1987	3.164	0.770
1955	2.554	0.800	1988	3.297	0.811
1956	2.589	0.808	1989	3.389	0.836
1957	2.602	0.803	1990	3.454	0.852
1958	2.578	0.780	1991	3.454	0.844
1959	2.631	0.796	1992	3.416	0.824
1960	2.754	0.847	1993	3.313	0.781
1961	2.806	0.861	1994	3.419	0.811
1962	2.841	0.866	1995	3.494	0.830
1963	2.876	0.872	1996	3.519	0.831
1964	2.937	0.890	1997	3.621	0.859
1965	2.949	0.884	1998	3.727	0.887
1966	2.931	0.865	1999	3.827	0.913
1967	2.910	0.845	2000	4.022	0.970
1968	2.994	0.872	2001	4.055	0.974
1969	3.068	0.894	2002	3.995	0.948
1970	3.126	0.909	2003	3.927	0.920
1971	3.071	0.874	2004	4.002	0.937
1972	3.084	0.870	2005	4.024	0.938
1973	3.177	0.899	2006	4.162	0.976
1974	3.094	0.854	2007	4.152	0.976
1975	2.872	0.753	2008	4.093	0.943
1976	2.953	0.777	2009	3.552	0.771
1977	2.962	0.772	2010	3.666	0.802
1978	2.984	0.773	2011	3.746	0.822
1979	3.049	0.790	2012	3.642	0.786
1980	3.008	0.766	2013	3.604	0.771
1981	2.928	0.727	2014	3.656	0.783
1982	2.891	0.705			

upper evolutionary branch. The crisis of 2008-2009 was accompanied by the fall of economic system on the lower evolutionary branch like the crisis of 1929-1933. The drift downwards of the lower evolutionary branch was strengthening the crises.

TYPES OF CRISES

Let's consider the types of crises in more details. The MSP-modelling of the economic complex adaptive system predicts the following types of crises.

The first type of crises corresponds to the crisis phase of evolutionary cycle in the MSP-model of ECAS. This is the fall of the economic system in the plane $(Z; R)$ from the upper evolutionary branch into the lower part of the lower evolutionary branch as it is depictured in Figure 2. This is always very deep and sever crisis like the crises of 1929-1933 and 2008-2009. As a rule, the rate of growth falls below zero. For example the rate of growth in the European economy catapulted in 2009 below than -4% (Figure 21).

The second type of the crises corresponds to the drift downwards of the economic system at the plane $(Z; R)$ due to the change of long-term productivity of capital. These crises are depictured in Figure 25. The growth of efficiency due to the motion of the system along evolutionary branch is stopped due to the drift downwards of the evolutionary branch. These crises are moderate. Although the rate of growth falls but this fall is still moderate as a rule. Often the rate of growth doesn't fall below zero as it took place in the years 1967, 1981, 2003 (Figure 21).

The third type of the crises are caused by the influence of external or internal adverse factors such as for example natural cataclysms or economic sanctions.

The crisis of the first type can be strengthened by the drift of the evolutionary branch. In this case crises of the first and of the second type happen simultaneously as it was in 1929-1933 and in 2007-2009. We see in Figure 25 that the European economic system was located on the lower evolutionary branch before 2007 year. The system moves onto the upper evolutionary branch in 2007. After that the system is falling into the lower evolutionary branch. This is a standard phase of the crisis of evolutionary cycle. However this description of the economic crisis in 2008-2009 suggests that parameter χ is more than zero. In this case, $\chi > 0$, the system can leap from the upper evolutionary branch into the lower part of the evolutionary branch. We choose the parameter $\chi = 0$ in a way to be the best fit as the parameter of linear approximation of the dependence $A_{m;fact}(P)$ but it is possible that this parameter may vary within some of the years.

First, let's consider a situation when $\chi = 0$. In this case the location of the evolutionary branches is depictured in Figure 5 from the Introduction and in Figure 25 (dashed and bold straight lines). Let's note that the lower branches in Figure 25 (dashed straight line) depict the increasing function of variable Z. It means that there are only two possible stationary states at the fixed value Z in this case ($\chi = 0$). If $\chi > 0$ there are three stationary states at the fixed value $Z_1 < Z < Z_0$ (Figure 2 of the Introduction). Consequently there are only two possibilities in this case ($\chi = 0$): the stable stationary states are located either at the upper or at the lower evolutionary branch. Therefore the MSP-system in this case $\chi = 0$ can be located only on the one of the evolutionary branches in this case $\chi = 0$. Until the equality $\chi = 0$ is fulfilled the leaps from one evolutionary branch into another branch are possible if only the stabilizing function changes in such a way that the former stable states become unstable and vice versa.

If the parameter χ can become more than zero during short interval of time the leap of the system from the upper into the lower evolutionary branch is possible. The period of the years 2007-2009 can be described as the short-term change of the stabilizing function which provoked the transitions from one evolutionary branch into another: "lower branch" (2006) → "upper branch" (2007) → "lower branch" (2008-2009). This period can be described also as the "crisis" stage of the evolutionary cycle. This interpretation suggests a very short-term change of the parameter χ. This period ($\chi > 0$) was sufficiently long in order to stimulate the leap of the system from the upper branch into the lower branch but the duration of this period wasn't sufficiently big to lead to the significant fall of the system. The process of the fall has stopped when the parameter χ again became zero ($\chi = 0$).

REFERENCES

Database of Central Intelligence Agency (CIA). (n.d.). Retrieved October 19, 2016: https://www.cia.gov/library

Feenstra, R. C., Inklaar, R., & Timmer, M. P. (2015). The Next Generation of the Penn World Table. *The American Economic Review*, *105*(10), 3150–3182. www.ggdc.net/pwt doi:10.1257/aer.20130954

Giussani, P. (2004). *Capitale Fisso e Guruismo*. Retrieved July 18, 2005, from: http://www.countdownnet.info/archivio/analisi/altro/326.pdf

Hochgraf, N. (1983), The future technological environment. *Proceedings of 11th World Petroleum Congress* (pp. 1-10). London: John Willey & Sons.

Kleinknecht, A. (1984). Prosperity, crisis, and innovation patterns. *Cambridge Journal of Economics*, *8*, 251–270.

Kleinknecht, A. (1987). *Innovation patterns in crisis and prosperity. Schumpeter's long cycle reconsidered*. London: the Macmillan Press Ltd.

Mensch, G. (1979). *Stalemate in technology*. Cambridge, MA: Ballinger.

Mitchell, W.C., (1928). *Business cycles. The problems and its setting*. New York: The National Bureau of Economic Research, Studies in business cycles, No. 1.

Mitchell, W.C., (1951). *What happens during business cycles?* New York: The National Bureau of Economic Research, Studies in Business Cycles, No.2.

Pushnoi, G. S. (2003). Dynamics of a system as a process of realization of its "potential". *Proceedings of*, (July), 20–24.

Pushnoi, G. S. (2004b, November). The Business Cycle Model on the Basis of Method of Systems Potential. *The Second Internet Conference on Evolutionary Economics and Econophysics*. Ekaterinburg, Russia: International A. Bogdanov Institute.

Pushnoi, G. S. (2010). *Crisis as Reconfiguration of the Economic Complex Adaptive System*. AAAI Fall CAS Symposium.

Solow, R. M. (1957). Technical change and production function. *The Review of Economics and Statistics*, *39*(3), 312–320. doi:10.2307/1926047

Van Duijn, J. (1983). *The long wave in economic life*. London: Allen and Unwin.

ENDNOTES

1.   The following MSP-parameters were used in Figure 1 and Figure 2 from the Introduction:

$$a = 0.05; d = 0.03; \Lambda = 0.08; \nu = 0.2; C_U = 6.0969; C_L = 0.9945$$

2.   U.S. Bureau of Economic Analysis (U.S. BEA): http://www.bea.gov/

3.   Federal Reserve Economic Data (FRED): https://fred.stlouisfed.org/series/TCU

4.   The chapters 2 and 3 contain findings which develop the ideas formulated earlier – Pushnoi (2005b; 2010).

5.   This is conditional extremum problem.

6.   Our calculations show that the basic results of MSP-analysis of European economy remain qualitatively same if even we shall add Greece in this list.

Chapter 3
The Great Depression of the 1930s Demonstrates Crisis and Depression of a Prolonged Evolutionary Cycle

MSP-ANALYSIS OF THE "GREAT DEPRESSION" OF THE 1930s

Dynamics of the economic indices reflects the influence of various factors. Pure picture of "evolutionary cycles" in the real dynamics is rare event because stochastic internal and external shocks perpetually influence onto both the position of long-term equilibrium point $(Z_0; R = 1)$ in the plane $(Z; R)$ and the geometric form of "evolutionary branches". Sometimes it is difficult to find an "evolutionary cycle" in an intricate pattern of change of eco-

DOI: 10.4018/978-1-5225-2170-9.ch003

nomic indexes. But there are situations when the "evolutionary cycle" becomes visible as the main trend of change of economic indicators. These are situations when point of long-term equilibrium quickly moves in the plane $(Z; R)$ and the dynamics of economic system takes the form of a typical evolutionary cycle.

We use below MSP-model of economic system for the analysis of stylized facts collected in the paper of Robert Solow (1957). Table 1 contains Solow' data for nonfarm industry of the U.S. economy. Share of property in income ω (column (2) in Table 1) is almost the constant.

Cobb-Douglas production function (18) in Chapter 2 contains parameter β which describes the share of capital (of property in wide sense) in income in optimally functioning economy (see for example Rabbani (2006)). Consequently Cobb-Douglas production function is the good theoretical approximation for the economy with constant share of capital in income.

Total factor productivity (Solow' technological factor) can be calculated by means of the equation (27) in Chapter 2 in which we substitute parameter

Table 1. Stylized facts for the U.S. economic system (1909-1949)

Year	Share of property in income; w	% labor force employed; f	Private nonfarm GNP per manhour; y	Employed capital per manhour; k	Rate of Growth of Technological Factor	Solow' Technological Factor; A	Normalized Technological Factor; An	A : An	Productivity of employed capital	Productivity of capital	Amax	Density of conditions; Z	Efficiency; R
(1)	(2)	(3)	(4)	(6)	(7)	(8)	(9)	(10)	(11)	(12)	(13)	(14)	(15)
	Solow (1957)	Solow (1957)	Solow (1957)	Solow (1957)	Solow (1957)	Solow (1957)	An =[y : k*w]	(8) : (9)	Pe ~ y : k	P ~ Pe * f		Z = K : Ym	R = P*Z
1909	0.335	91.1	0.623	2.06	-0.018	1.000	0.489	2.045	0.302	0.276			
1910	0.330	92.8	0.616	2.10	0.039	0.982	0.482	2.037	0.293	0.272	Amax = 0.6 (1920 - 1929)		
1911	0.335	90.6	0.647	2.17	0.002	1.021	0.499	2.045	0.298	0.270	Amax ~ 0.82 * Exp[0.01 * t] (1930 - 1945)		
1912	0.330	93.0	0.652	2.21	0.040	1.022	0.502	2.037	0.295	0.274			
1913	0.334	91.8	0.680	2.23	0.007	1.063	0.520	2.044	0.305	0.280			
1914	0.325	83.6	0.682	2.20	-0.028	1.071	0.528	2.029	0.310	0.259			
1915	0.344	84.5	0.669	2.26	0.034	1.041	0.505	2.060	0.296	0.250			
1916	0.358	93.7	0.700	2.34	-0.010	1.077	0.516	2.086	0.299	0.280			
1917	0.370	94.0	0.679	2.21	0.072	1.066	0.506	2.105	0.307	0.289			
1918	0.342	94.5	0.729	2.22	0.014	1.143	0.555	2.059	0.328	0.310			
1919	0.354	93.1	0.767	2.47	-0.076	1.158	0.557	2.080	0.311	0.289			
1920	0.319	92.8	0.721	2.58	-0.072	1.073	0.533	2.009	0.279	0.259	0.600	3.178	0.824
1921	0.369	76.9	0.770	2.55	0.032	1.147	0.545	2.105	0.302	0.232	0.600	3.009	0.699
1922	0.339	81.7	0.788	2.49	0.010	1.184	0.578	2.047	0.316	0.259	0.600	3.046	0.788
1923	0.337	92.1	0.809	2.61	0.017	1.196	0.586	2.043	0.310	0.285	0.600	3.148	0.899
1924	0.330	88.0	0.836	2.74	0.035	1.216	0.599	2.029	0.305	0.268	0.600	3.274	0.879
1925	0.336	91.1	0.872	2.81	-0.011	1.258	0.616	2.042	0.310	0.283	0.600	3.310	0.936
1926	0.327	92.5	0.869	2.87	-0.005	1.245	0.616	2.022	0.303	0.280	0.600	3.388	0.949
1927	0.323	90.0	0.871	2.93	-0.006	1.239	0.615	2.013	0.297	0.268	0.600	3.451	0.923
1928	0.338	90.0	0.874	3.02	0.020	1.231	0.602	2.047	0.289	0.260	0.600	3.464	0.902
1929	0.332	92.5	0.895	3.06	-0.043	1.255	0.617	2.033	0.292	0.271	0.600	3.518	0.952
1930	0.347	88.1	0.880	3.30	0.024	1.202	0.582	2.066	0.267	0.235	0.820	2.659	0.625
1931	0.325	78.2	0.904	3.33	-0.023	1.231	0.611	2.012	0.271	0.212	0.828	2.720	0.577
1932	0.397	67.9	0.879	3.28	0.010	1.202	0.549	2.192	0.268	0.182	0.837	2.447	0.445
1933	0.362	66.5	0.869	3.10	0.072	1.215	0.577	2.106	0.280	0.186	0.845	2.436	0.454
1934	0.355	70.9	0.921	3.00	0.039	1.302	0.624	2.088	0.307	0.218	0.853	2.380	0.518
1935	0.351	73.0	0.943	2.87	0.060	1.353	0.651	2.077	0.329	0.240	0.862	2.300	0.552
1936	0.357	77.3	0.982	2.72	-0.010	1.434	0.687	2.087	0.361	0.279	0.871	2.186	0.610
1937	0.340	81.0	0.971	2.71	0.021	1.420	0.692	2.052	0.358	0.290	0.879	2.196	0.637
1938	0.331	74.7	1.000	2.78	0.048	1.450	0.713	2.033	0.360	0.269	0.888	2.231	0.599
1939	0.347	77.2	1.034	2.66	0.050	1.520	0.736	2.064	0.389	0.300	0.897	2.111	0.634
1940	0.357	80.6	1.082	2.63	0.044	1.596	0.766	2.083	0.411	0.332	0.906	2.055	0.681
1941	0.377	86.8	1.122	2.58	0.004	1.666	0.785	2.122	0.435	0.377	0.915	1.972	0.744
1942	0.356	93.6	1.136	2.64	0.041	1.672	0.804	2.080	0.430	0.403	0.925	2.021	0.814
1943	0.342	97.4	1.180	2.62	0.071	1.741	0.849	2.051	0.450	0.439	0.934	2.018	0.885
1944	0.332	98.4	1.265	2.63	0.021	1.864	0.918	2.032	0.481	0.473	0.943	2.023	0.957
1945	0.314	96.5	1.296	2.66	-0.044	1.903	0.953	1.997	0.487	0.470	0.953	2.054	0.966
1946	0.312	94.8	1.215	2.5	-0.017	1.820	0.913	1.994	0.486	0.461	0.962	1.952	0.899
1947	0.327	95.4	1.194	2.5	0.016	1.789	0.885	2.021	0.478	0.456	0.972	1.906	0.869
1948	0.332	95.7	1.221	2.55	0.025	1.817	0.895	2.031	0.479	0.458	0.982	1.904	0.872
1949	0.326	93	1.275	2.7		1.862	0.922	2.019	0.472	0.439	0.992	1.970	0.865

Source: Solow (1957).

β with annual share of property in income ω. The following chain of formulas was used as algorithm for calculation of "efficiency" and "density of conditions" of the U.S. economy.

$$A_N = \frac{y}{k^\omega} \text{ (from the equation (27) in Chapter 2)} \tag{1}$$

$$f_L \approx f_K \equiv f \tag{2}$$

$$Z = \frac{K}{Y_m} = \frac{f \cdot K}{A_m K_e^\omega L_e^{1-\omega}} = \frac{K_e}{A_m K_e^\omega L_e^{1-\omega}} = \frac{k^{1-\omega}}{A_m} \tag{3}$$

$$R = P \cdot Z = \frac{Y}{K} \cdot \frac{K_e}{A_m K_e^\omega L_e^{1-\omega}} = \frac{f \cdot Y}{f \cdot A_m K^\omega L^{1-\omega}} = \frac{Y}{Y_m} = \frac{f \cdot A}{A_m} \tag{4}$$

Technological factor A_N (the equation (1)) is normalized factor. Solow' (1957) normalization of technological factor ($A(1909) = 1$) don't consistent with equality (1). Ratio $A : A_N$ is almost constant (Table 1; column (10) and Figure 1). Equality (2) was proposed by Solow (1957) for approximate estimate of employed capital. This assumption is valid only if capital intensity don't change significantly. Solow' (1957) computations (column (6) of his paper) demonstrate that capital intensity actually changes between 2.06 and 3.3). Therefore the equality (2) is fulfilled only approximately. The calculation of efficiency and density of conditions (equations (3) and (4)) can't be fulfilled until we didn't define maximal technological factor A_m. Growth of factor A_m describes the progress in science and technologies which were not embodied in real production yet as possible (potential) technological progress. Let's model function $A_m(t)$ as exponential function:

$$A_m(t) = A_m(0) \cdot Exp(n \cdot t) \tag{5}$$

Figure 1. Non-normalized per normalized total factor productivity (TFP) ratio; $\dfrac{A}{A_n}$

(Table 5; column (10)). Non-farm industry of the U.S. economy; 1909-1949.

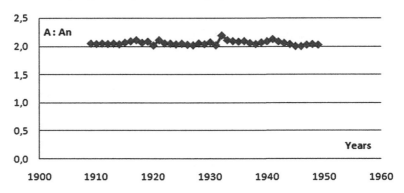

We shall consider below two periods: (1) the period of prosperity of 1920s (1920-1929) and (2) the period of "Great Depression" (1930-1945). These are two qualitatively different epochs in economic life of America. Indexes of exponent n in these periods must be different. Unique method doesn't exist for the exact determination of these indices. Period of "Great Depression" and the Second World War is obviously the period of deep transformations in the U.S. economic system. Therefore we assumed that the following inequality takes place:

$$n\left(1921-1929\right) << n\left(1930-1945\right) \tag{6}$$

Initial values $A_m\left(0\right)$ were taken in such a way that maximal efficiency of the economic system in each period equals almost unit. The simplest choice of index of exponent in the first period is:

$$n\left(1921-1929\right) = 0$$

We can vary index $n\left(1930-1945\right)$ observing how the curve $R\left(Z\right)$ is deforming. Values R and Z can be computed via the equations (3)-(4) in Chapter 2. Geometric forms of these curves are identical. Therefore we consider as example curve $R\left(Z\right)$ for $n\left(1930-1945\right) = 0.01$. Requirement $R_{\max}\left(1921-1929\right) \approx 1$ is fulfilled if we choose the following value $A_m\left(0\right) = 0.6$.

In this case we have $R_{\max} = R(1929) \approx 0.952$ (Table 1; column (15)). Requirement $R_{\max}(1930 - 1945) \approx 1$ is fulfilled if we choice the following value $A_m(0) = 0.82$. In this case we have $R_{\max} = R(1945) \approx 0.966$ (Table 1; column (15)). Curve $R(Z)$ is depictured in Figure 2. We can separate two evolutionary cycles: (1) 1920-1929 and 1933-1945 but evolutionary curves of these cycles have different location in the plane $(Z; R)$. Evolutionary branches for the second case (1933-1945) are shifted to the left relatively of evolutionary branches of the first cycle (1920-1929). Point of long-term equilibrium drifts to the left after 1929.

Two processes determine dynamics after 1929: (1) motion of economic system along evolutionary branch and (2) drift of evolutionary branch in the plane $(Z; R)$ - Figure 3. Trajectory of the economic system is the motion along moving evolutionary branch. If evolutionary branch climbs in the plane $(Z; R)$ (Figure 4) the efficiency of the economic system increases quicker than in the case of motionless evolutionary branch. The equation (7) describes time dependence of efficiency:

Figure 2. Drift of long-term equilibrium point during "Great Depression" (Table 1; columns (14) and (15)). Evolutionary branches correspond to the following evolutionary parameters: (1) period 1920-1929: $Z_0 = 3.7; \chi = 2.2; C_U = 100; C_L = 50$; (2) period 1933-1945: $Z_0 = 2.1; \chi = 0.3; C_U = 20; C_L = 2.6$.

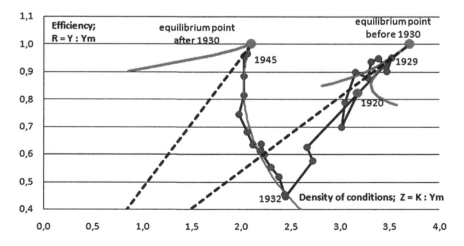

Figure 3. Great Depression of 1930s as imposition of two processes: (1) the "crisis" stage of evolutionary cycle and (2) the shift of the global equilibrium point $\left(Z_0; R = 1\right)$

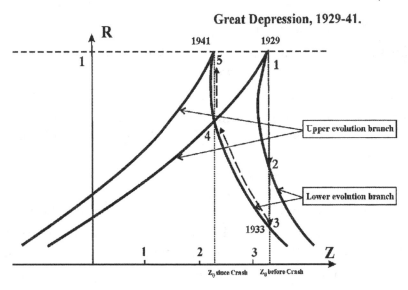

Figure 4. Dynamics of economic system as motion along moving evolutionary branch

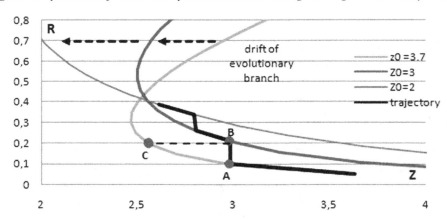

$$R(t) = \frac{1}{1 + \left[\dfrac{1 - R(0)}{R(0)}\right] \cdot e^{-(a+d) \cdot t}} \tag{7}$$

Time dependence of productivity of capital is described by the following equation:

$$P(t) = \frac{P_0}{1 + \left[\dfrac{P_0 - P(0)}{P(0)}\right] \cdot e^{-(a+\Lambda) \cdot t}} \tag{8}$$

$$P_0 = \frac{1}{Z_0} = \frac{a + \Lambda}{\nu} \tag{9}$$

Productivity of capital in our model equals tangent of angle of inclination of radius-vector connecting origin of coordinates of the plane $(Z; R)$ with point located at evolutionary branch.

$$P = \frac{R}{Z} = \frac{Y}{K} \tag{10}$$

We can calculate productivity of capital using equations (8) or (10). We used data for efficiency from column (15) in Table 1. Density of conditions was calculated by means of the equation (20) from the Introduction with parameters $Z_0 = 2.1; \chi = 0.3; C_L = 2.6$. Theoretical values $P(t)$ were calculated on the basis of the equation (10) and they almost coincides with factual data for productivity of capital (Figures 5-6).

In order that estimate parameters $\{a; \Lambda; \nu; d\}$ we used Kendrick (1961) data about the U.S. economy (Table 2). Depreciation rate changes insignificantly $(0.028 \div 0.04)$ during 1933-1945 years. Rate of growth is very unstable (-0.03 $\div$ 0.15). Mean value of rate of growth can be taken as the first crude approximate estimate for the economic parameter a. Mean values of parameters $\{a; \Lambda; \nu\}$ are collected in the Table 3. Drift of long-term equilibrium point means that economic parameters were not constant after 1929. The

Table 2. Stylized facts for the U.S. economic system (1909-1949)

Year	GNP	GNP Growth Rate	Gross Domestic Investment, GDI			Capital Consumption Allowance	Real Capital Stock in Domestic Economy	Depreciation Rate	Investment Rate
			Total	New Construction and Equipment	Change in Business Inventories				
(1)	(2)	(3)	(4)	(5)	(6)	(7)	(8)	(9)	(10)
	Kendrick (1961), Table A-I.	from (2)	(5) + (6)	Kendrick (1961), Table A-IIa	Kendrick (1961), Table A-IIa	Kendrick (1961), Table A-I.	Kendrick (1961), Table A-XV	(7) : (8)	(4) : (2)
1909	53.615		12.624	11.229	1.395	5.920	221.809	0.0267	0.2355
1910	54.263	0.012	12.470	11.595	0.875	6.158	228.359	0.0270	0.2298
1911	55.341	0.020	11.206	10.500	0.706	6.403	235.136	0.0272	0.2025
1912	58.171	0.051	12.900	11.741	1.159	6.637	240.387	0.0276	0.2218
1913	60.828	0.046	13.842	12.684	1.158	6.886	247.125	0.0279	0.2276
1914	55.755	-0.083	9.813	9.786	0.027	7.109	253.657	0.0280	0.1760
1915	57.434	0.030	9.635	9.406	0.229	7.285	259.727	0.0280	0.1678
1916	66.356	0.155	12.893	11.226	1.667	7.489	264.460	0.0283	0.1943
1917	64.692	-0.025	11.914	11.428	0.486	7.754	269.779	0.0287	0.1842
1918	63.640	-0.016	11.994	11.465	0.529	8.019	274.337	0.0292	0.1885
1919	70.271	0.104	14.614	11.749	2.865	8.650	278.121	0.0311	0.2080
1920	71.383	0.016	15.039	10.726	4.313	8.603	282.540	0.0304	0.2107
1921	68.355	-0.042	9.769	9.891	-0.122	8.183	286.280	0.0286	0.1429
1922	73.150	0.070	13.197	12.944	0.253	8.663	290.436	0.0298	0.1804
1923	82.994	0.135	18.210	15.435	2.775	8.905	298.526	0.0298	0.2194
1924	85.222	0.027	15.209	16.193	-0.984	9.043	308.547	0.0293	0.1785
1925	87.359	0.025	19.624	18.022	1.602	9.407	319.226	0.0295	0.2246
1926	93.438	0.070	20.469	19.312	1.157	10.086	332.064	0.0304	0.2191
1927	94.161	0.008	19.163	18.785	0.378	10.163	344.133	0.0295	0.2035
1928	95.715	0.017	18.346	18.763	-0.417	10.592	354.809	0.0299	0.1917
1929	101.444	0.060	20.352	18.678	1.674	10.994	365.089	0.0301	0.2006
1930	91.513	-0.098	14.870	15.428	-0.558	10.902	373.097	0.0292	0.1625
1931	84.300	-0.079	10.862	11.579	-0.717	10.862	376.298	0.0283	0.1288
1932	70.682	-0.162	4.050	7.318	-3.268	10.246	373.175	0.0275	0.0573
1933	68.337	-0.033	3.022	6.370	-3.348	9.960	365.427	0.0273	0.0442
1934	74.609	0.092	5.306	8.096	-2.790	9.995	358.425	0.0279	0.0711
1935	85.808	0.150	12.432	9.881	2.551	10.188	356.808	0.0286	0.1449
1936	95.798	0.116	14.840	14.123	0.717	10.563	358.540	0.0295	0.1549
1937	103.917	0.085	19.261	14.717	4.544	10.884	364.078	0.0299	0.1853
1938	96.670	-0.070	12.006	12.963	-0.957	10.923	368.057	0.0297	0.1242
1939	103.736	0.073	15.426	14.788	0.638	11.086	370.930	0.0299	0.1487
1940	112.961	0.089	19.310	16.201	3.109	11.401	379.162	0.0301	0.1709
1941	126.237	0.118	26.826	21.007	5.819	12.457	389.744	0.0320	0.2125
1942	122.571	-0.029	26.548	24.157	2.391	13.934	396.616	0.0351	0.2166
1943	121.918	-0.005	25.049	26.006	-0.957	14.785	396.195	0.0373	0.2055
1944	126.633	0.039	26.077	27.113	-1.036	15.907	391.997	0.0406	0.2059
1945	130.218	0.028	22.256	23.531	-1.275	16.217	387.229	0.0419	0.1709
1946	151.895	0.166	25.923	19.705	6.218	14.658	390.287	0.0376	0.1707
1947	153.515	0.011	22.321	23.118	-0.797	16.558	400.991	0.0413	0.1454
1948	158.828	0.035	29.944	25.879	4.065	18.012	415.492	0.0434	0.1885
1949	153.970	-0.031	22.877	25.667	-2.790	19.014	430.424	0.0442	0.1486

Source: Kendrick (1961).

U.S. economic system was transforming qualitatively during 1930-1945 years. Therefore we must take into account drift of long-term equilibrium point $\left(Z_0; R = 1 \right)$ and the change of the economic parameters. All the equations of MSP-model of ECAS were deduced for the case of constant evolutionary parameters. If parameters are changing the trajectory of economic

Table 3. Mean values of economic parameters before and after Great Crash; mean values are calculated on the base of data in Table 1.

Period	a	Λ	V	Z_0	P_0
1920-1929	0.038	0.0297	0.1971	2.8946	0.3455
1933-1945	0.050	0.0323	0.1581	1.9179	0.5214

system intersects many evolutionary branches with different values of economic parameters.

We can interpret this process as sequence which consists of stages of short-term stays on the different evolutionary branches and transitions of system from one evolutionary branch into another evolutionary branch (Figure 4). Formally we can approximate this complex trajectory intersecting many evolutionary branches with different parameters as some kind of "evolutionary branch" with definite parameters $\{C_L; \chi; Z_0\}$. We can use theoretical equation (20) from the Introduction for this pseudo evolutionary branch as it is depictured in Figure 2 but time-dependence for a pseudo-evolutionary-branch differs from theoretical dependences (7)-(8) deduced for true evolutionary branches.

There is no unique algorithm for modeling of trajectory of economic system in situation of transitional period (1933-1945) with moving point of long-term equilibrium. We consider simplest case when long-term equilibrium point Z_0 drifts uniformly from value $Z_0 = 3.7$ in 1932 to value $Z_0 = 2.0$ in 1945 (Table 4). Mean value for rate of growth in 1933-1945 equals 0.05 and mean value for depreciation rate equals 0.0323 (Table 2). We can use these mean values as approximate estimates for parameters $\{a; \Lambda\}$. We fix these parameters as constant parameters of our model of transition period 1933-1945. Parameter ν in our model changes and can be calculated as $\nu = Z_0 \cdot (a + \Lambda)$. Parameter χ is parameter of lower evolutionary pseudo-branch $\chi = 0.3$. Parameter d can be calculated from formula $\chi \equiv \dfrac{\Lambda - d}{a + d}$ as follows:

$$d = \frac{\Lambda - a\chi}{1 + \chi} \tag{11}$$

Results of calculations are represented in Table 4. True dynamics of economic system in transitional period 1933-1945 is the motion along moving (changing) evolutionary branch. But nevertheless we can describe this process by standard MSP-equations (7)-(8) if we assume that it is the process of motion along motionless evolutionary branch is occurring in course of time with other scale. Factual drift of evolutionary branch upwards with time increases speed of growth of efficiency and productivity of capital (Figure 4).

For example the time required for the definite increment of efficiency when the system is driving along motionless evolutionary branch (motion along segment of branch A → C in Figure 4) is larger than the time required for the same increment of efficiency when the system moves upward being on the evolutionary branch rising up (motion A → B in Figure 4). If we consider all points A; B;... as the points of some evolutionary branch we must take into account the change in speed of process in order that ordinary MSP-equations of dynamics (7)-(8) can be applied in this case also. We can achieve this goal if we shall change the scale of time i.e. if we simply multiply time in the equations (7)-(8) by some scale factor, s. The climb of the

Table 4. Evolutionary parameters (1933-1945) for the U.S. nonfarm industry

	Depreciation Rate	Rate of growth	Investment Rate	Long-term equilibrium point	Parameter d	Parameter kappa
Designation	Λ	a	v			
Column	(1)	(2)	(3)	(4)	(6)	(7)
Comments:	Table 3	Table 3	$Z_0 \cdot (a + \Lambda)$	Unoform Drift	$\dfrac{\Lambda - a\chi}{1+\chi}$	Fixed
1932	0.0323	0.05	0.305	3.700	0.0133	0.3
1933	0.0323	0.05	0.294	3.569	0.0133	0.3
1934	0.0323	0.05	0.283	3.438	0.0133	0.3
1935	0.0323	0.05	0.272	3.308	0.0133	0.3
1936	0.0323	0.05	0.261	3.177	0.0133	0.3
1937	0.0323	0.05	0.251	3.046	0.0133	0.3
1938	0.0323	0.05	0.240	2.915	0.0133	0.3
1939	0.0323	0.05	0.229	2.785	0.0133	0.3
1940	0.0323	0.05	0.218	2.654	0.0133	0.3
1941	0.0323	0.05	0.208	2.523	0.0133	0.3
1942	0.0323	0.05	0.197	2.392	0.0133	0.3
1943	0.0323	0.05	0.186	2.262	0.0133	0.3
1944	0.0323	0.05	0.175	2.131	0.0133	0.3
1945	0.0323	0.05	0.165	2.000	0.0133	0.3
1946	0.0323	0.05	0.154	1.869	0.0133	0.3
1947	0.0323	0.05	0.143	1.738	0.0133	0.3
1948	0.0323	0.05	0.132	1.608	0.0133	0.3
1949	0.0323	0.05	0.122	1.477	0.0133	0.3

system along evolutionary branch with changing parameters mathematically can be described as motion of this system along motionless evolutionary branch but motion occurring in the new scale of time ($t \rightarrow s \cdot t$). Results of calculation of efficiency and productivity of capital according to the equations (7)-(8) with scale factor $s = 1.15$ are represented in Table 5.

Figures 5-6 demonstrates theoretical time dependence (8)-(9) for productivity of capital within both ordinary and new scale ($P(0) = 0.2$;

$P_0 = \dfrac{1}{Z_0} = 0.476$). Figures 7-8 demonstrates theoretical dependence (7) from

the Introduction for efficiency on time within both ordinary and new scales ($R(0) = 0.47$).

Table 5. Theoretical and factual productivity of capital and efficiency of economic system. Dynamics of economic system can be represented as motion along evolutionary pseudo-branch in time with new scale; scale factor equals 1.15

Year	Time in new scale	Theoretical productivity of capital	Theoretical Efficiency	Factual productivity of capital	Factucal Efficiency
	t	P	R	Table 1; column (12)	Table 1; column (15)
1932	0.00	0.200	0.470	0.182	0.445
1933	1.15	0.211	0.489	0.186	0.454
1934	2.47	0.224	0.510	0.218	0.518
1935	3.99	0.239	0.534	0.240	0.552
1936	5.74	0.256	0.562	0.279	0.610
1937	7.75	0.275	0.594	0.290	0.637
1938	10.07	0.297	0.630	0.269	0.599
1939	12.73	0.321	0.669	0.300	0.634
1940	15.79	0.346	0.711	0.332	0.681
1941	19.30	0.371	0.755	0.377	0.744
1942	23.35	0.396	0.800	0.403	0.814
1943	28.00	0.419	0.844	0.439	0.885
1944	33.35	0.437	0.884	0.473	0.957
1945	39.50	0.452	0.919	0.470	0.966
1946	46.58	0.462	0.947	0.461	0.899
1947	54.72	0.469	0.968	0.456	0.869
1948	64.08	0.473	0.982	0.458	0.872
1949	74.84	0.475	0.991	0.439	0.865

Figure 5. Productivity of capital in the U.S. nonfarm industry; theoretical curve $P(t)$ corresponds to the following parameters $P(0) = 0.2$; parameters $a; \Lambda$ are in Table 4.

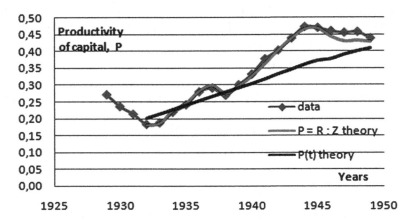

Figure 6. Productivity of capital in the U.S. nonfarm industry; theoretical curve $P(t)$ is depictured for new scale of time

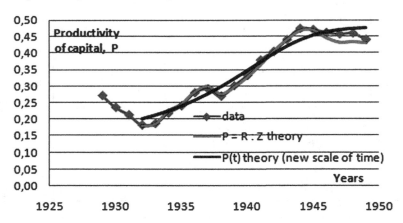

So, according to MSP-model of the U.S. economy the period of Great Depression is a transitional period to new long-term equilibrium state. Point of long-term equilibrium $(Z_0; R = 1)$ was drifting to the left in the plane $(Z; R)$ during this period (1933-1945). Comparison of economic parameters before and after 1930 (Table 3) show that the economy become more strong and successful after this hard and dramatic period of life of the United States. Rate of growth a and long-term productivity of capital P_0 had been increas-

Figure 7. Efficiency of the U.S. economic system in nonfarm industry (details in Table 3; column (14)); theoretical curve $R(t)$ is depictured for the following parameters: $R(0) = 0.47$; parameters $a; d$ are in Table 4.

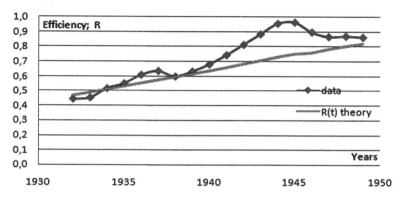

Figure 8. Efficiency of the U.S. economic system in nonfarm industry; theoretical curve $R(t)$ is depictured for new scale of time.

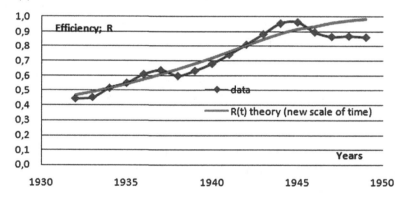

ing. The growth of productivity of capital is consequence of shift of long-term equilibrium point. Logistical law (8) of this growth follows from MSP-equations. Aulin (1997) proposed the model of economic growth with a logistic law of growth of productivity of employed capital. In our model this law describes the growth of productivity of total capital. It is remarkable that we can use standard MSP-formulas deduced for motionless evolutionary branch even in the case of moving evolutionary branch. Change of the scale of time mathematically describes influence of drift of evolutionary branch on dynamics of system. The increment of efficiency (and of productivity of capital) is a sum of increment for account of the motion along evolutionary branch and increment for account of climb of evolutionary branch. Trajectory of the system in this case is not pure evolutionary branch. However, this trajectory can be approximated with good accuracy by some kind of evolutionary branch, and we can use standard equations of time dynamics (7)-(8) via change of the scale of time. This method (the change of the scale of time) spreads the possibilities of MSP-model in applications to the systems with changing economic parameters[1].

WHAT WAS THE CAUSE OF "GREAT DEPRESSION" OF 1930S? OVERVIEW OF HISTORICAL EVENTS AND INTERPRETATIONS.

According to MSP-model the instability of global equilibrium state of the economic system is the cause of "crisis" stage of evolutionary cycle. This is mathematical cause of "crisis". Economy evolves cyclically via the sequence of evolutionary cycles with different durations. The process of economic oscillations is a normal law of the economic development. If amplitudes of these oscillations at the "crisis" stage are small people don't think about it as a "catastrophe". However of course it is a "catastrophe" mathematically, a small catastrophe. The role of the "crisis" is similar to the role of the disease in human life. "Crisis" initiates and stimulates the upgrade within economic system just like a non dangerous short-term disease strengthens human organism and like the vaccination strengthens immunity. However there are special situations when depth and duration of crisis suddenly increase over a ordinary values. The depth of crisis could increase due to the deformation of "evolutionary branches" of the economic CAS and/or due to the adverse shift of global equilibrium point in the plane of a "density of conditions" – "efficiency". The reasons which lead to the changes of evolutionary branches, apparently, are connected with features of a system's configuration. Just like a course of a disease depends on internal state of an organism, on internal hidden imbalances of work of different inner systems, on the "inner harmony" of their work, the depth and duration of a crisis in the economy in the same way depends on the internal chronic system imbalances, on the state of "inner harmony" within the economic system. Each crisis initiates and stimulates reconfiguration (upgrade) of a system and restoration of "internal harmony" within economic system. It means that old institutions, laws, and rules of behaviour are rapidly changing during and after crisis. The phenomenon "Great Depression" of 1930s is the unique example which illustrates both the existence of evolutionary branches and the influence of configuration of the economic system on the disposition and geometric form of evolutionary branches. The depth of crisis was strengthened by rapid adverse shift of long-term equilibrium point $\left(Z_0; R = 1\right)$ (Figure 3). This shift increased productivity of capital P_0 and have eliminated deep internal tensions in a system configuration.

The striving for gaining maximum profit has always been a dominant factor of economic growth. Let us call this factor "economic selfishness". A selfishness in economic systems is not only a condition of personal welfare growth, but also a force retaining personal selfish behavior in economics in certain limits.

The situation changes cardinally when each segment of the market is controlled by several most powerful economic agents (stakeholders) that rule the game for all market participants. Selfish force dominates in those systems. Economic selfishness of those stakeholders suppresses economic initiative of other economic agents.

A good example of this type of economy is the economy of the United States in early thirties. Prosperity of the twenties was sustained by routines of behaviour of economic agents which in fact were violating the principle of "inner harmony" in society. The system of resources distribution became extremely unbalanced when a small group of stakeholders became very reach, and many others became very poor and barely could make ends meet. Economically strong units were ruling over economically weak units. Stakeholders didn't have any interest in collaboration with the rest of population; they didn't even understand that interests of others need to be taken into account also.

There were three basic forms of economic selfishness at different levels of society:

1. Large businesses put too much pressure on individual small producers. This pressure was especially strong in the farm industry.
2. Business owners put too much pressure on their employees.
3. The United States put too much pressure on other countries which became their debtors after the First World War.

This infringement of "internal harmony" principle that finally ended up in unprecedented depression that paralysed national economy for nearly ten years. We do not mean to say that the violation of moral laws was the reason of crisis. There is no any direct interrelation between morality and economy. However, ignorance of the problems of economic disballances and inability to solve them timely was the main cause of the deep and long crisis in 1930s.

Business is based on selfishness; therefore only governments and civil societies can ensure the state of "internal harmony" within the economic system via civil codes. A new reality emerged in twenties: large corporations started to control economy. This new economy needed a new social system which is able to restrict the economic selfishness of corporations and solve inequality problems in society. Such system did not exist in twenties. That's why problems were accumulating and finally this burden of unsolved problems have led to a crisis.

Let's list factors which caused long-term excess of rate of investment ν over the level required for the normal development in twenties.

Large business (corporations) dictated prices and conditions of sales to the other producers. Corporations were establishing ungrounded high prices and were making super profits. The monopolies and large corporations were growing enormously rich which caused profits decrease in dispersed individual manufacturers.

Gardiner C. Means (1934) told at the annual meeting of the American Statistical Association:

… The last century has seen a steadily increasing shift from market coordination to administrative coordination… As a result of this shift from market to administration, the area of coordination remaining to the market has been greatly reduced while the increased bargaining power of the big administrative units has induced the counter concentration in the form of cooperative bargaining organizations, farm cooperatives, labor unions… thus reducing the number of separate units interacting though the market… Prices have become problems of administration. (Himmelberg, 1968; p.30)

The prices fixed administratively mismatched the costs. These were rigid (fixed) prices. These prices lost the capacity to regulate the market and started to dominate in economy by the end of twenties. Means (1935) said:

Very many of our wholesale prices are administrated. Administrated prices are to be found in a great many highly competitive industries… Inflexible administrated prices are a major factor in our economy. This is heightened when we add relative inflexibility of railroad and utility rates, or salaries and often of labor rates, of many commercial loan rates, and of many government services…But ever in the … competitive industries such as automobiles, the rigidity of prices is evident while in the dispersed industries like farming… prices are extremely flexible…(1) Inflexible administrated prices are a major factor in our economy, (2) they constitute a serious impediment to balanced economic functioning, (3) they result primarily from and are inherent in economic concentration and modern industrial organization... (Ibid., 1968; p.29-30)

McCracken (1938) noted in his paper devoted to the influence of monopolies upon the crisis:

...We do not live in a frictionless world of free competition and flexible price... Our modern economy is marked by frictions of many types, by rigid prices administered by government or business organizations sufficiently unified and powerful to control supply and regulate prices.... Whereas one of the major functions of competition is to keep price related to cost the major purpose of monopoly is to break the connection between cost and price... Monopolistic competition tends to achieve equilibrium by holding prices relatively rigid and restricting the output to the demand which will be effective at the predetermined price. (Ibid., 1968; p. 34-35)

Pressure of corporations upon farmers was especially strong. Farm prices discrimination is the most outstanding example of economic inequality. Adams (1932) wrote:

The large business enterprises particularly in the fields of mining, manufacturing and trade through monopolies, cartels, and trade associations have been able in great measure to hold the prices of their products at relatively stable points in the face of an increasing output and lower costs... The farmers... partly because of the lack of joint ability to control output and the marketing of their products have little power to hold up the prices of their products. Producers' control of the prices of one class of products and the lack of control by producers of another class of products have thrown the price system out of adjustment and have caused an unbalanced development of industry. (Ibid., 1968; p.18-19)

The farmers' fate was disastrous in 1920-ies. Ostrolenk (1932) in New York Times, September 25, 1932 wrote:

The Most Superficial study of the statistics reveals that while industry reached a new peak of prosperity between 1920 and 1929, the farmer met with one financial setback after another, that he was becoming poorer and poorer, that the disaster of 1920 was followed by an even greater financial catastrophe in 1930. (Shannon, 1960; p.17)

The price level for agriculture goods was too low as compared with the industrial products. This resulted in serious migration of the rural population. The industrialization of America in the twenties was based upon the influx of cheap labor from villages and upon low prices for raw materials and staple foodstuffs. In this sense the city is growing rich while agriculture is becoming poorer. In this sense industry in cities was growing richer while agriculture in rural areas was becoming poorer.

Adams (1932) wrote:

The small purchasing power of the farming population (due to relatively low prices of agricultural products) since 1920 has adversely affected the demand for consumers' goods in the United States. In spite of this fact, however, the low prices of agricultural products were one of the forces upon which our great industrial expansion (1922-29) fed. The relatively low prices of agricultural products gave manufacturers cheaper raw materials and relieved them of stronger pressure for increases in wages of workers. Low agricultural prices also provided cheap food for the urban population, adding to their relative power to purchase other commodities. (Himmelberg, 1968; p.17-18)

Many economists were indicating that administrative inflexible prices one of the causes of the crisis of thirties. Means (1935) said:

The most significance of these inflexible prices lies in their disruptive effect on the functioning of our economy", "if all prices had been flexible it is doubtful if we would have had a serious depression after the stock crash of 1929. Instead of producing lower prices, the drop demand produces a drop in sales and in production. Workers and machines are thrown out of use and both owners and workers have less to spend, thus amplifying the original drop in demand. In this manner, rigid prices can expand an initial small fluctuation of industrial activity into a cataclysmic depression. (Ibid.; p.29)

Adams (1932) wrote:

I agree with those who hold that both individual prices and the system of prices have lost some the elasticity they used to have, and that this change has contributed to our present difficulties... I believe that... if prices had generally followed the lead of declining costs, we should have had today only a very mild business depression, or, no at all, instead of the very severe one we now have. (Ibid.; p.18)

The privileged position of the United States as compared to the other countries after the First World War guaranteed extremely favourable trade balance. The United States became a world creditor. The entire country was growing due to privileged position of the United States in the World. The countries - debtors were either had to expand their export, pay with gold, or take new loans.

This policy eventually disturbed the balance in the world stock markets. The change in the world prices distorted the price structure within the country. Benkert (1933) in pamphlet "How to Restore Values…" wrote:

It is evident that the existing paralysis of business in the United States is due primarily to a break down of fair price interrelationships among commodities, raw materials, manufactured goods and services… The present price level of commodities and raw materials in contrast with the price level of essential services as expressed in taxes, interest and maturing debts, rents, transportation and utility rates… Many commodity and raw material prices… are at the lowest level in a century. Essential services depending on contract or government fixation still enjoy the peak price level of recent years… What has caused the present disparity in prices? …
During the war the United States had changed from a debtor to a preponderant creditor nation. During the past-war decade … most of the civilized nations of the world became our debtors… Foreign nations were therefore compelled to curtail imports and expand exports to provide funds for service charges on these external loans… In many of these countries programs were initiated to reduce the quantity of commodities used by their own populations in order to have a greater supply for export and at the same time their own manufactures were stimulated so as to reduce imports and provide additional exports to equalize their balance of payments… These policies initiated even before the crash of 1929, started a worldwide downward trend of commodity prices…" and "…compelled our foreign debtor nations to bid for gold… This procedure… broke down world price levels and flooded all markets with cheaper and cheaper goods… Our price level for commodities, raw materials and other goods in world competition… declined proportionately. Our domestic price levels for services and goods depending on contract, governmental fixation, usage, trade combinations, etc., remained where they were. Thus was brought about the disparity in price levels within our own country. (Ibid.; p.1-3)

Gordon (1952) describes the crash of the "debt bondage" policy carried out in the twenties.

During the First World War, the United States became a creditor of international account. In the decade following, the surplus of exports over imports had paid the interest and principal on loans from Europe continued. The high tariffs, which restricted imports and helped to create this surplus of exports, remained... Other countries, which were buying more than they sold, and had debt payments to make in addition, had somehow to find the means for making up the deficit in their transactions with United States.

During most of the twenties the difference was covered by cash – i.e., gold payments to the United States – and by new private loans by the United States to other countries. Most of the loans were to governments... and a large proportion were to Germany and Central and South America... Countries could not cover their adverse trade balance with the United States with increased payments of gold... This meant that they had either to increase their exports to the United States or reduce their imports or default on their past loans... Accordingly, debts, including war debts, went into default and there was a precipitate fall in American exports... It contributed to the general distress and was especially hard on farmers. (Ibid.; p.92-93)

The redistribution of national income in favor of proprietors occurred in twenties. The share of wage in national income was diminishing during 1920s. This eventually disrupted the demand for consumer goods artificially maintained by means of the crediting system (instalment buying). Those who lived on income from property grew relatively rich while those who lived on earnings.

Adams (1932) wrote:

The pursuit of profits was the underlying incentive which brought into action the forces which increased our power of production. From the standpoint of production of economic goods and services, we have today, the most effective industrial system the world has been seen.

But in this system one outstanding weakness is now apparent. We have failed to develop effective methods of the distribution of money income to the mass of consumers. The money income received by consumers is not sufficiently large to enable them to purchase at prevailing prices the consumers' goods and services, which our economic system produces. This outstanding weakness is a result largely of the desire for high profits on the part of managers. (Ibid.; p.19)

From 1923 to 1929 our economic system was trough out of balance. During this period we increased our power to produce goods, especially per worker, while at the same time the distribution of the current money income or power to purchase these goods became more unequal and maladjusted. This lack of balance was overcome temporarily through the unsound use of bank credit in creating buying power and therefore the demand for goods. The artificial prosperity thus generated could not last forever. The maladjustment between the production of goods and the distribution of income finally showed itself in the present depression. (Ibid.; p.15).

Galbraith (1955) notes in book *"The Great Crash, 1929"*:

In 1929... 5% of the population with the highest incomes received approximately one third of all personal income. The proportion of personal income received in the form of interest, dividends, and rent... was about twice as great as in the years following the Second World War. This highly unequal income distribution meant that the economy was depend on a high level of investment. (Ibid.; p.90)

The reasons for growth of the share of property in national income during 1920s are: (1) the excess profit of corporations that was backed administratively by the system of fixed prices, (2) the speculative boom at the end of twentieth that was followed by surge of frauds and swindles. John Galbraith writes:

American enterprise in the twenties had opened its hospitable arms to an exceptional number of promoters, gaffers, swindlers, impostors, and frauds. (Ibid.; p.91)

The Banking Act of 1933; Securities Act of 1933; and Securities and Exchange Act of 1934 that drastically restricted the possibility of financial manipulations was the first step undertaken by the government as soon as the society recovered from the crisis.

John K.G's opinion summarizes all the above:

In 1929... the economy was fundamentally unsound. (Ibid.; p.90)

Let us list the principal items of this "disease" once again:

1. Large-scale businesses had a huge advantage over non-united dispersed manufacturers for increasing profits; figuratively speaking, they

were making their profits basically "at the expense" of those small manufactures.

2. Urban setting prospered "at the expense" of rural settings.
3. The country in general was making profit due to privileged position among other countries.
4. The group of proprietors were increasing their own part of national income by reducing shares of workers.

The economic system suffered from the excessive selfishness. The crisis of the 1930s was the direct consequence of infringement of ballance in distribution of incomes between different social groups both within country and between countries. The fundamental principle of internal harmony has been broken. In this sense the economic situation in twenties contadicted religious and ethical principles of human life. Respected orthodox priest Nikolay Serbian characterizes those events in one of his letters in the following way:

"Crisis" is a Greek word (χρισισ); it means "court" in translation... In earlier times the Europeans, if struck by misfortune, used the word "court"... Now the word court is substituted by the word "crisis"... You ask about the cause of the present crisis, or the God's court? The cause is always the same – ... recreancy from God... Lord used modern instruments to talk some sense contemporary people. He struck a blow on banks, stock exchanges and the whole financial system. He overturned the tables of moneychangers all over the world, as He once did in the Jerusalem Temple. He spread unheard-of panic among the dealers and moneychangers. He disturbed everything, overthrew, confused, and aroused fear... (Serbian, 2003; p. 17)

Below are the evidence of witnesses of those events, the economists, well-known political figures, and ordinary people. People thoght about it as a catastrophe. David A. Shannon, the editor of collected articles *"The Great Depression"*, in 1961, assesses the events of those years like this:

...The Great Depression was a traumatic experience. It was all the more traumatic because the immediately preceding years had been quite comfortable once on the whole and the American mood had been, unusually optimistic. During the 1920' business and political leaders spoke of the New Era... An ever-expanding economy, full employment, and the elimination of poverty were permanent futures, many believed, of the New Era. (Shannon, 1960; p. IX)

In twenties the business was prospering, the incomes were growing, and nothing foreboded the thunderstorm. John Kenneth Galbraith characterizes the economic situation on the eve of the crisis as follows:

In 1929 the labor force was not tired, it could have continued to produce indefinitely at the best 1929 rate. The capital plant of the country was not depleted. In the proceeding years of prosperity, plant had been renewed and improved. In fact, depletion of the capital plant occurred during the ensuring years of idleness when new investment was sharply curtailed. Raw materials in 1929 were ample for the current rate of production. Entrepreneurs were never more eupeptic. Obviously if men, materials, plant and management were all capable of continued and even enlarged exertions a refreshing pause was not necessary. (Himmelberg, 1968; p.88)

Robert A. Gordon (1952) notes the following in his detailed research:

From 1923 though 1929, business remained at a high level and tended to increase still further… We thus have a picture of a prolonged investment boom, which supported a steady expansion in incomes and consumers' demand and at same time provided the enlarged capacity necessary to meet the rising demand for goods and services. (Ibid.; p.104)
There was overinvestment in the late 1920's in the sense that capacity… had been expanding at a rate that could not be indefinitely maintained… The chief immediate cause of the downturn, then, was probably the impact of "partial overinvestment" on business expectations. This, however, is not sufficient to account for the length or severity of the depression… (Ibid.; p.108)

There is not so far a common opinion so far among the economists about the reasons that engendered this stagnation in economy, unprecedented in terms of gravity and duration. The fact of stagnation was unusual because it happened without any visible external reasons: there were no wars, droughts or any natural disasters, or social cataclysms.

According to Arthur B. Adams (1932):

The economic conditions which led up to the depression were somewhat similar to those which have led up to other business depressions: were increase in production, increase in trade, and considerable inflation in bank credit. (Ibid.; p.15)

John Kenneth Galbraith (1955) writes:

But unlike these other occasions in 1929 the recession continued and contin-
ued and got violently worse. This is unique feature of the 1929 experience.
This is what we need really to understand. (Ibid.; p.90)
What... are plausible causes of the depression the task of answering can be
simplified somewhat by dividing the problem into two parts. First there is
the question of why economic activity turned down in 1929. Second there
is the vastly more important question of why, having started down, on this
unhappy occasion it went down and down and down and remained low for
a full decade. (Ibid.; p.89)

David A. Shannon named the events of 1930s a "catastrophe that paralyzed
America for more than a decade". This is mathematically exact definition of
a sequence of the events during those years. The crisis of 30-ies was in fact
a catastrophe in mathematical sense, a jump of the economic system from
the "upper evolutionary branch" into the "lower evolutionary branch". However, this time the jump was accompanied by a rapid growth of long-term
productivity of the capital. This resulted a shift of point Z_0 to the left in the
plane $\left(Z;R\right)$. Therefore the crisis became much deeper and longer than normal stage of crisis in course of the usual business cycle. (Figure 3).

The growth of long-term productivity of capital had being forming for a
long time and was a direct consequence of industrialisation in twenties.
However, the adaptation of the economic system to new level of productivity of the capital was requiring the reduction of investment rate ν in accor-
dance with the equation, $P_0 = \dfrac{1}{Z_0} = \dfrac{a + \Lambda}{\nu}$, so it contradicted the interest of
those who lived on excessive investment rate (speculators and brokers at the
stock exchange).

The high speed of shift of the point $\left(Z_0;R=1\right)$ after the "Black Tuesday"
is the direct consequence of the situation when the force maintained the
stable location of that point in the place $\left(Z;R\right)$ lost its effect, and the economic system was able to begin the structural change that had been matured
for a long time.

Robert A. Gordon (1952) expressed the widespread point of view of later
economists regarding the events of those years:

Investment opportunities (30th) were restricted then because they had been so
thoroughly exploited in the 1920's and because the severity of the financial

liquidation after 1929 led businessmen and investors to view with a jaundiced eye the opportunities that were available. (Ibid.; p.110)

"Black Tuesday" changed the long-term expectations radically. Unreasonably overestimated expectations of super profits disappeared. A possibility to adjust the economic system to new level of long-term productivity of the capital came into being. However, in order to make this happen, it was necessary to eliminate the inner economic misbalances accumulated in the twenties. Roosevelt's policy of New Deal was the system of measures that managed to solve this problem.

Joseph A. Schumpeter (1939) in His book *"Business Cycles"* writes:

"Objectively" – i.e. irrespectively of intentions harbored by any individuals – they (investors) amounted to systematic attack on investment opportunity all round: it was frontally attacked by direct reduction of revenues – or the operative part of total net revenues – though taxation, which would have been only the more effective if there really had been also an inherent tendency for investment opportunity to shrink; simultaneously, it was attacked in the rear by increasing costs; and both attacks were supplemented by a third – the attack on those traditional methods of management, pricing, and financing in the sphere of "big business", which were associated with the latter's emergence and successes. (Ibid.; p.67)

The crisis of the 1930s started as a normal "jump" of the economic system from the "upper evolutionary branch" towards the "lower evolutionary branch". Mathematically, jumps like that underlie the business cycles. According to our hypothesis, they represent regularly occurring micro-catastrophes which stimulate qualitative upgrade and progress of economic system. However this time the jump downwards turned out to be a catastrophe in every sense of the word.

David A. Shannon describes the events of that time as follows:

After several months of depression America was indeed a place turned topsy-turvy. Even the surface appearance of the cites changed. Former bond sales-men were on the sidewalks trying to sell apples. Former clerks roamed the business districts in attempts to make a living by shining shoes. Unemployed and homeless men welcomed arrests for vagrancy and the warmth and food to be had in jail. Over a hundred thousand American workers applied for jobs in the Soviet Union. Shanty towns appeared in and around the industrial cities,

and the inhabitants of these housing developments born desperation bitterly named them for the President of the United States. (Shannon, 1960; p.1)
It is difficult to say whether the unemployed urban worker or the farmer suffered the more from the depression. (Ibid.; p.16)
Forlorn, down-and-out men shuffled hopeless through bread lines. (Ibid.; p. IX)
Industrial workers and farmers dearly suffered more from want during the depression than other economic groups. Nevertheless, the deprivations of middle-class families were serious. Most people who made their living from their invested capital, from their business, or from their professional work did not go hungry – although some did – but many lost a considerable part of their fortune and took a major loss of income. (Ibid.; p.72)

New York Times, June 5, 1932 was writing:

Darwin's theory that man can adopt himself to almost any new environment is being illustrated, in this days of economic change, by thousands of New Yorkers who have discovered new ways to live and new ways to earn a living since their formerly placid lives were thrown into chaos by unemployment or kindred exigencies. (Ibid.; p.10)

John Kenneth Galbraith is characterizing the overall atmosphere of 1930-ies as follows:

When the misfortune had struck, the attitudes of the time kept anything from being done about it. This, perhaps, was the most disconcerting feature of all. Some people were hungry in 1930 and 1931 and 1932. Others were tortured by the fear that they might go hungry. Yet others suffered the agony of the descent from the honor and respectability that goes with income into poverty. And still others feared that they would be next. Meanwhile everyone suffered from a sense of utter hopelessness. (Himmelberg, 1968; p.95)

David A. Shannon writes:

In 1931 and 1932 talk of social revolution become common. Surely though thousands of people the dispossessed and the hungry will revolt against the government and the economic system that had brought them to their desperate situation. But no revolution came. At least there was no revolution such as many anticipated, with rioting, blood in the gutters and violent overthrow of government. Instead a majority of the electorate switched its allegiance from the party of Herbert Hoover to the party of Franklin Delano Roosevelt. (Shannon, 1960; p. X)

A change of power took place instead of revolution. Roosevelt's New Deal policies removed the economy from crisis. Different economists assess the importance of this policy in the recovery process in different ways. But despite of shortcomings of specific acts, New Deal policies objectively promoted overcoming the crisis.

It was a rigid policy of restricting of economic selfishness: (1) establishing of control over the banks and stock markets activity (The Banking and Securities Acts of 1933 and Securities and Exchange Act of 1934), (2) establishing of the control over prices and wage rates (National Industrial Recovery Act (June, 1933) – NIRA and National Labor Relation Act (Jule, 1935); Public Utility Act of 1935), and (3) introduction of higher taxes on corporate profit.

John Chamberlain, a journalist and commentator on the economic and political scene, wrote in his book *"The Enterprising Americans: A Business History of the United States"*, 1963:

The first important domestic creation the New Deal, the NRA, was a total abnegation of the competitive market economy... With its price-fixing and market-allocating codes the NRA was a denial of the free system... Businessmen came to ask themselves whether Roosevelt really understood a system where the hope of profit sparks expansion and investment. (Shannon, 1960; p.96)

The policy of redistribution of national income made possible to increase share of labor. John Chamberlain gives the following figures:

... Money wage rates in manufacturing advanced some 43 per cent between 1933 and 1939 and real wages by an extraordinary 34 per cent... Some of this rise was no doubt to be expected in a period of partial recovery but much of it followed out of government-blessed wage boosts from an unprecedented surge of union organization. (Ibid.; p.97)

Relief, Housing and Social Security Programs (NIRA, Emergency Relief Act of 1932, National Housing Act of 1934; Social Security Act of 1935), Public Works, government intervention "for getting agriculture into a better balance with the rest of the economy" (Soil Conservation and Domestic Allotment Act of 1936 and the Agricultural Adjustment Act of 1938) and other measures taken by the government made it possible to relax the social tension. It was a policy of moderate socialist reforms, mild expropriation of the share of income of the society's richest section.

Franklin D. Roosevelt in 1934 had explained the essence of New Deal as follows:

What we seek is balance in our economic system – balance between agriculture and industry and balance between the wage earner, the employer, and the consumer. (Faulkner, 1949; p.199)

It is understandable that the bourgeoisie did not like these measures, but they were compelled to accept them (being afraid to lose everything otherwise).

In judgement of Joseph A. Schumpeter:

… Behind these measures, administrative acts, and anticipations there is something much more fundamental, viz., an attitude hostile to the industrial bourgeoisie… They (businessmen) are not only, but they feel threatened. (Himmelberg, 1968; p.68)

The willingness of government to find reasonable consensus that would suit all the parties and policies restricted the economic salfishness in society stabilized economy of the country. Timely return to the principle of "internal harmony" in politics helped to prevent the revolution and withdraw the country from chaos.

According to David A. Shannon:

Roosevelt and his party succeeded in partially alleviating the personal distress of the Great Depression and in effecting a partial economic recovery. (Shannon, 1960;; p. X)

Franklin D. Roosevelt in 1938 in his public speech on the radio expressed the close relationship of his politics with the principle of "internal harmony" as follows:

No doubt you will be told that the Government spending program of the past five years did not cause the increase in our national income… That is true in part, for the Government spent only a small part of the total. But Government spending acted as trigger to set off private activity…
The Government contribution of land that we once made to business was the land of all the people. And the Government contribution of money, which we now make to business ultimately, comes out of the labor of all the people. It

is therefore, only sound morality, as well as a sound distribution of buying power, that the benefits of the prosperity coming from this use of the money of all the people should be distributed among all the people – at the bottom as well as at the top. (Ibid.; p.27).

After the Great Crash at the New York Stock Exchange, the "Black Tuesday", as this unfortunate day will be called later, a catastrophe was developing as an avalanche. Let's note just some of the facts, illustrating them with statistical data. The next day after the collapse a regular issue of New York Times was released with a bombastic title: *"Worst Stock Crash stemmed by banks. 12,894,650 – Share Day Swamps Market Leaders Confer, Find Conditions Sound":*

The most disastrous decline in the biggest and broadest stock market at history... The total losses cannot be accurately calculated because of the large number of markets and the thousands of securities not listed on any exchange. However, they were staggering, running into billions of dollars. (Ibid.; p.2)

Monstrous in its scale fall of shares was really a serious blow to stability of the economy. However, some cases of large-scale collapse in stock markets were happening before; this has always seriously affected the economic activity, but in reality the economy was adjusting to the changes in the stock market after a while. Therefore no one could expect that the Wall Street collapse would cause those consequences.

On the day of crash, October 24, after an emergency meeting at the office of J.P. Morgan & Co. five most influential bankers assured citizens:

... That the market smash has been caused by technical rather than fundamental consideration and that many sound stocks are selling too low. (Ibid.; p.2)

Also, in 6 days New York Times informed that:
Stock Prices virtually collapsed yesterday, swept downward with gigantic losses in the most disastrous trading day in the stock market's history. (Ibid.; p.4)

The economic indices of 1929 did not cause any serious anxiousness although there were some indicators of weakening of business activity. John Kenneth Galbraith inform, for instance:

Federal Reserve indexes of industrial activity and of factory production... reached a peak in June. They then turned down and continued to decline throughout the rest of the year…The turning point in other indicators – factory payrolls, freight-car loadings and department store sales – came later, and it was October or after before the trend in all of them was clearly down… the summer of 1929 marked the beginning of the familiar inventory recession. (Himmelberg, 1968; p.89)

However the economy overall seemed to be stable. Broadus Mitchell, a distinguished economic historian writes about economic situation shortly before "Black Tuesday" in his book *"Depression Decade: From New Era through New Deal, 1929-1941"*:

The White House reported the President as considering "that business could look forward to the coming year with greater assurance". H. Booth, president of the Merchants' Association of New York, saw "no fundamental reason why business should not find itself again on the upgrade early in 1930… (Shannon, 1960; p.5)

Public authorities did not believe in a possibility of a serious crisis and reassured the people that it wasn't anything significant.
According to Broadus Mitchell (1947):

The Guaranty Trust Company of New York expressed qualified hope: "Although there is no failure to appreciate the importance of the collapse of stock prices as an influence on general business or to ignore the historical fact that such a collapse has almost invariably been followed by a major business recession, emphasis has… been placed on certain fundamental differences between the conditions that exist at present and these that have usually been witnessed at similar times in past. (Ibid.; p.5)

However, inspite of all forecasts and expectations, the crisis was developing. The economy not just did not recover after a shock but continued to fall despite of all assurances and conjurations. According to David A. Shannon:

The Wall Street debacle directly and immediately affected only a relatively small part of the American population, but a new and dismal era had began. Despite the assurance – or incantations – of business and political leaders that the stock market crash did not reflect upon the health of the economy in general, it was not long before almost every indication of the nation's economic welfare showed trouble. (Ibid.; p.1)

People did not realize immediately that the shares drop that time was radically different than ever. They did not realize right away that the downfall of the stock market was a certain kind of "perturbance" of economic system, and after that the system is not able to return to its former equilibrium state.

John Kenneth Galbraith noted:

On the whole, the great stock market crash can be more readily explained than the depression that followed it. And among the problems involved in assessing the causes of depression none is more intractable than the responsibility to be assigned to the stock market crash. Economics still does not allow final answers on these matters... After the Great Crash came the Great Depression which lasted, with varying severity, for ten years... It is easier to account for the boom and crash in the market than to explain their bearing on the depression, which followed. The causes of the Great Depression are still far from certain. (Himmelberg, 1968; p.86-87)

Let's formulate once again our interpretation of the crisis of the 1930s. Its main feature is the fact that the recession was unusual, significantly strengthened by considerable and fast change of the parameters of the system, namely, by rapid reduction of "density of conditions" Z_0.

This considerable reduction was a consequence of two reasons: 1) a growth of long-term productivity of the capital during the twenties and 2) excessive investment rate in this period above the level that would match this new, higher long-term productivity of the capital.

Banking system closely connected with the stock market was the first who have suffered because of the events of Black Tuesday.

According to David A. Shannon:

Banks began to fail at an alarming rate. (Shannon, 1960; p. IX)
...More than 5,000 banks closed their doors in the three years, 1930-1932. (Ibid., p.72)

Harold U. Faulkner in His book *"Labor in America"*, informs:

In the two years, 1930-31, 3,750 banks failed. (Faulkner, 1949; p.195)

William Greenleaf (1968), in book *"American Economic Development Since 1860"*, describes the banking system collapse as follows:

The real run on the American banks can be dated from the failure of the Bank of the United States in New York in December, 1930. From that time... failures continued at an increasing rate... The R.F.C. (Reconstruction Finance Corporation, based in January 1932) succeeded in slackening the pace of failures, though they continued throughout 1932 at the average rate of 40 banks and $2 million of deposits every each... Towards the end of the year the final collapse began. The first state moratorium was declared on October 31st; the Detroit banks closed on February 14, 1933, and within three weeks the bank "holiday' had spread to every state in the Union. (Greenleaf, 1968; p.193-194)

Default hit the real economy as well by rapid fall of demand for the investment goods.

According to John Kenneth Galbraith:

The collapse in securities values affected in the first instance the wealthy and the well-to-do. But... in the world of 1929 this was a vital group. The members disposed of a large proportion of the consumer income; they were the source of a lion's share of personal saving and investment. Anything that struck of the spending or investment by this group would of necessity have broad effects on expenditure and income in the economy at large. Precisely such a blow was struck by the stock market crash... (Himmelberg, 1968; p.95)

David A. Shannon notes:

The Wall Street panic triggered a general collapse. Within only a few months unemployment becomes a serious problem. (Shannon, 1960; p. IX)

Webbink (1941) published the following facts about the increase of unemployment in 1930s.

Within a few months after the stock market collapse of October, 1929, unemployment had been catapulted from its status of a vague worry to be considered some future day into position of one of the country's foremost preoccupation. Unemployment increased steadily... from the fall of 1929 to the spring of 1933. (Shannon, 1960; p.VI)

According to Paul Webbink (1941), the unemployment has doubled from March 1930 to March 1931, and the next year - by 50 more percent. By March 1932 the unemployment by different estimates had reached from 11,250,000 to 12,500,000. The peak of unemployment was in winter 1932-1933. Different sources give approximately the same numbers. According to Robert Nathan, by March 1933 the country had 13,577,000 unemployed. According to National Industrial Conference Board, the number of unemployed at that moment was 14,586,000. American Federation of Labor and Congress of Industrial Organizations provide still greater values - 15,389,000 and 16,000,000 respectively.

According to John Kenneth Galbraith:

In 1933 nearly thirteen million were out of work, or about one in every four in the labor force. (Himmelberg, 1968; p.86)

The drop in production reached catastrophic scale. The curtailment of production entailed the fall in prices, reduction of hourly wages of industrial workers and employees' salaries.

John Kenneth Galbraith informs:

In 1933 GNP... was nearly a third less than in 1929. Not until 1937 did the physical volume of production recover to the levels of 1929, and then it promptly slipped back again. Until 1941 the dollar value of production remained below 1929. Between 1930 and 1940 only once, in 1937, did the average number unemployed during the year drop below eight million. (Ibid.; p.86)

We could proceed with adducing another facts and figures describing the huge catastrophe that happened in America in the thirties. The scope of the tragedy may be evidenced by the figures of increment of population (Table 6) given by Alvin H. Hansen (1951) in book "Business Cycles and National Income" (p. 76):

It is clear that the "Black Tuesday" engendered this catastrophe but didn't cause it. It was already mentioned that the cause was infringement of principle of "internal harmony" in twenties. This disharmony created a gap between the potential and actual productivity of capital. This gap was growing during twenties. The rate of the investments in 1920s was overestimated due to speculative boom in stock markets and seemed to guarantee a welfare of the investors.

The collapse in stock market was the incitement that caused the fall of the economic system from the "upper evolutionary branch" into the "lower branch". In this sense it was simply the influence that stimulates the jump downwards i. e. the "crisis" stage of evolutionary cycle. But "Black Tuesday" didn't meet the expectations as well. It caused a rapid shift of the point

Table 6. The increase in population in the United States (ten-year data)

Decade	Increase in population (Millions of persons). Source: Hansen (1951).
1900-1909	16
1910-1919	13.7
1920-1929	17
1930-1939	8.9
1940-1949	18

$\left(Z_0; R = 1\right)$ which became the reason of unusual depth and unusual duration of this crisis.

The high rate of investment was sustained in the twenties due to the following properties of economy:

1.   Privileged financial position of the country in the world,
2.   Low share of labor in the national income,
3.   Disproportion of prices for the products of big and small business,
4.   Too high prices for the products of monopolies.

All these factors created the situation of long-term implicit misbalance in the economic system. "Internal tensions" between different parts within system's configuration were accumulated during long time period. Collapse of stock market was only trigger that activated and transformed these "inner tensions" into the actual process of destruction of previous configuration of the economic system.

If the investment rate had lowered smoothly in twenties within several cycles, the Great Depression wouldn't have happened. The economy would continuously shift to a new level of productivity of the capital. Each separate crisis would be somewhat more profound, but overall the transition would be less painful. However, such a route demanded a restriction for the "economic selfishness" on the part of the society. A social system that could have taken the role of such a restricting factor was not built yet in twenties.

REFERENCES

Adams, A. B. (1932). *Trends of business 1922-1932*. Harper & Brothers.

Aulin, A. (1997). *The origins of economic growth. The fundamental interaction between material and nonmaterial values*. Berlin: Springer - Verlag.

Benkert, A. W. (1933). *How to restore values. The quick safe way out of the Depression, The John Day Pamphlets, No. 23*. New York: The John Day Co.

Chamberlain, J. (1963). *The enterprising Americans: a business history of the United States*. New York: Harper Colophon Books.

Faulkner, H. U. (1949). *Labor in America*. New York: Harper & brothers.

Galbraith, J. K. (1955). *The Great Crash 1929*. Boston: Houghton Mifflin Company.

Gordon, R. A. (1952). *Business fluctuations*. New York: Harper & Row.

Greenleaf, W. (1968). *American economic development since 1860*. New York: Harper & Row.

Hansen, A. H. (1951). *Business cycles and national income*. New York: W.W. Norton & Co.

Himmelberg, R. F. (1968). *The Great Depression and American capitalism*. Boston: D.C. Heath and Co.

Kendrick, J. W. (1961). *Productivity trends in the United States*. Princeton, NJ: The National Bureau of Economic Research (NBER), General Series, No.71.

McCracken, H. L. (1938, October). Monopolistic competition and business fluctuations. *Southern Economic Journal, 2*(2), 158–178. doi:10.2307/1052445

Means, G. C. (1935). Price inflexibility and the requirements of a stabilizing monetary policy. *Journal of the American Statistical Association, 30*(June), 401–413. doi:10.1080/01621459.1935.10502286

Mitchell, B. (1947). *Depression decade: from New Era through New Deal, 1929-1941*. New York: Rinehart & Co., Inc.

Ostrolenk, B. (1932, September 25). The farmer's plight: a far-reaching crisis. *New York Times*.

Rabbani, S. (2006). *Deviation of constant labor and capital share from the Cobb-Douglas production function.* Retrieved October 19, 2016 from: http://srabbani.com/

Schumpeter, J. A. (1939). *Business cycles.* New York: McGraw-Hill Book Company.

Serbian, N. (2003). *Missionary letters.* Publishing house of the Moscow farmstead of the Trinity Lavra of St. Sergius.

Shannon, D. A., (1960). *The Great Depression.* Prentice-Hall, Inc.

Solow, R. M. (1957). Technical change and production function. *The Review of Economics and Statistics*, *39*(3), 312–320. doi:10.2307/1926047

Webbink, P. (1941). Unemployment in the United States, 1930-1940. *Papers and Proceedings of the American Economic Association.* American Economic Association.

ENDNOTE

[1]   Economic systems with changing economic parameters are considered in Chapter 4.

Chapter 4
MSP–Systems with Variable Parameters

MSP-EQUATIONS AND PRINCIPLE OF MAXIMIZATION

In this chapter we consider generalization of Method of Systems Potential for the case of systems with variable evolutionary parameters. At first we consider general mathematical formulation of this task. In MSP-model of economic CAS evolutionary parameters of economic system, economic parameters, change with time. Rate of growth, a, is very unstable value. The norm of investment (investment as a percentage of GDP) ν and depreciation rate Λ are much more stable values.

Although variation of parameters obviously depends partially from random factors we think that this is not a unique cause. By using stylized facts for the U.S. economy we shall show below that correlation between variations of different parameters exists in economy. Therefore the model with constant evolutionary parameters is only approximate, rough model of reality.

MSP-equations were deduced from Lamarck's evolutionary laws. We didn't use assumption about constancy of evolutionary parameters when we

DOI: 10.4018/978-1-5225-2170-9.ch004

deduced MSP-equations (E1)-(E7) (Introduction). Assuming constancy of evolutionary parameters we obtained analytical solutions (13)-(21) of the equations (E1)-(E7) (Introduction).

Thus MSP-equations (E1)-(E7) are fulfilled even if evolutionary parameters are not constants. We interpret these equations as mathematical expressions of fundamental laws of evolution. These are laws which regulate the development of complex adaptive systems at macroscopic level. As a rule, fundamental laws in science express the action of the principle of maximization or of optimization of some criteria. For example laws of motion in physics follows from the principle of least action. Many of equations in economic modelling follows from the principle of maximization (of utility, profit, welfare and so on) or from the principle of minimization (of cost, expenditures and so on). Therefore it will be natural to assume that MSP-equations also can be deduced from the principle of maximization or minimization. Let's assume that MSP-equations follow from the principle of maximization of a goal-function. We don't discuss what sense this function makes until the application of MSP-model with variable parameters in economics will be considered.

Let' designate goal-function as $\Omega\left(\Phi;U;\Phi_R\right)$. We consider only a system of independent MSP-equations (E1), (E3) and (E4) (Introduction) for variables $\left(\Phi;U;\Phi_R\right)$. The equation (E2) follows from the equations (E1) and (E3). The equation (E5) follows from the equations (E1) and (E3). The equation (E6) follows from the equations (E3) and (E4). The equation (E7) follows from the equations (E5) and (E6). Graphically a goal-function $\xi=\Omega\left(\Phi;U;\Phi_R\right)$ is some kind of surface in 4-dimensional space $\left(\xi;\Phi;U;\Phi_R\right)$. Vector of gradient,

$$\nabla\Omega\equiv\left\{\frac{\partial\Omega}{\partial\Phi};\frac{\partial\Omega}{\partial U};\frac{\partial\Omega}{\partial\Phi_R};\right\}$$ in definite point of 3-dimensional space $\left(\Phi;U;\Phi_R\right)$

points in the direction of the greatest rate of increase of the goal-function. Vector $\left(\dot{\Phi};\dot{U};\dot{\Phi}_R\right)$ describes the shift of location of the system in space $\left(\Phi;U;\Phi_R\right)$ in unit of time. If we fix the length of this vector then vector of gradient for the goal-function determines the direction of the most rapid increase of this function. Let's assume that MSP-equations describe motion of the system along the vector of gradient $\left(\dot{\Phi};\dot{U};\dot{\Phi}_R\right)$ of the goal-function. It means that vectors $\nabla\Omega$ and $\left(\dot{\Phi};\dot{U};\dot{\Phi}_R\right)$ are collinear. Moreover we can always normalize the goal-function in such a way that these vectors will be equal.

It gives us the following system of the equations in partial derivatives:

$$\dot{\Phi} = -d \cdot \Phi + \left(a + d\right) \cdot \Phi_R = \frac{\partial \Omega}{\partial \Phi} \qquad (1)$$

$$\dot{U} = -\Lambda \cdot U + \nu \cdot \Phi_R = \frac{\partial \Omega}{\partial U} \qquad (2)$$

$$\dot{\Phi}_R = a \cdot \Phi_R = \frac{\partial \Omega}{\partial \Phi_R} \qquad (3)$$

We can consider the case when parameters Λ and d are the constant whereas parameters a and ν are variable values. This assumption is suitable for the economic model in which parameters Λ and d are much stable than parameters a and ν. Moreover these parameters, Λ and d, describe the rate of decrease of potential and conditions of realization influenced by action of the entropy principle. This is the fundamental principle of nature and we reasonably assume that these parameters most likely are almost constant values.

In order that to simplify the equations we use the following designations in this chapter:

$$\Phi \to x; \ U \to y; \ \Phi_R \to z \qquad (4)$$

The equations (1)-(3) can be rewritten as follows:

$$\frac{\partial \Omega}{\partial x} = -d \cdot x + \left(a + d\right) \cdot z \qquad (5)$$

$$\frac{\partial \Omega}{\partial y} = -\Lambda \cdot y + \nu \cdot z \qquad (6)$$

$$\frac{\partial \Omega}{\partial z} = a \cdot z \qquad (7)$$

This is the system of three equations in partial derivatives for three variables. This system has solution if only mixed second-order derivatives are equal:

$$\frac{\partial^2 \Omega}{\partial x \partial y} = \frac{\partial^2 \Omega}{\partial y \partial x} \tag{8}$$

$$\frac{\partial^2 \Omega}{\partial x \partial z} = \frac{\partial^2 \Omega}{\partial z \partial x} \tag{9}$$

$$\frac{\partial^2 \Omega}{\partial y \partial z} = \frac{\partial^2 \Omega}{\partial z \partial y} \tag{10}$$

EQUATIONS FOR PARAMETERS a AND ν

Let parameters $a = a\left(x; y; z\right)$ and $\nu = \nu\left(x; y; z\right)$ are functions of variables $\left(x; y; z\right)$. Conditions (8)-(10) will be fulfilled if parameters a and ν are satisfying to the following equations in partial derivatives:

$$a'_y - \nu'_x = 0 \tag{11}$$

$$\left(a'_x - a'_z\right)z - a = d \tag{12}$$

$$\left(a'_y - \nu'_z\right)z - \nu = 0 \tag{13}$$

The following equation for function $\nu = \nu\left(x; y; z\right)$ follows from the equations (11) and (13):

$$\left(\nu'_x - \nu'_z\right)z - \nu = 0 \tag{14}$$

Particular solutions of this equation are solutions of the following kind:

$$\nu\left(x;y;z\right) = \frac{B\left(y\right)\cdot H\left(x+z\right)}{z} \tag{15}$$

Particular solutions of the equation (12) are solutions of the following kind:

$$a\left(x;y;z\right) = \frac{Y\left(y\right)\cdot A\left(x+z\right)}{z} + \frac{d\cdot x}{z} \tag{16}$$

Functions $B\left(y\right)$, $H\left(x+z\right)$, $Y\left(y\right)$ and $A\left(x+z\right)$ are arbitrary differentiable functions. The equation (11) gives the following equality:

$$\frac{B\left(y\right)\cdot H'\left(x+z\right)}{z} = \frac{Y'\left(y\right)\cdot A\left(x+z\right)}{z} \tag{17}$$

Sign "touch" means a derivative with respect to variable of function. For example $H'\left(x+z\right)$ means derivative with respect to variable $x+z$. We can rewrite the equation (17) as equation with separable variables:

$$\frac{A\left(x+z\right)}{H'\left(x+z\right)} = \frac{B\left(y\right)}{Y'\left(y\right)} = \alpha \tag{18}$$

Number α is the constant because left part of the equation (18) depends only on variable $x+z$ whereas right part of this equation depends only on variable y. It is only possible if number α is a constant.

We can rewrite the solutions (15)-(16) using the equalities (18) as follows:

$$\nu\left(x;y;z\right) = \frac{\alpha Y'\left(y\right)\cdot H\left(x+z\right)}{z} \tag{19}$$

$$a\left(x;y;z\right) = \frac{\alpha Y\left(y\right)\cdot H'\left(x+z\right)}{z} + \frac{d\cdot x}{z} \tag{20}$$

The first item at the right part of the equation (20) is a solution of the equation (12) with the right part which equals zero and the second item at the right part of the equation (20) is the particular solution of this equation. Linearity of the equation (12) with the right part which equals zero means that any combination of kind $\dfrac{\alpha Y(y) \cdot H'(x+z)}{z}$ can be added to the right part of the equation (20) without violation of equality (12). Linearity of the equation (14) means that any combination of kind $\dfrac{\alpha Y'(y) \cdot H(x+z)}{z}$ can be added to the right part of the equation (19) without violation of equality (14). Therefore general solutions of the equations (12) and (14) are the solutions of the following kind:

$$\nu = C_1 \cdot \frac{B(y) H(x+z)}{z} + C_2 \cdot \frac{H_1(x+z)}{z} + C_3 \cdot \frac{B_1(y)}{z} + C_4 \cdot \frac{B}{z} \tag{21}$$

$$a = C_5 \cdot \frac{Y(y) \cdot A(x+z)}{z} + C_6 \cdot \frac{A_1(x+z)}{z} + C_7 \cdot \frac{Y_1(y)}{z} + C_8 \cdot \frac{A}{z} + \frac{d \cdot x}{z} \tag{22}$$

Variables $x; y; z$ grow with time whereas parameters a and ν are located within limited intervals $a_{\min} < a < a_{\max}$ and $\nu_{\min} < \nu < \nu_{\max}$. We can satisfy this condition if functions at the right parts of the equalities (21) and (22) are linear fractional functions.

According to the equalities (21)-(22) these functions can be only functions of the following kind:

$$\nu = \frac{b_1 y + b_2(x+z)}{z} = b_1 \cdot \frac{y}{z} + b_2 \cdot \frac{x}{z} + b_2 \tag{23}$$

$$a = \frac{b_4 y + b_3(x+z)}{z} + \frac{d \cdot x}{z} = b_4 \cdot \frac{y}{z} + (b_3 + d) \cdot \frac{x}{z} + b_3 \tag{24}$$

Really ratios $\dfrac{x}{z} = \dfrac{1}{R}$ and $\dfrac{y}{z} = \dfrac{Z}{R}$ are variables which change in localized region of the plane $(Z;R)$ and b_2, b_3 are some constants. We still can add some constants to the numerators of fractions (23) and (24) but if variable z unlimitedly grows the influence of this additional constant is negligible. Therefore the equalities (23) and (24) are unique equalities which describe parameters a and ν changing within limited intervals $a_{\min} < a < a_{\max}$ and $\nu_{\min} < \nu < \nu_{\max}$. The next equality follows from the equation (11):

$$b_2 = b_4 \equiv \mu \tag{25}$$

Finally the equations (23)-(24) for parameters a and ν can be rewritten as follows:

$$\nu = \frac{b_1 y + \mu (x + z)}{z} \tag{26}$$

$$a = \frac{\mu y + b_3 (x + z)}{z} + \frac{d \cdot x}{z} \tag{27}$$

These formulas in standard designations can be written as:

$$\nu = \mu \left(1 + \frac{1}{R}\right) + \frac{b_1 Z}{R} \tag{28}$$

$$a = b_3 \left(1 + \frac{1}{R}\right) + \frac{\mu Z + d}{R} \tag{29}$$

Let's designate these parameters in the point of long-term equilibrium $(Z_0; R = 1)$ as ν_0 and a_0. We can express parameters b_1 and b_3 from these equations as follows:

$$b_1 = \frac{\nu_0 - 2\mu}{Z_0} \tag{30}$$

$$b_3 = \frac{a_0 - \mu Z_0 - d}{2} \tag{31}$$

GOAL-FUNCTION FOR MSP-SYSTEMS

The goal-function for parameters (28)-(29) can be found from the equations (5)-(7):

$$\Omega\left(x;y;z\right) = d \cdot xz + \frac{\left(b_1 - \Lambda\right)y^2}{2} + \mu \cdot y\left(x + z\right) + \frac{b_3 \cdot \left(x + z\right)^2}{2} \tag{32}$$

The graph of function $\Omega\left(x;y;z\right) = Const \equiv \Omega$ is a surface of the second order. The quadratic form (32) can be represented in the canonical form:

$$\frac{X^2}{P_1} + \frac{Y^2}{P_2} + \frac{Z^2}{P_3} = 1 \tag{33}$$

The signs of coefficients $P_1; P_2; P_3$ determine the type of a surface. Signatures of kind {--+},{-+-}{+--} correspond to a two-sheet hyperboloid. Signatures {-++},{++-}{+-+} correspond to a one-sheet hyperboloid. Signature of the kind {+++} corresponds to an ellipsoid.

The quadratic form (32) can be reduced to a canonical form via the following coordinate transformation:

$$X = x + \frac{\mu}{b_3}y + \left(1 + \frac{d}{b_3}\right)z \tag{34}$$

$$Y = y + \frac{Q}{2P} \cdot z \tag{35}$$

$$\tilde{Z} = z \tag{36}$$

$$P = -\frac{\mu^2}{2b_3} + \frac{b_1 - \Lambda}{2} \, ; \; Q = -\frac{\mu d}{b_3} \tag{37}$$

We have a canonical quadratic form in new variables:

$$\frac{X^2}{P_1} + \frac{Y^2}{P_2} + \frac{Z^2}{P_3} = 1 \tag{38}$$

$$P_1 = \frac{2\Omega}{b_3} \, ; \; P_2 = \frac{\Omega}{P} \, ; \; P_3 = -\frac{\Omega}{d + \dfrac{d^2}{2b_3} + \dfrac{Q^2}{4P}} \, . \tag{39}$$

The MSP-equations describe motion of a MSP-system in the direction of gradient of a goal-function. The goal-function in standard variables can be rewritten as follows:

$$\Omega\left(x; y; z\right) = \Phi^2 \cdot \left\{ d \cdot R + \frac{b_1 - \Lambda}{2} \cdot Z^2 + \mu \cdot Z \cdot \left(1 + R\right) + \frac{b_3}{2} \cdot \left(1 + R\right)^2 \right\} \tag{40}$$

The multiplier in braces is a limited value whereas potential increases with time. Therefore goal-function grows together with the potential.

EQUATIONS FOR FUNCTIONS $x\left(t\right)$, $y\left(t\right)$, $z\left(t\right)$, $R\left(t\right)$, $Z\left(t\right)$, $R\left(Z\right)$ FOR MSP-SYSTEMS WITH VARIABLE PARAMETERS

Equations for functions $x\left(t\right); y\left(t\right); z\left(t\right)$ follow from the equations (E1), (E3) and (E4) (Introduction) after substitution of the expressions (28)-(29):

$$\dot{x} = d \cdot z + \mu \cdot y + b_3 \cdot \left(x + z\right) \tag{41}$$

$$\dot{y} = \left(b_1 - \Lambda\right) \cdot y + \mu \cdot \left(x + z\right) \tag{42}$$

$$\dot{z} = d \cdot x + \mu \cdot y + b_3 \cdot \left(x + z\right) \tag{43}$$

$$\dot{R} = \left(1 - R\right)\left[\mu Z + \left(b_3 + d\right)\left(1 + R\right)\right] \tag{44}$$

$$\dot{Z} = -\mu Z^2 + Z\left[d - \Lambda + b_1 - \left(1 + R\right)\left(b_3 + d\right)\right] + \mu\left(1 + R\right) \tag{45}$$

We omit long calculations and give here only final result.
Solution of the equations (41)-(43)

$$x(t) = \left(\frac{\lambda_1 + p}{2\mu}\right)C_1 e^{\lambda_1 t} + \left(\frac{\lambda_2 + p}{2\mu}\right)C_2 e^{\lambda_2 t} + \left(\frac{x(0) - z(0)}{2}\right)e^{-d \cdot t} \tag{46}$$

$$y(t) = C_1 e^{\lambda_1 t} + C_2 e^{\lambda_2 t} \tag{47}$$

$$z(t) = \left(\frac{\lambda_1 + p}{2\mu}\right)C_1 e^{\lambda_1 t} + \left(\frac{\lambda_2 + p}{2\mu}\right)C_2 e^{\lambda_2 t} + \left(\frac{z(0) - x(0)}{2}\right)e^{-d \cdot t} \tag{48}$$

Constants in these formulas depend on parameters as follows:

$$\lambda_1 = \frac{q - p + \sqrt{\left(q - p\right)^2 + 4\left(2\mu^2 + pq\right)}}{2} \tag{49}$$

$$\lambda_2 = \frac{q - p - \sqrt{\left(q - p\right)^2 + 4\left(2\mu^2 + pq\right)}}{2} \tag{50}$$

$$p = \Lambda - b_1 \tag{51}$$

$$q = d + 2b_3 \tag{52}$$

$$C_1 = \frac{y(0) \cdot (\lambda_2 + p) - \mu \cdot (z(0) + x(0))}{\lambda_2 - \lambda_1} \tag{53}$$

$$C_2 = \frac{\mu \cdot (z(0) + x(0)) - y(0) \cdot (\lambda_1 + p)}{\lambda_2 - \lambda_1} \tag{54}$$

Solutions of the equations (42)-(43) follow from definitions:

$$R(t) = \frac{z(t)}{x(t)} \tag{55}$$

$$Z(t) = \frac{y(t)}{x(t)} \tag{56}$$

The equation for evolutionary branches follows from the equations (44)-(45):

$$\frac{dR}{dZ} = \frac{\dot{R}}{\dot{Z}} = \frac{(1-R)\left[\mu Z + \tilde{d}(1+R)\right]}{(-\mu)\left[(Z - Z_0)(Z - Z_1) + (1-R)\left(1 - \frac{\tilde{d} \cdot Z}{\mu}\right)\right]} \tag{57}$$

$$\tilde{d} = d + b_3 \tag{58}$$

$$Z_1 = \frac{-\tilde{p} - \sqrt{\tilde{p}^2 + 8}}{2} < 0 \tag{59}$$

$$Z_0 = \frac{\nu_0}{a_0 + \Lambda} \tag{60}$$

$$\tilde{p} = \frac{d + \Lambda + 2b_3 - b_1}{\mu} \tag{61}$$

The equation (57) is a kind of Jacobi' differential equation:

$$\frac{dy}{dx} = \frac{Axy + By^2 + ax + by + c}{Ax^2 + Bxy + \alpha x + \beta y + \gamma} \tag{62}$$

$$A = -\mu \,;\; B = -\tilde{d} \,;\; a = \mu \,;\; b = \tilde{d} \,;\; c = \tilde{d}$$

$$\alpha = -\left(Z_0 + Z_1\right) + \tilde{d} \,;\; \beta = \mu \,;\; \gamma = \left(-\mu\right)\left(Z_0 Z_1 + 1\right) \tag{63}$$

This equation can be reduced to a linear equation by the following variable substitution:

$$\xi = \frac{R - 1}{Z - Z_0} \quad \zeta = \frac{1}{Z - Z_0} \tag{64}$$

We obtain the following linear equation:

$$\xi\left(A_1 + A_2\xi\right)\frac{d\zeta}{d\xi} - \left(A_3 + A_2\xi\right)\zeta = \mu + \xi\tilde{d} \tag{65}$$

$$A_1 = -\left(2\tilde{d} + \mu Z_1\right) \; A_2 = \tilde{d} \cdot Z_0 - \mu \; A_3 = \mu\left(Z_0 - Z_1\right) \tag{66}$$

$$A_1 \neq 0 \; A_2 \neq 0 \; A_3 \neq 0 \tag{67}$$

Solution expressed via variables $Z; R$ describes evolutionary branches of MSP-system with variable parameters:

$$Z = Z_1 + \frac{(1 - R)(\mu - \tilde{d} \cdot Z_1)}{(2\tilde{d} + \mu Z_0)} - $$
$$-C_0 \cdot (Z_1 - Z_0) \cdot |1 - R|^\chi \cdot |(1 - R)(\mu - \tilde{d} \cdot Z_0) - (Z - Z_0)(2\tilde{d} + \mu Z_1)|^{1-\chi} \tag{68}$$

$$\chi \equiv \frac{\mu(Z_1 - Z_0)}{(2\tilde{d} + \mu Z_1)} \tag{69}$$

A special solution of the equations (44)-(45) exists in addition to solution (68) if the following equalities are fulfilled:

$$\frac{2Z(0)}{Z_0} - 1 - R(0) = 0 \tag{70}$$

$$\mu = \frac{(\lambda_2 + p)Z(0)}{1 + R(0)} < 0 \tag{71}$$

$$\lambda_2 = \frac{q - p - \sqrt{(q + p)^2 + 8\mu^2}}{2} \tag{72}$$

$$p = \Lambda - b_1 \tag{73}$$

$$q = d + 2b_3 \tag{74}$$

In this case dependence $R(Z)$ is the following linear function:

$$R = \frac{2Z}{Z_0} - 1 \qquad (75)$$

Initial conditions in this solution satisfy to the equality (70). Analysis of behavior of functions $x(t); y(t); z(t)$ finds that any small deviation of MSP-system from the trajectory (75), i.e. a small violation of condition (70), create the situation of degradation when one (or several) from the set of variables $x(t); y(t); z(t)$ tends to a zero if $t \rightarrow \infty$. Solutions with growing functions $x(t); y(t); z(t)$ are possible if $\mu > 0$. The equalities (70) and (71) are mathematically equivalent equalities. Therefore a small deviation from the trajectory (75) is equivalent of a small violation of the equality (71). However negative sign of the parameter μ does not change if the violation of equality (71) is small. Therefore the trajectory (75) is not a stable trajectory of development: small deviations from this trajectory are growing with time. A stabilizing feedback must exist in order to this trajectory to became stable.

Evolutionary branches (68) and trajectory (75) are depictured in Figure 1. We see that the stright line (189) is tangent of the evolutionary branches

Figure 1. Evolutionary branches of MSP-system with variable parameters; the following parameters were used in calculation: $a_0 = 0.031$; $\nu_0 = 0.17$; $\mu = 0.1$; $d = 0.1$; $\Lambda = 0.04796$; $C_U = 0.6$; $C_L = 0.8$; $Z_0 = 2.153$

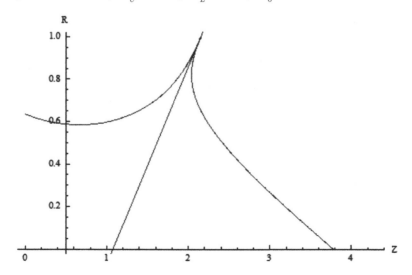

in the point of a long-term equilibrium $(Z_0; R = 1)$. A geometric shape of the evolutionary branches for MSP-systems with variable parameters is similar to the geometric shape of branches for systems with constant parameters. However there are two differences: (1) the lower evolutionary branch intersects abscissa axes and (2) function which corresponds to the upper evolutionary branch can decrease. It means that density of conditions satisfies the inequality: $Z < Z_{\max}$ ($Z_{\max} = 0.38$ in Figure 1).

Second, it means that motion of MSP-system along upper evolutionary branch when density of condition is small can be followed by efficiency falling. These are new features in configuration of evolutionary branches and dynamics of MSP-system.

STABILIZING FUNCTION OF MSP-SYSTEMS WITH VARIABLE PARAMETERS

Stabilizing function for MSP-systems with constant parameters does not take into account the existence of a special solution $Z = Z_0 \cdot R$. Upper evolutionary branch and the lower part of lower evolutionary branch are locuses of the points of minimum of stabilizing function whereas the points of maximum of this function are located at the upper part of lower evolutionary branch. The accounting of trajectory $Z = Z_0 \cdot R$ in construction of stabilizing function doesn't make essential changes to the dynamics of the system because this trajectory almost coincides with upper evolutionary branch in neighborhood of long-term equilibrium point (trajectory $Z = Z_0 \cdot R$ is tangent to upper evolutionary branch in this point). The accounting of trajectory $Z = Z_0 \cdot R$ in construction of stabilizing function changes the locuses of stable equilibrium points: points of this trajectory in this case be the points of stable equilibrium whereas the points of upper evolutionary branch became the points of unstable equilibrium. MSP-system displays evolutionary cycle but instead of jumps of MSP-system between lower and upper evolutionary branches we have now jumps of MSP-system between lower evolutionary branch and trajectory $Z = Z_0 \cdot R$. The changes in dynamics are insignificant.

Locus of stable and unstable equilibrium states in the plane $(Z; R)$ is depictured in Figure 2. Points of stable equilibrium are located at the low part of lower evolutionary branch and at the right line (75). Stabilizing function is the function of the following type:

Figure 2. Evolutionary branches of MSP-system with variable parameters as locus of stable and unstable temporary equilibrium

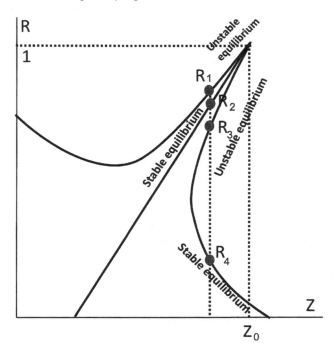

$$W\left(R;Z\right) = C_0 \cdot \left[\frac{R^5}{5} + A_1\frac{R^4}{4} + A_2\frac{R^3}{3} + A_3\frac{R^2}{2} + A_4R + A_5\right] \qquad (76)$$

$$A_1 = -\left(R_1 + R_2 + R_3 + R_4\right) \qquad (77)$$

$$A_2 = R_1\left(R_2 + R_3 + R_4\right) + R_2\left(R_3 + R_4\right) + R_3R_4 \qquad (78)$$

$$A_3 = -\left(R_1\left(R_2R_3 + R_2R_4 + R_3R_4\right) + R_2R_3R_4\right) \qquad (79)$$

$$A_4 = R_1R_2R_3R_4 \qquad (80)$$

$$C_0 < 0 \tag{81}$$

A constant A_5 is arbitrary number. Quantities R_k ($k = 1; 2; 3; 4$) depend on Z and are located at the evolutionary branches as it is depictured in Figure 2. Stabilizing function is depictured in Figure 3. We see that the graph of this function does not have deep holes. Therefore we can expect that the effect from stabilization will be weak. Random impacts will move MSP-system within region limited by upper and lower evolutionary branches. Therefore we can conclude that the dynamics of MSP-system is similar to the process of random walk within this region. However it is not absolutely random walk. The potential barriers created by relief of stabilizing function rigidly limit the region of random walk of MSP-system.

APPLICATION OF MSP-MODEL WITH VARIABLE PARAMETERS FOR ANALYSIS OF THE U.S. ECONOMY (1950-2014)

We use standard economic interpretations (12)-(15) from Chapter 1 of MSP-variables considered in chapter 2. Variables Z and R are interconnected by the equation of evolutionary branches (68). The equations (28)-(29) connect variables Z and R with parameters a (rate of growth) and ν (investment rate). Therefore must be interdependence between rate of growth and invest-

Figure 3. Stabilizing function $W\left(R; Z\right)$ *of MSP-system with variable parameters*

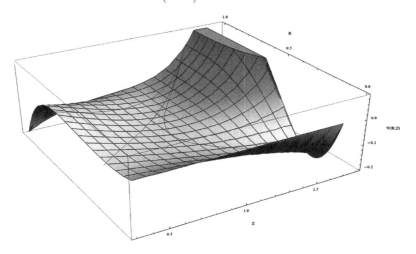

ment rate if the economic system does not deviate from definite evolutionary branch. We can verify this theoretical conclusion using economic stylized facts.

We used interactive data: Tables 1a-1b (Current Cost Net Stock of Fixed Assets and Consumer Durable Goods); Table 1.3 (Current-Cost Depreciation of Fixed Assets and Consumer Durable Goods); Table 1.5 (Investment in Fixed Assets and Consumer Durable Goods), and Table 1.17.5 (Gross Domestic Product, Gross Domestic Income, and Other Major NIPA Aggregates) from database of the U.S. Bureau of Economic Analysis (BEA). Data for the U.S. economy (1950-2014) are represented in Table 11. Efficiency and density of conditions of MSP-system can be calculated by means the following equalities which follows from the equations (28)-(29):

$$R = \frac{\mu^2 - b_1\left(d + b_3\right)}{\mu\left(\nu - \mu\right) - b_1\left(a - b_3\right)} \tag{82}$$

$$Z = \frac{\mu\left(a + d\right) - \nu\left(d + b_3\right)}{\mu\left(\nu - \mu\right) - b_1\left(a - b_3\right)} \tag{83}$$

We used the following values for parameters of MSP-system of ECAS:

$$\mu = 0.1 \,;\; d = 0.1 \,;\; a_0 = 0.031 \,;\; \nu_0 = 0.17 \,;\; \Lambda = 0.04796 \,; \tag{84}$$

$$b_1 = -0.01393 \,;\; b_3 = -0.14214 \,;\; C_U = 0.6 \,;\; C_L = 0.8 \,. \tag{85}$$

Parameters (84) were chosen in such a way that locations of evolutionary branches were in accordance with values of efficiency and density of conditions calculated on the basis of statistical data. Parameters b_1 and b_3 were calculated on the basis of the equalities (30)-(31). Constants C_U and C_L and parameters (84) were taken in such a way that the cusp of evolutionary branches coincides with cusp of factual values (columns (9)-(10) in Table 1). The rate of growth a was calculated as a percentage increment of GDP in next year in relation to current year. The investment rate ν was calculated as percentage of investment in gross domestic product (the details in Table

1a-1b). Dependence ν versus a is depictured in Figure 4. We see a sharp peak directed down and to the left. Moreover the location of points is not random distribution. Points are located within limited area with frontier of type of the cusp directed down and to the left.

In order to find theoretical dependence between parameters a and ν we use the equation of evolutionary branches (68). We substitute the right parts of the equalities (82) and (83) instead of efficiency and density of conditions. Theoretical dependence $\nu(a)$ represents evolutionary branches in coordinates $(a; \nu)$. Factual values $(a; \nu)$ and theoretical dependence $\nu(a)$ are depictured in Figure 5. We see that factual values are located within region limited by evolutionary branches. Dispersion of the points along an axis a is large but it is limited by the definite frontiers which almost coincide with upper and lower evolutionary branches in coordinates $(a; \nu)$. Figure 5 demonstrates that the high level of efficiency (near of cusp) corresponds to the moderate levels of the investment rate and the rate of growth.

Evolutionary branches (equation (68)) and factual values $(Z; R)$ (Table 1; columns (9)-(10)) are depictured in Figure 6. We see that factual values $(Z; R)$ are located within region limited by evolutionary branches. Large values of efficiency correspond to the peak of evolutionary branches. Dispersion along Z-axes sharply decreases near this peak.

Figure 4. Investment rate versus rate of growth for the U.S. economy (1950-2014)
Source: the U.S. Bureau of Economic Analysis (interactive Tables 1.1; 1.3; 1.5; 1.17.5).

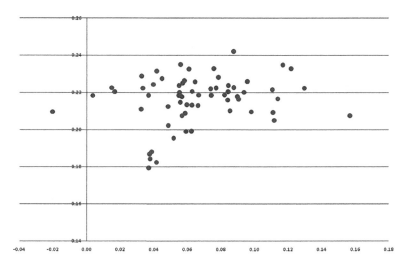

Table 1a. Stylized data for the U.S. economy (1950-2014)

Year	Billions of dollars				Share of investment in GDP (nu)	Rate of Growth (a)	Rate of Depreciation	R	Z	Producti- vity of Capital (2) : (4)	R/Z
	GDP	Invest- ment in fixed assets	Net Stock of Fixed Assets	Deprecia- tion of Fixed Assets							
(1)	(2)	(3)	(4)	(5)	(6)	(7)	(8)	(9)	(10)	(11)	(12)
	BEA; Table 1.17.5	BEA; Table 1.5	BEA; Table 1.1	BEA; Table 1.3	(3) : (2)		(5) : (4)				
1950	300.2	62.3	871.9	33.5	0.2075	0.1569	0.0384	0.6309	2.3080	0.3443	0.2733
1951	347.3	72.5	957.7	37.8	0.2088	0.0587	0.0395	0.6883	1.8042	0.3626	0.3815
1952	367.7	78.5	1012.5	40.6	0.2135	0.0598	0.0401	0.6646	1.7637	0.3632	0.3768
1953	389.7	85.1	1051.6	43.5	0.2184	0.0036	0.0414	0.6787	1.4106	0.3706	0.4812
1954	391.1	85.2	1099.4	46	0.2178	0.0897	0.0418	0.6268	1.8750	0.3557	0.3343
1955	426.2	93	1196.3	48.9	0.2182	0.0561	0.0409	0.6455	1.7009	0.3563	0.3795
1956	450.1	100.7	1301	54.1	0.2237	0.0551	0.0416	0.6225	1.6492	0.3460	0.3774
1957	474.9	105.7	1368.6	58.9	0.2226	0.0150	0.0430	0.6516	1.4450	0.3470	0.4509
1958	482	104.1	1414.8	62.5	0.2160	0.0840	0.0442	0.6382	1.8648	0.3407	0.3422
1959	522.5	117.2	1471.3	65.5	0.2243	0.0398	0.0445	0.6289	1.5658	0.3551	0.4017
1960	543.3	118.7	1521.4	67.9	0.2185	0.0368	0.0446	0.6563	1.5960	0.3571	0.4112
1961	563.3	123.1	1581.3	70.6	0.2185	0.0742	0.0446	0.6331	1.7911	0.3562	0.3535
1962	605.1	133.2	1653.5	74.1	0.2201	0.0554	0.0448	0.6375	1.6805	0.3660	0.3793
1963	638.6	141.8	1717	78	0.2220	0.0739	0.0454	0.6186	1.7580	0.3719	0.3519
1964	685.8	153.5	1829.9	82.4	0.2238	0.0844	0.0450	0.6057	1.7938	0.3748	0.3377
1965	743.7	168	1953.8	88	0.2259	0.0959	0.0450	0.5918	1.8299	0.3806	0.3234
1966	815	183.4	2119.4	95.3	0.2250	0.0573	0.0450	0.6159	1.6499	0.3845	0.3733
1967	861.7	189.7	2284	103.5	0.2201	0.0938	0.0453	0.6151	1.8726	0.3773	0.3285
1968	942.5	206.1	2510.4	113.3	0.2187	0.0821	0.0451	0.6278	1.8295	0.3754	0.3432
1969	1020	222.9	2742	124.8	0.2186	0.0549	0.0455	0.6447	1.6918	0.3720	0.3811
1970	1076	226	2988.6	136.8	0.2101	0.0854	0.0458	0.6640	1.9324	0.3600	0.3436
1971	1168	244.7	3293.2	148.9	0.2095	0.0981	0.0452	0.6581	2.0028	0.3546	0.3286
1972	1282	277.8	3619	160.9	0.2166	0.1139	0.0445	0.6180	2.0040	0.3544	0.3084
1973	1429	315	4102.1	178	0.2205	0.0842	0.0434	0.6190	1.8227	0.3482	0.3396
1974	1549	335.1	4876	206	0.2164	0.0905	0.0422	0.6327	1.8931	0.3176	0.3342
1975	1689	346.1	5267.8	237.5	0.2049	0.1117	0.0451	0.6709	2.1246	0.3206	0.3158
1976	1878	393	5738	259.1	0.2093	0.1110	0.0452	0.6510	2.0694	0.3272	0.3146
1977	2086	463.8	6408.3	288.2	0.2223	0.1297	0.0450	0.5875	2.0186	0.3255	0.2910
1978	2357	553.1	7241.3	325	0.2347	0.1169	0.0449	0.5511	1.8491	0.3254	0.2980
1979	2632	637.1	8343.6	371.1	0.2421	0.0875	0.0445	0.5408	1.6635	0.3155	0.3251
1980	2863	666.3	9494.9	425.8	0.2328	0.1217	0.0448	0.5552	1.8865	0.3015	0.2943
1981	3211	743	10476.9	484.9	0.2314	0.0417	0.0463	0.5995	1.5237	0.3065	0.3934
1982	3345	744.7	11065.2	534.2	0.2226	0.0876	0.0483	0.6087	1.8199	0.3023	0.3344
1983	3638	805.8	11448.5	560.4	0.2215	0.1107	0.0489	0.6006	1.9398	0.3178	0.3096
1984	4041	940.4	12081.7	594.2	0.2327	0.0757	0.0492	0.5771	1.6789	0.3344	0.3438
1985	4347	1021.3	12723.9	636.6	0.2350	0.0560	0.0500	0.5790	1.5688	0.3416	0.3691
1986	4590	1067.8	13524.6	682.1	0.2326	0.0610	0.0504	0.5849	1.6096	0.3394	0.3634

Source: Interactive Tables 1.1; 1.3; 1.5; 1.17.5 of database of the U.S. Bureau of Economic Analysis.

Table 1b. Stylized data for the U.S. economy (1950-2014)

Year	Billions of dollars				Share of investment in GDP (nu)	Rate of Growth (a)	Rate of Depreciation	R	Z	Producti-vity of Capital (2) : (4)	R/Z
	GDP	Invest-ment in fixed assets	Net Stock of Fixed Assets	Deprecia-tion of Fixed Assets							
(1)	(2)	(3)	(4)	(5)	(6)	(7)	(8)	(9)	(10)	(11)	(12)
	BEA; Table 1.17.5	BEA; Table 1.5	BEA; Table 1.1	BEA; Table 1.3	(3) : (2)		(5) : (4)				
1987	4870	1111.5	14320.6	727.7	0.2282	0.0785	0.0508	0.5921	1.7280	0.3401	0.3427
1988	5253	1168.1	15201.4	782.1	0.2224	0.0771	0.0514	0.6155	1.7709	0.3455	0.3475
1989	5658	1231.7	16067.4	835.8	0.2177	0.0569	0.0520	0.6472	1.7096	0.3521	0.3786
1990	5980	1261.7	16828.8	886.6	0.2110	0.0325	0.0527	0.6955	1.6362	0.3553	0.4251
1991	6174	1228.6	17252.2	930.9	0.1990	0.0592	0.0540	0.7409	1.9129	0.3579	0.3873
1992	6539	1278	17978.9	959.5	0.1954	0.0519	0.0534	0.7686	1.9128	0.3637	0.4018
1993	6879	1369.9	18883.3	1003.5	0.1992	0.0625	0.0531	0.7373	1.9304	0.3643	0.3819
1994	7309	1477.8	20010.7	1055.3	0.2022	0.0486	0.0527	0.7309	1.8158	0.3652	0.4026
1995	7664	1590.5	20980.1	1122.6	0.2075	0.0569	0.0535	0.6959	1.8066	0.3653	0.3852
1996	8100	1726.9	21976.9	1175.9	0.2132	0.0628	0.0535	0.6641	1.7821	0.3686	0.3726
1997	8609	1848	23119.4	1240.2	0.2147	0.0558	0.0536	0.6617	1.7314	0.3723	0.3821
1998	9089	2004.9	24411	1310.6	0.2206	0.0629	0.0537	0.6311	1.7153	0.3723	0.3679
1999	9661	2181	25974.3	1401.1	0.2258	0.0646	0.0539	0.6089	1.6805	0.3719	0.3624
2000	10285	2352.6	27695.3	1514.9	0.2287	0.0328	0.0547	0.6147	1.4967	0.3714	0.4107
2001	10622	2361.5	29244.4	1604.5	0.2223	0.0335	0.0549	0.6412	1.5476	0.3632	0.4143
2002	10978	2332	30682.8	1662.4	0.2124	0.0486	0.0542	0.6771	1.7128	0.3578	0.3953
2003	11511	2451.2	32367.4	1727.5	0.2129	0.0664	0.0534	0.6628	1.8037	0.3556	0.3675
2004	12275	2683.5	35681.5	1831.9	0.2186	0.0667	0.0513	0.6372	1.7522	0.3440	0.3637
2005	13094	2965	39294.7	1982.3	0.2264	0.0582	0.0504	0.6098	1.6432	0.3332	0.3711
2006	13856	3152	42506.5	2136.4	0.2275	0.0449	0.0503	0.6130	1.5679	0.3260	0.3910
2007	14478	3192	44400.8	2264.3	0.2205	0.0166	0.0510	0.6601	1.4695	0.3261	0.4492
2008	14719	3084.5	45856.4	2363.8	0.2096	-0.0204	0.0515	0.7439	1.3273	0.3210	0.5605
2009	14419	2655.2	44944.9	2368.8	0.1841	0.0378	0.0527	0.8617	1.9725	0.3208	0.4369
2010	14964	2683.1	45859.5	2382.3	0.1793	0.0370	0.0519	0.9028	2.0387	0.3263	0.4428
2011	15518	2829.4	47313.6	2450.6	0.1823	0.0416	0.0518	0.8721	2.0237	0.3280	0.4309
2012	16163	3018.5	48711.9	2530.1	0.1868	0.0374	0.0519	0.8421	1.9336	0.3318	0.4355
2013	16768	3152.9	50949.1	2627.1	0.1880	0.0388	0.0516	0.8312	1.9255	0.3291	0.4317
2014	17419	**3358.5**			0.1928						

Source: Interactive Tables 1.1; 1.3; 1.5; 1.17.5 of database of the U.S. Bureau of Economic Analysis.

Figure 5. Theoretical dependence $\nu(a)$ *and factual values*

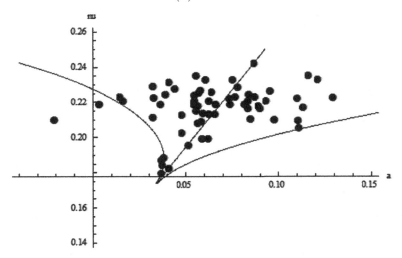

Figure 6. Theoretical dependence $R(Z)$ *and factual values (Table 1a-1b; columns (9)-(10))*

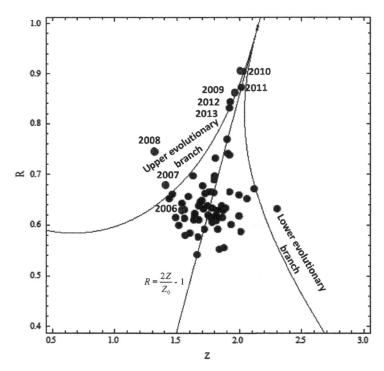

In the new version of MSP-model of ECAS the role of stochastic impacts in dynamics of the system is not negligible. Therefore the system influenced by stochastic shocks wanders along the surface of stabilizing function within the area limited by some barriers (Figure 3). As a rule the system wanders along the almost flat plateau of this surface but this plateau is limited by barriers which restrict the system from leaving the plateau. We can interpret plateau as the area of quasi-stable states of MSP-system ("plateau of stability").

In 2007 the U.S. economic system overcomes one of barriers of limiting plateaus for the first time ever (Figure 6). After that the system is moving down along the opposite side of this barrier. Therefore the distance between the location of the economic system and the plateau on the surface of the stabilizing function increases after year 2007. The rate of growth of GDP and the share of investment in GDP for the area located outside of the barrier limiting "plateau of stability" on the surface of stabilizing function are very small (Figures 5; 7). Therefore as soon as the economic system gets into the area located behind the barrier the rate of growth of economy and share of investment in GDP rapidly falls. This is the situation of a deep crisis. We see that crisis of 2008 can be explained in MSP-model with variable parameters as an exit of economic system out potential barrier which is located along upper evolutionary branch. If economic system for some reason manages to overcome this barrier (upper evolutionary branch) then this system quickly rolls down from it into the area with small rate of growth.

The equations (28)-(29) and (68) can be used for deduction of theoretical dependencies between any pair of variables: $R(Z); \nu(a); \nu(Z); \nu(R); a(Z); a(R)$. For example dependence $a(R)$ and factual values (Table 1a-1b; columns (7) and (9)) are depictured in Figure 7

The goal-function (32) for economic system can be rewritten via economic variables as follows:

$$\Omega\left(x; y; z\right) = d \cdot Y_m Y + \frac{\left(b_1 - \Lambda\right) K^2}{2} + \mu \cdot K\left(Y_m + Y\right) + \frac{b_3 \cdot \left(Y_m + Y\right)^2}{2} \qquad (86)$$

$$\Omega\left(x; y; z\right) = d \cdot \frac{Y^2}{R} + \frac{\left(b_1 - \Lambda\right) K^2}{2} + \mu \cdot K\left(\frac{Y}{R} + Y\right) + \frac{b_3 \cdot \left(\frac{Y}{R} + Y\right)^2}{2} \qquad (87)$$

Figure 7. Theoretical dependence $a(R)$ *and factual values (Table 1a-1b; columns (7) and (9))*

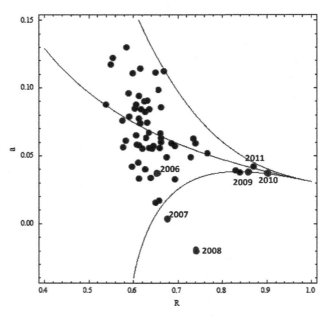

A goal-function is a some kind of criteria of optimality for economic system. The goal-function (87) show how the basic economic variables (the capital, output, and maximal output) determine criteria of optimality of economic system as a whole.

We used the data of the Table 1a-1b (columns (2), (4), and (9)) for calculation of goal-function of the U.S. economy. The results of calculation are depictured in Figure 8. We see that goal-function grows during almost the entire period. The goal-function decreases only during 2008-2009 crisis years. The rate of growth of the goal-function is depictured in Figure 9. Crisis of 2008-2009 qualitatively differs from any other crisis of this period (1950-2013) because the goal-function begins to fall during this crisis for the first time ever. According to analysis of historical data similar falling of goal-function was observed only in 1930-1932 years. Perhaps, it is just an accidental coincidence but it might be not only a coincidence. Perhaps, the falling of goal-function in 2008-2008 testifies about some serious problems within the U.S. economic system.

Figure 8. Goal-function for the U.S. economy (1950-2013)

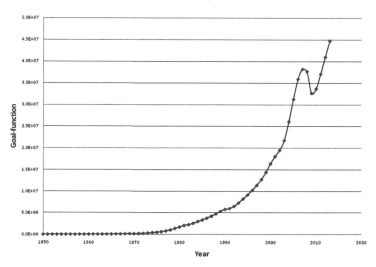

Figure 9. Rate of growth for goal-function of the U.S. economy (1950-2013)

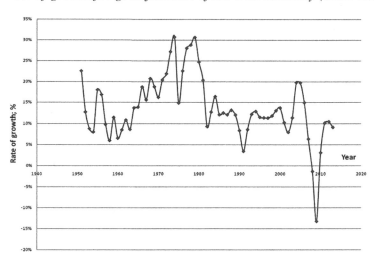

Conclusion

In this book we considered some possible applications of the MSP-approach in economics. General MSP-principles and MSP-equations are the basis of these particular models. However there are various ways to create working MSP-models of economy. We can choose to fix or not fix the economic parameters of the model. MSP-models can differ by the choice of specification of the model. For example we can choose the various types of production functions and specify time-dependence of some variables such as, for example, maximal total factor productivity. The change of long-term productivity of capital can be described either via the model with fixed parameters on the basis of the methods of comparative statics or via the model with changing parameters.

The MSP-model with slowly changing economic parameters was applied for the analysis of the European economic system during the years 1950-2014 (Chapter 2). Stylized data (Penn Tables; version 9.0) confirm the MSP-equations for the dependence between the productivity of labor and the productivity of capital very well. A linear dependence between maximal total factor productivity and productivity of capital was found via application of the MSP-equations for productivity of capital to statistical data. The theoretical MSP-dependence for productivity of labor excellently reproduces dynamics of factual productivity of labor during the years 1950-2014.

The MSP-model with slowly varying economic parameters was also applied for the analysis of the U.S. economic system during the years 1909-1948 (Chapter 3). In this case we have modeled maximal total factor productivity as an exponential function of time. MSP-analysis explains dramatic events of 1930s as phases of crisis and depression of evolutionary cycle. This crisis was strengthened by the rapid drift of long-term equilibrium state of the economic system.

The MSP-model with varying economic parameters is applied for the description of the U.S. economic dynamics (Chapter 4). This specification of the MSP-model explains the crisis of 2008-2009 as the exit of economic system out of frontiers of the plateau of stability at the surface of stabilizing function.

We believe that the MSP-modelling of the economic complex adaptive systems opens new possibilities for research and forecasting of economic processes.

Many economists and authorities in business and policy indicate even more often onto the necessity of application of new methods for economic analysis and forecasting. President of the ECB (European Central Bank) at the ECB Central Banking Conference Frankfurt, 18 November 2010 in the speech 'Reflections on the nature of monetary policy non-standard measures and finance theory' resumed the lessons of the crisis of 2008-2009 by the following conclusions:

When the crisis came, the serious limitations of existing economic and financial models immediately became apparent.... Macro models failed to predict the crisis and seemed incapable of explaining what was happening to the economy in a convincing manner. As a policy-maker during the crisis, I found the available models of limited help. In fact, I would go further: in the face of the crisis, we felt abandoned by conventional tools.

Axtell et al. (2016) write in published recently book Wilson & Kirman (2016) "Complexity and evolution":

We find that the methods of evolutionary analysis and of complex systems will be extremely useful in capturing the open-ended, evolving nature of an economy composed of interactive agents. (Axtel et al., 2016; p. 81)

Penn (2016) writes:

Many of the grand challenges that society faces are concerned with understanding, managing and indeed creating complex living, lifelike or hybrid systems at multiple scales. Conventional approaches have often been unsuccessful in dealing with the inherent non-linearity, adaptability and self-organised behaviours of these systems. (In Gershenson, 2016; p. 26)

Multiple new projects that aim to the creation of agent-based macro-economic models have been initiated last few years: Mandel' et al. (2009) agent-based "Lagom" model of national economy (Germany), Dawid' et al. (2013) agent-based the Eurace@Unibi Model designed for applications to the European economy and others.

Application of the Method of Systems Potential in economics opens new possibilities for economic analysis, economic modelling and economic forecasting. The results presented in this book apparently indicate that MSP-modelling can be successfully used as new Method of the economic analysis. MSP-model of the economic system explains non-trivial dependencies in stylized facts about productivity of capital, productivity of labor, and capital intensity. MSP-model explains (and describes quantitatively!) phenomenon of "Great Depression" and crisis of 2008-2009 years.

Since 2003 this Method was included into the online-course of system dynamics (Garcia, 2011). This Method is used also as the tool for the analysis and the forecasting in the Center of military-political researches of MGIMO Russian Foreign Ministry (http://prognoz.eurasian-defence.ru/?q=node/70916).

Last few years this Method is used more often as a general methodology in various areas of system explorations: general system analysis (Barashko, 2015), manufacturing systems and enterprises (Hanafy, 2010, Chutchenko, 2011, Kladchenko, 2012, Novikova, 2012, Zaharchyn and Andreychuk, 2014, Tsepov, 2014, 2015), finance markets and investments (Dubrovsky and Kuzmin, 2011, Beseda, 2012), economic systems (Kochetkov and Kochetkova, 2010, Herman, 2012, Babyna and Karpenko, 2013, Babyna, 2014, Nazmeev et al., 2014), linguistic systems (Skybina, 2012, 2016), territorial and regional socioeconomic systems (Kuzmin, 2011, Zavyalov, 2012), pension systems (Visotskaia and Linev, 2014), adaptive control systems (Vasilenko, 2011), systems of federal and regional management (Koroluk, 2010, 2016, Ablaev, 2015) educational systems (Schumann at al., 2014, Makarov et al., 2014), information systems (Danish, 2007), adaptive management systems (Zhmurko, 2013), computer systems and networks (Mukhin et al., 2014) and others. The Method generally is applied as a logical scheme for the qualitative description of the system processes.

There are two puzzles concerning the application of this Method for exploration of the real complex adaptive systems.

The first puzzle concerns the right interpretation of MSP-notions when we consider a certain system. The basic notions of the Method are very abstract. It is not always possible to find the right rules of interpretation quickly. As a rule, a rigorous qualitative and quantitative preliminary analysis of data is needed in order to find the right interpretation rules. Creation of mathematical MSP-model of a certain object is possible only after the right choice of interpretation of the basic MSP-terms. Although this task is difficult, I think this Method can be applied not only for deeper understanding of system processes at a qualitative level but also as a new quantitative method for description and forecasting of these processes.

The second puzzle concerns interrelation between MSP-modelling and Multi-Agent Modelling (MAM). Although MSP-notions describe macroscopic characteristics of ensemble of interacting adaptive agents it is not always clear, how to connect mathematically these two ways of the modeling in certain cases. MSP-MAM interrelation is similar to interrelation between thermodynamics and molecular theory. Just as interaction of molecules creates macroscopic thermodynamic dependencies between macroscopic parameters of a physical system, interaction of adaptive agents creates macroscopic regularities between macroscopic properties of a system as a whole. Method of Systems Potential describes these macroscopic (thermodynamic) properties of the whole system. MSP-approach explains why very dissimilar systems evolve cyclically and why quality of a system (its internal configuration) changes suddenly after each cycle. Spiral of development and sudden changes of quality of object are the main laws of Hegel's dialectics. In this sense the Method of Systems Potential can be treated also as a method for analytical description of dialectical laws which rule the development of real complex adaptive systems.

REFERENCES

Ablaev, I. M. (2015). The model of state regulation of development of innovative clusters in regional economy of Russia. *Proceedings of X International Scientific Conference of the Euroasian Scientific Association* (pp. 85-88). Moscow: ESA.

Axtell, R., Kirman, A., Couzin, I. D., Fricke, D., Hens, T., Hochberg, M. E., . . . Sethi, R. (2016). Challenges of Integrating Complexity and Evolution into Economics. In Complexity and evolution: towards to new synthesis for economics (pp. 65-81). Cambridge, MA: MIT Press.

Babyna, O. (2014). Conceptual modeling framework of formation and implementation processes of enterprise potential. *Actual Problems of International Relations, 118*(2), 60–69.

Babyna, O., & Karpenko, O. (2013). Development of an economic system as a process of implementation of its capacity. Economic Development, 4(68), 57-61.

Barashko, O. G. (2015). Procedure of amplification of weak signals in complex adaptive systems. *Reports of 79th scientific and technical conference of Belarusian State Technological University* (p. 14).

Beseda, Y. K. (2012). Peculiarities in manifestation of adapting capabilities of financial and investment potential of real economic subjects. *Actual Problems of Economy, 5*(131), 8–17.

Chutchenko, S. G. (2011). *The concept of providing regional competitiveness of a building company on information and economic basis.* Maykop State Technological University.

Danish, A. G. (2007). *Organizational and economic tools of increase in competitiveness of the entities on the basis of cost methods and information systems* (Doctoral Dissertation). Novocherkassk.

Dawid, H., Gemkow, S., Harting, P., van der Hoog, S., & Neugartd, M. (2013). Agent-Based Macroeconomic Modeling and Policy Analysis: The Eurace@Unibi Model. In Handbook on Computational Economics and Finance. Oxford University Press.

Dubrovsky, V. Zh., & Kuzmin, Ye. A. (2011, February). Adaptive approach to portfolio management of public-private partnership projects: Regional implementation aspects. *Izvestiya of the Urals State University of Economics, 1*(33), 53–62.

Garcia, J. M. (2011). Internet online-course on system dynamics. Polytechnic Institute of Catalonia. Retrieved from http://www.system-dynamics-courses.com/cde.htmhttp://www.dinamica-de-sistemas.com/

Gershenson, C., Froes, T., Siqueiros, J. M., Aguilar, W., Isquierdo, E. J., & Sayama, H. (Eds.). (2016). *Proceedings of the ALife 2016, the Fifteenth International Conference on the Synthesis and Simulation of Living Systems.* Academic Press.

Hanafy, M., & AlGeddawy, T. N. & EiMaraghy, H. A. (2010). Complex adaptive systems. Applications in manufacturing systems modeling. *3rd CIRP Conference on Assembly Technology Systems - CATS 2010.*

Herman, S. A. (2012). *Adaptability and survival in populations of small and medium enterprises* (Doctoral dissertation). University of Hertfordshire, UK.

Kladchenko, I. S. (2012). Balance as a condition for effective performance of the modern industrial enterprise. *Economic Bulletin of the National Mining University N, 4*(40), 36–40.

Kochetkov, S. V., & Kochetkova, O. V. (2010). Intellectual resource as contour of new economy. *Proceedings of VII International Kondratieff's Conference: Future Economy Contours* (pp. 128-131). Moscow: International Fund of N. D. Kondratieff.

Koroluk, Yu. G. (2010). Main aspects of application-oriented use of the concept "Potential" as target category of regional government. *Investment: Practice and Experience, 2010*(9), 78–81.

Koroluk, Yu. G. (2016). *Regional development potential in the scenario management mechanisms.* Academy of Municipal Management, DKS Center LLC.

Kristinevich, S. A. (2011a). The measurement of adaptive efficiency of human capital exploitation on the basis of Method of Systems Potential. *Proceedings of VII International Kondratieff's Conference. Contours of Future Economy* (pp. 131-136). Moscow: International Kondratieff's Fund.

Kristinevich, S. A. (2011b). Measurement of institutional efficiency of development of a human capital: Conceptual Approaches. *Vestnik BGEU*, (1), 17-23.

Kuzmin, Ye. A. (2011). Processes of innovative development of territorial systems on the basis of public-private partnership in risk - managerial approach. In I. V. Naumov (Ed.), *Problems and Prospects of Innovative Development of Territorial Socio-economic Systems* (pp. 229–256). Yekaterinburg, Russia: Institute of Economics, Ural Branch of Russian Academy of Sciences.

Makarov, A.N., & Nazmeev, E.F., Maksutina, E.V., & Alpatova, E.S. (2014). Education reform in context of innovative development of the Russian economy. *Life Science Journal, 11*(6s), 372–375.

Mandel, A., Furst, S., Lass, W., Meissner, F., & Jaeger, C. (2009). *Lagom generiC: an agent-based model of growing economies.* ECF Working Paper 1/2009.

Mukhin, V. Ye., Kornaga, Y. I., & Steshyn, V. V. (2014). Adaptive safety mechanisms for computer systems based on the modified Kohonen neural networks. St. Petersburg State Polytechnical University Journal, 2(193), 31-38.

Nazmeev, E. F., Maksutina, E. V., Makarov, A. N., Alpatova, E. S., & Galimov, A. Z. (2014). Agglomerative effects in economic development (on the example of regions of Russia). *Life Science Journal, 11*(6s), 380–383.

Novikova, N. B. (2012). *Organizational and economic tools of management of upgrade of industrial enterprise as instrument ensuring the stability of its functioning and development* (Doctoral Dissertation). Southern Russian State Technical University.

Penn, A. (2016). Artificial life and society: philosophies and tools for experiencing, interacting with and managing real world complex adaptive systems. *Proceedings of the ALife 2016, the Fifteenth International Conference on the Synthesis and Simulation of Living Systems*, 26-27.

Schumann, C. A., Gerischer, H., Tittmann, C., Orth, H., Xiao, F., Schwarz, B., & Schumann, M.-A. (2014, March). Development of international educational systems by competence networking based on project management. *Procedia: Social and Behavioral Sciences*, *119*(19), 192–201. doi:10.1016/j.sbspro.2014.03.023

Skybina, V. I. (2012). On developmental mechanisms in pluricentric languages. Canadian Academy of Independent Scholars, Zaporizhey State Medical University. *Bulletin of Philology of Ukrainian Academy of Sciences*, *14*(1), 121-137.

Skybina, V. I. (2016). What it takes to become a pluricentric language. In *Schedule of Abstracts, CIEL8, 8th International Conference in Evolutionary Linguistics* (pp. 91-93). Indiana University.

Tsepov, A. U. (2014). *Models, method and the structurally functional organization of system of handling of diverse data for management of investment of small innovative industrial enterprise* (Doctoral Dissertation). Kursk, Southwest University.

Tsepov, A. U. (2015). Methods for evaluating the risks of investing small innovative business as an adaptive system by information criterion. Provincial Scientific Notes, (1), 146-149.

Vasilenko, O. B. (2011). Adaptation and adaptive control systems: problems, directions, prospects. Oil and Gas Industry, (4), 57-61.

Visotskaia, N. V., & Linev, I. V. (2014). System of investment of pension accumulation as difficult (complex) adaptive system. Scientific Notes of the Russian Academy of Entrepreneurship, 38, 26-37.

Wilson, D. S., & Kirman, A. (Eds.). (2016). *Complexity and evolution: towards to new synthesis for economics. Strüngmann Forum Reports 19.* Cambridge, MA: MIT Press.

Zaharchyn, G., & Andreychuk, J. (2015). The conceptual model of essential expression of innovative activity adaptive planning mechanism at the mechanical engineering enterprises. *New Technologies and Modelling Processes, 4*(1), 97–103.

Zavyalov, A. Yu. (2012). About internal innovative adaptation of regional social and economic system. *Proceedings of XI International Conference: Economy and Modern Management: Theory and Practice*, (pp. 64-67). Novosibirsk: SibAS.

Zhmurko, D. J. (2013). The concept, essence and classification of adaptive management systems with organizational complexity. *Scientific Journal of Kuban State Agricultural University, 90*(06), 970–988.

Related Readings

To continue IGI Global's long-standing tradition of advancing innovation through emerging research, please find below a compiled list of recommended IGI Global book chapters and journal articles in the areas of economics, global economies, and business markets. These related readings will provide additional information and guidance to further enrich your knowledge and assist you with your own research.

Abdul-Mohsin, A. (2017). The Relationship between Entrepreneurial Competencies, Competitive Intelligence, and Innovative Performance among SMEs from an Emerging Country: Competitive Intelligence in SMEs. In I. Hosu & I. Iancu (Eds.), *Digital Entrepreneurship and Global Innovation* (pp. 37–58). Hershey, PA: IGI Global. doi:10.4018/978-1-5225-0953-0.ch003

Abubakre, M., Coombs, C. R., & Ravishankar, M. N. (2017). The Impact of Salient Cultural Practices on the Outcome of IS Implementation. *Journal of Global Information Management*, 25(1), 1–20. doi:10.4018/JGIM.2017010101

Agrawal, H. O. (2016). An Approach to Business Strategy. In U. Panwar, R. Kumar, & N. Ray (Eds.), *Handbook of Research on Promotional Strategies and Consumer Influence in the Service Sector* (pp. 154–182). Hershey, PA: IGI Global. doi:10.4018/978-1-5225-0143-5.ch009

Allegreni, F. (2017). Crowdfunding as a Marketing Tool. In W. Vassallo (Ed.), *Crowdfunding for Sustainable Entrepreneurship and Innovation* (pp. 187–203). Hershey, PA: IGI Global. doi:10.4018/978-1-5225-0568-6.ch011

Ambani, P. (2017). Crowdsourcing New Tools to Start Lean and Succeed in Entrepreneurship: Entrepreneurship in the Crowd Economy. In W. Vassallo (Ed.), *Crowdfunding for Sustainable Entrepreneurship and Innovation* (pp. 37–53). Hershey, PA: IGI Global. doi:10.4018/978-1-5225-0568-6.ch003

Related Readings

Amone, W. (2015). Global Market Trends. In B. Christiansen (Ed.), *Handbook of Research on Global Business Opportunities* (pp. 37–58). Hershey, PA: IGI Global. doi:10.4018/978-1-4666-6551-4.ch002

Aryanto, V. D. (2017). The Role of Local Wisdom-Based e-Eco-Innovation to Promote Firms Marketing Performance. *International Journal of Social Ecology and Sustainable Development*, 8(1), 17–31. doi:10.4018/IJSESD.2017010102

Asturias, L. R. (2016). Business Development Opportunities and Market Entry Challenges in Latin America. In M. Garita & J. Godinez (Eds.), *Business Development Opportunities and Market Entry Challenges in Latin America* (pp. 256–271). Hershey, PA: IGI Global. doi:10.4018/978-1-4666-8820-9.ch012

Ayari, A. (2016). Corporate Social Responsibility in the Bahraini Construction Companies. In M. Al-Shammari & H. Masri (Eds.), *Ethical and Social Perspectives on Global Business Interaction in Emerging Markets* (pp. 40–51). Hershey, PA: IGI Global. doi:10.4018/978-1-4666-9864-2.ch003

Baporikar, N. (2017). Business Excellence Strategies for SME Sustainability in India. In P. Ordóñez de Pablos (Ed.), *Managerial Strategies and Solutions for Business Success in Asia* (pp. 61–78). Hershey, PA: IGI Global. doi:10.4018/978-1-5225-1886-0.ch004

Baranowska-Prokop, E., & Sikora, T. (2017). Competitiveness of Polish International New Ventures from Managerial Perspective. In A. Vlachvei, O. Notta, K. Karantininis, & N. Tsounis (Eds.), *Factors Affecting Firm Competitiveness and Performance in the Modern Business World* (pp. 83–107). Hershey, PA: IGI Global. doi:10.4018/978-1-5225-0843-4.ch003

Bartens, Y., Chunpir, H. I., Schulte, F., & Voß, S. (2017). Business/IT Alignment in Two-Sided Markets: A COBIT 5 Analysis for Media Streaming Business Models. In S. De Haes & W. Van Grembergen (Eds.), *Strategic IT Governance and Alignment in Business Settings* (pp. 82–111). Hershey, PA: IGI Global. doi:10.4018/978-1-5225-0861-8.ch004

Beharry-Ramraj, A. (2016). Business Strategies Creating Value for Social Entrepreneurs. In Z. Fields (Ed.), *Incorporating Business Models and Strategies into Social Entrepreneurship* (pp. 80–96). Hershey, PA: IGI Global. doi:10.4018/978-1-4666-8748-6.ch005

Bernardino, J., & Neves, P. C. (2016). Decision-Making with Big Data Using Open Source Business Intelligence Systems. In H. Rahman (Ed.), *Human Development and Interaction in the Age of Ubiquitous Technology* (pp. 120–147). Hershey, PA: IGI Global. doi:10.4018/978-1-5225-0556-3.ch006

Bodea, C., Stelian, S., & Mogos, R. (2017). E-Learning Solution for Enhancing Entrepreneurship Competencies in the Service Sector. In I. Hosu & I. Iancu (Eds.), *Digital Entrepreneurship and Global Innovation* (pp. 225–244). Hershey, PA: IGI Global. doi:10.4018/978-1-5225-0953-0.ch011

Bojorges Moctezuma, N. P. (2017). Consumer Impetuosity in M-Commerce: Designing Scale to Measure the Shopping Behavior. In Rajagopal, & R. Behl (Eds.), Business Analytics and Cyber Security Management in Organizations (pp. 84-105). Hershey, PA: IGI Global. doi:10.4018/978-1-5225-0902-8.ch007

Bowen, G., & Bowen, D. (2017). Strategist: Role and Attributes. In V. Wang (Ed.), *Encyclopedia of Strategic Leadership and Management* (pp. 1745–1757). Hershey, PA: IGI Global. doi:10.4018/978-1-5225-1049-9.ch121

Breuer, W., Quinten, B., & Salzmann, A. J. (2015). Bank vs. Bond Finance: A Cultural View of Corporate Debt Financing. In B. Christiansen (Ed.), *Handbook of Research on Global Business Opportunities* (pp. 289–315). Hershey, PA: IGI Global. doi:10.4018/978-1-4666-6551-4.ch014

Bruno, G. (2017). A Dataflow-Oriented Modeling Approach to Business Processes. *International Journal of Human Capital and Information Technology Professionals*, *8*(1), 51–65. doi:10.4018/IJHCITP.2017010104

Can, M., & Doğan, B. (2017). The Effects of Economic Structural Transformation on Employment: An Evaluation in the Context of Economic Complexity and Product Space Theory. In F. Yenilmez & E. Kılıç (Eds.), *Handbook of Research on Unemployment and Labor Market Sustainability in the Era of Globalization* (pp. 275–306). Hershey, PA: IGI Global. doi:10.4018/978-1-5225-2008-5.ch016

Carvalheira, A. M., & Moreira, A. C. (2016). Searching for Opportunities and Trust in International Markets: Entrepreneurial Perspective of a Traditional Industry SME. In L. Carvalho (Ed.), *Handbook of Research on Entrepreneurial Success and its Impact on Regional Development* (pp. 675–701). Hershey, PA: IGI Global. doi:10.4018/978-1-4666-9567-2.ch028

Carvalho, L., Camacho, N., Amorim, G., & Esperança, J. P. (2016). Transnational Acceleration of Local Startups: Portugal's Building Global Innovators (BGI) Model. In L. Carvalho (Ed.), *Handbook of Research on Entrepreneurial Success and its Impact on Regional Development* (pp. 41–71). Hershey, PA: IGI Global. doi:10.4018/978-1-4666-9567-2.ch003

Related Readings

Castro, O. A., Arias, C. L., Ibañez, J. E., & Bulla, F. J. (2017). Universities Fostering Business Development: The Role of Education in Entrepreneurship. In I. Hosu & I. Iancu (Eds.), *Digital Entrepreneurship and Global Innovation* (pp. 193–224). Hershey, PA: IGI Global. doi:10.4018/978-1-5225-0953-0.ch010

Chaudhuri, S. (2016). Application of Web-Based Geographical Information System (GIS) in E-Business. In U. Panwar, R. Kumar, & N. Ray (Eds.), *Handbook of Research on Promotional Strategies and Consumer Influence in the Service Sector* (pp. 389–405). Hershey, PA: IGI Global. doi:10.4018/978-1-5225-0143-5.ch023

Chauhan, R. S., & Das, R. (2017). Entrepreneurship Policy Framework: Understanding Cultural and Educational Determinants for Entrepreneurship. In G. Afolayan & A. Akinwale (Eds.), *Global Perspectives on Development Administration and Cultural Change* (pp. 95–139). Hershey, PA: IGI Global. doi:10.4018/978-1-5225-0629-4.ch005

Chen, Y. (2017). Sustainable Supply Chains and International Soft Landings: A Case of Wetland Entrepreneurship. In B. Christiansen & F. Kasarcı (Eds.), *Corporate Espionage, Geopolitics, and Diplomacy Issues in International Business* (pp. 232–247). Hershey, PA: IGI Global. doi:10.4018/978-1-5225-1031-4.ch013

Choudhury, M. A. (2017). Cybernetic Approach for the Stock Market: An Empirical Study of Bangladesh. In I. Oncioiu (Ed.), *Driving Innovation and Business Success in the Digital Economy* (pp. 193–210). Hershey, PA: IGI Global. doi:10.4018/978-1-5225-1779-5.ch013

Christansen, B., Dirikan, T., Dirikan, C., & Kasarcı, F. (2016). Turkey's Economic Sustainability in Global Hypercompetition. In N. Zakaria, A. Abdul-Talib, & N. Osman (Eds.), *Handbook of Research on Impacts of International Business and Political Affairs on the Global Economy* (pp. 173–184). Hershey, PA: IGI Global. doi:10.4018/978-1-4666-9806-2.ch009

Cinelli, S. A. (2017). The World's Oldest Profession - Now and Then: Disruption of the Commercial Banking Model. In W. Vassallo (Ed.), *Crowdfunding for Sustainable Entrepreneurship and Innovation* (pp. 78–89). Hershey, PA: IGI Global. doi:10.4018/978-1-5225-0568-6.ch005

Cvijanovic, D., & Mihailović, B. (2016). Effects of Globalization on Economies in Transition. In V. Erokhin (Ed.), *Global Perspectives on Trade Integration and Economies in Transition* (pp. 26–44). Hershey, PA: IGI Global. doi:10.4018/978-1-5225-0451-1.ch002

Daidj, N. (2015). A Dynamic Vision of Value Chains: From Value Chains to Business Models (BM). In *Developing Strategic Business Models and Competitive Advantage in the Digital Sector* (pp. 156–182). Hershey, PA: IGI Global. doi:10.4018/978-1-4666-6513-2.ch006

Daidj, N. (2015). Disruptive Technologies, Innovation, and Competition in the Digital Economy. In *Developing Strategic Business Models and Competitive Advantage in the Digital Sector* (pp. 183–211). Hershey, PA: IGI Global. doi:10.4018/978-1-4666-6513-2.ch007

Dau, L. A., Moore, E. M., Soto, M. A., & LeBlanc, C. R. (2017). How Globalization Sparked Entrepreneurship in the Developing World: The Impact of Formal Economic and Political Linkages. In B. Christiansen & F. Kasarcı (Eds.), *Corporate Espionage, Geopolitics, and Diplomacy Issues in International Business* (pp. 72–91). Hershey, PA: IGI Global. doi:10.4018/978-1-5225-1031-4.ch005

de Burgh-Woodman, H., Bressan, A., & Torrisi, A. (2017). An Evaluation of the State of the CSR Field in Australia: Perspectives from the Banking and Mining Sectors. In D. Jamali (Ed.), *Comparative Perspectives on Global Corporate Social Responsibility* (pp. 138–164). Hershey, PA: IGI Global. doi:10.4018/978-1-5225-0720-8.ch007

De Moraes, A. J., Ekanem, I., & Osabutey, E. (2017). New Perspectives on the Internationalisation of Micro-Businesses. In S. Ojo (Ed.), *Diasporas and Transnational Entrepreneurship in Global Contexts* (pp. 115–129). Hershey, PA: IGI Global. doi:10.4018/978-1-5225-1991-1.ch007

Demiray, M., Burnaz, S., & Aslanbay, Y. (2017). The Crowdfunding Market, Models, Platforms, and Projects. In W. Vassallo (Ed.), *Crowdfunding for Sustainable Entrepreneurship and Innovation* (pp. 90–126). Hershey, PA: IGI Global. doi:10.4018/978-1-5225-0568-6.ch006

Di Fatta, D., Musotto, R., D'Aleo, V., Vesperi, W., Morabito, G., & Lo Bue, S. (2017). Weak Ties and Value of a Network in the New Internet Economy. In S. Hai-Jew (Ed.), *Social Media Data Extraction and Content Analysis* (pp. 66–84). Hershey, PA: IGI Global. doi:10.4018/978-1-5225-0648-5.ch003

Diehl, M. (2016). Financial Market Infrastructures: The Backbone of Financial Systems. In M. Diehl, B. Alexandrova-Kabadjova, R. Heuver, & S. Martínez-Jaramillo (Eds.), *Analyzing the Economics of Financial Market Infrastructures* (pp. 1–19). Hershey, PA: IGI Global. doi:10.4018/978-1-4666-8745-5.ch001

Related Readings

Eftonova, T., Kiran, M., & Stannett, M. (2017). Long-term Macroeconomic Dynamics of Competition in the Russian Economy using Agent- based Modelling. *International Journal of System Dynamics Applications*, 6(1), 1–20. doi:10.4018/IJSDA.2017010101

Ekanem, I., & Uwajeh, N. J. (2017). Transnational Entrepreneurs and Their Global Market Entry Modes. In S. Ojo (Ed.), *Diasporas and Transnational Entrepreneurship in Global Contexts* (pp. 130–151). Hershey, PA: IGI Global. doi:10.4018/978-1-5225-1991-1.ch008

El Dessouky, N. F. (2016). Corporate Social Responsibility of Public Banking Sector for Sustainable Development: A Comparative Study between Malaysia and Egypt. In M. Al-Shammari & H. Masri (Eds.), *Ethical and Social Perspectives on Global Business Interaction in Emerging Markets* (pp. 52–73). Hershey, PA: IGI Global. doi:10.4018/978-1-4666-9864-2.ch004

Encinas-Ferrer, C. (2017). Currency Parity and Competitiveness: The Case of Greece. In A. Vlachvei, O. Notta, K. Karantininis, & N. Tsounis (Eds.), *Factors Affecting Firm Competitiveness and Performance in the Modern Business World* (pp. 282–299). Hershey, PA: IGI Global. doi:10.4018/978-1-5225-0843-4.ch010

Firdhous, M. F. (2015). Strategies for Evaluating Cloud System Providers during the Transformation of Businesses. In F. Soliman (Ed.), *Business Transformation and Sustainability through Cloud System Implementation* (pp. 58–77). Hershey, PA: IGI Global. doi:10.4018/978-1-4666-6445-6.ch005

Garo, E. (2017). Gap Between Theory and Practice in Management Education: Teaching Entrepreneurship Through Practice. In D. Latusek (Ed.), *Case Studies as a Teaching Tool in Management Education* (pp. 264–277). Hershey, PA: IGI Global. doi:10.4018/978-1-5225-0770-3.ch014

Gençer, M., & Oba, B. (2017). Taming of "Openness" in Software Innovation Systems. In I. Oncioiu (Ed.), *Driving Innovation and Business Success in the Digital Economy* (pp. 26–40). Hershey, PA: IGI Global. doi:10.4018/978-1-5225-1779-5.ch003

Gianni, M., & Gotzamani, K. (2016). Integrated Management Systems and Information Management Systems: Common Threads. In P. Papajorgji, F. Pinet, A. Guimarães, & J. Papathanasiou (Eds.), *Automated Enterprise Systems for Maximizing Business Performance* (pp. 195–214). Hershey, PA: IGI Global. doi:10.4018/978-1-4666-8841-4.ch011

Goerlach, C., Brehm, A., & Lonnen, B. (2016). FMIs – Knights in Shining Armour? In M. Diehl, B. Alexandrova-Kabadjova, R. Heuver, & S. Martínez-Jaramillo (Eds.), *Analyzing the Economics of Financial Market Infrastructures* (pp. 71–89). Hershey, PA: IGI Global. doi:10.4018/978-1-4666-8745-5.ch004

Hamidi, H. (2017). A Model for Impact of Organizational Project Benefits Management and its Impact on End User. *Journal of Organizational and End User Computing*, 29(1), 51–65. doi:10.4018/JOEUC.2017010104

Hartlieb, S., & Silvius, G. (2017). Handling Uncertainty in Project Management and Business Development: Similarities and Differences. In Y. Raydugin (Ed.), *Handbook of Research on Leveraging Risk and Uncertainties for Effective Project Management* (pp. 337–362). Hershey, PA: IGI Global. doi:10.4018/978-1-5225-1790-0.ch016

Haynes, J. D., Arockiasamy, S., Al Rashdi, M., & Al Rashdi, S. (2016). Business and E Business Strategies for Coopetition and Thematic Management as a Sustained Basis for Ethics and Social Responsibility in Emerging Markets. In M. Al-Shammari & H. Masri (Eds.), *Ethical and Social Perspectives on Global Business Interaction in Emerging Markets* (pp. 25–39). Hershey, PA: IGI Global. doi:10.4018/978-1-4666-9864-2.ch002

Heuver, R., & Heijmans, R. (2016). Using FMI Transaction Data in Simulations: Less Is More? In M. Diehl, B. Alexandrova-Kabadjova, R. Heuver, & S. Martínez-Jaramillo (Eds.), *Analyzing the Economics of Financial Market Infrastructures* (pp. 102–123). Hershey, PA: IGI Global. doi:10.4018/978-1-4666-8745-5.ch006

Homata, A., Mihiotis, A., & Tzortzaki, A. M. (2017). Franchise Management and the Greek Franchise Industry. In A. Vlachvei, O. Notta, K. Karantininis, & N. Tsounis (Eds.), *Factors Affecting Firm Competitiveness and Performance in the Modern Business World* (pp. 251–281). Hershey, PA: IGI Global. doi:10.4018/978-1-5225-0843-4.ch009

Huang, L. K. (2017). A Cultural Model of Online Banking Adoption: Long-Term Orientation Perspective. *Journal of Organizational and End User Computing*, 29(1), 1–22. doi:10.4018/JOEUC.2017010101

Hunter, M. G. (2015). Adoption. In *Strategic Utilization of Information Systems in Small Business* (pp. 136–169). Hershey, PA: IGI Global. doi:10.4018/978-1-4666-8708-0.ch005

Hunter, M. G. (2015). E-Business. In *Strategic Utilization of Information Systems in Small Business* (pp. 241–256). Hershey, PA: IGI Global. doi:10.4018/978-1-4666-8708-0.ch011

Hunter, M. G. (2015). Entrepreneurs' Contributions to Small Business: A Comparison of Success and Failure. In B. Christiansen (Ed.), *Handbook of Research on Global Business Opportunities* (pp. 168–198). Hershey, PA: IGI Global. doi:10.4018/978-1-4666-6551-4.ch008

Hunter, M. G. (2015). Information Systems. In *Strategic Utilization of Information Systems in Small Business* (pp. 78–108). Hershey, PA: IGI Global. doi:10.4018/978-1-4666-8708-0.ch003

Hunter, M. G. (2015). Management Processes. In *Strategic Utilization of Information Systems in Small Business* (pp. 211–225). Hershey, PA: IGI Global. doi:10.4018/978-1-4666-8708-0.ch009

Hunter, M. G. (2015). Theories for Investigations. In *Strategic Utilization of Information Systems in Small Business* (pp. 109–135). Hershey, PA: IGI Global. doi:10.4018/978-1-4666-8708-0.ch004

Ianole, R. (2014). An Empirical Exploration of Mental Representations in the Individual Saving Decision Process. *International Journal of Applied Behavioral Economics*, *3*(3), 48–63. doi:10.4018/ijabe.2014070104

Igbinakhase, I. (2017). Responsible and Sustainable Management Practices in Developing and Developed Business Environments. In Z. Fields (Ed.), *Collective Creativity for Responsible and Sustainable Business Practice* (pp. 180–207). Hershey, PA: IGI Global. doi:10.4018/978-1-5225-1823-5.ch010

Iwaloye, O. O., & Shi, G. J. (2016). Market Receptiveness and Product Positioning Model of Chinese Firms in Emerging Markets. In A. Gbadamosi (Ed.), *Handbook of Research on Consumerism and Buying Behavior in Developing Nations* (pp. 99–119). Hershey, PA: IGI Global. doi:10.4018/978-1-5225-0282-1.ch005

Iwata, J. J., & Hoskins, R. G. (2017). Managing Indigenous Knowledge in Tanzania: A Business Perspective. In P. Jain & N. Mnjama (Eds.), *Managing Knowledge Resources and Records in Modern Organizations* (pp. 198–214). Hershey, PA: IGI Global. doi:10.4018/978-1-5225-1965-2.ch012

Jain, P. (2017). A Crowd-Funder Value (CFV) Framework for Crowd-Investment: A Roadmap for Entrepreneurial Success in the Contemporary Society. In W. Vassallo (Ed.), *Crowdfunding for Sustainable Entrepreneurship and Innovation* (pp. 288–309). Hershey, PA: IGI Global. doi:10.4018/978-1-5225-0568-6.ch016

Jasmine, K. S., & Sudha, M. (2015). Business Transformation though Cloud Computing in Sustainable Business. In F. Soliman (Ed.), *Business Transformation and Sustainability through Cloud System Implementation* (pp. 44–57). Hershey, PA: IGI Global. doi:10.4018/978-1-4666-6445-6.ch004

Jihene, M. (2016). Women's Empowerment and Socio-Economic Development in MENA Region: Adaptation to Trade Policies and Access to Market for Promoting Entrepreneurship. In S. Sen, A. Bhattacharya, & R. Sen (Eds.), *International Perspectives on Socio-Economic Development in the Era of Globalization* (pp. 113–128). Hershey, PA: IGI Global. doi:10.4018/978-1-4666-9908-3.ch007

Kamasak, R., & Yavuz, M. (2016). Economic Development, Market Characteristics and Current Business Conditions in Turkey: A Guide for Successful Business Operations. In B. Christiansen & M. Erdoğdu (Eds.), *Comparative Economics and Regional Development in Turkey* (pp. 336–354). Hershey, PA: IGI Global. doi:10.4018/978-1-4666-8729-5.ch016

Kaplan, Z. (2017). The EU's Internal Market and the Free Movement of Labor: Economic Effects and Challenges. In F. Yenilmez & E. Kılıç (Eds.), *Handbook of Research on Unemployment and Labor Market Sustainability in the Era of Globalization* (pp. 61–75). Hershey, PA: IGI Global. doi:10.4018/978-1-5225-2008-5.ch005

Kasemsap, K. (2016). Exploring the Roles of Entrepreneurship and Internationalization in Global Business. In L. Carvalho (Ed.), *Handbook of Research on Entrepreneurial Success and its Impact on Regional Development* (pp. 481–512). Hershey, PA: IGI Global. doi:10.4018/978-1-4666-9567-2.ch021

Kasemsap, K. (2017). Mastering Business Process Management and Business Intelligence in Global Business. In M. Tavana, K. Szabat, & K. Puranam (Eds.), *Organizational Productivity and Performance Measurements Using Predictive Modeling and Analytics* (pp. 192–212). Hershey, PA: IGI Global. doi:10.4018/978-1-5225-0654-6.ch010

Kasemsap, K. (2017). The Importance of Entrepreneurship in Global Business. In B. Christiansen & F. Kasarcı (Eds.), *Corporate Espionage, Geopolitics, and Diplomacy Issues in International Business* (pp. 92–115). Hershey, PA: IGI Global. doi:10.4018/978-1-5225-1031-4.ch006

Kaushal, L. A. (2016). Multinational Corporations: A Boon or Bane for a Developing Economy – A Study in Indian Context. In N. Zakaria, A. Abdul-Talib, & N. Osman (Eds.), *Handbook of Research on Impacts of International Business and Political Affairs on the Global Economy* (pp. 154–172). Hershey, PA: IGI Global. doi:10.4018/978-1-4666-9806-2.ch008

Related Readings

Kavoura, A., & Koziol, L. (2017). Polish Firms' Innovation Capability for Competitiveness via Information Technologies and Social Media Implementation. In A. Vlachvei, O. Notta, K. Karantininis, & N. Tsounis (Eds.), *Factors Affecting Firm Competitiveness and Performance in the Modern Business World* (pp. 191–222). Hershey, PA: IGI Global. doi:10.4018/978-1-5225-0843-4.ch007

Khalique, M., Shaari, J. A., & Isa, A. H. (2015). A Descriptive Study of Intellectual Capital in SMEs Operating in Electrical and Electronics Manufacturing Sector in Malaysia. In P. Ordoñez de Pablos, L. Turró, R. Tennyson, & J. Zhao (Eds.), *Knowledge Management for Competitive Advantage During Economic Crisis* (pp. 1–15). Hershey, PA: IGI Global. doi:10.4018/978-1-4666-6457-9.ch001

Khan, I. U., Hameed, Z., & Khan, S. U. (2017). Understanding Online Banking Adoption in a Developing Country: UTAUT2 with Cultural Moderators. *Journal of Global Information Management*, 25(1), 43–65. doi:10.4018/JGIM.2017010103

Kiregian, E. (2017). The Transformation of Russian Business Education and Its Outcomes: How Russia Moved Away from Marxism toward a Market Economy through Revitalized Business Education. In F. Topor (Ed.), *Handbook of Research on Individualism and Identity in the Globalized Digital Age* (pp. 457–477). Hershey, PA: IGI Global. doi:10.4018/978-1-5225-0522-8.ch020

Kofahi, I., & Alryalat, H. (2017). Enterprise Resource Planning (ERP) Implementation Approaches and the Performance of Procure-to-Pay Business Processes: (Field Study in Companies that Implement Oracle ERP in Jordan). *International Journal of Information Technology Project Management*, 8(1), 55–71. doi:10.4018/IJITPM.2017010104

Kożuch, B., & Jabłoński, A. (2017). Adopting the Concept of Business Models in Public Management. In M. Lewandowski & B. Kożuch (Eds.), *Public Sector Entrepreneurship and the Integration of Innovative Business Models* (pp. 10–46). Hershey, PA: IGI Global. doi:10.4018/978-1-5225-2215-7.ch002

Kumar, M. (2017). A Panel Data Analysis for Exploring the New Determinants of Growth in Small and Medium Sized Enterprises in India. *International Journal of Asian Business and Information Management*, 8(1), 1–23. doi:10.4018/IJABIM.2017010101

Kumar, M. (2017). Profitability of Indian Firms in Foreign Direct Investment. *International Journal of Asian Business and Information Management*, 8(1), 51–67. doi:10.4018/IJABIM.2017010104

Laine, T. A., & Korpinen, K. (2016). Exploiting Parallelization to Increase the Performance of Payment Systems Simulations. In M. Diehl, B. Alexandrova-Kabadjova, R. Heuver, & S. Martínez-Jaramillo (Eds.), *Analyzing the Economics of Financial Market Infrastructures* (pp. 91–101). Hershey, PA: IGI Global. doi:10.4018/978-1-4666-8745-5.ch005

Lavassani, K. M., & Movahedi, B. (2017). Applications Driven Information Systems: Beyond Networks toward Business Ecosystems. In I. Oncioiu (Ed.), *Driving Innovation and Business Success in the Digital Economy* (pp. 159–171). Hershey, PA: IGI Global. doi:10.4018/978-1-5225-1779-5.ch011

Le, N., Li, X., & Yukhanaev, A. (2015). Locational Determinants of Foreign Direct Investment in the Vietnamese Economy. In B. Christiansen (Ed.), *Handbook of Research on Global Business Opportunities* (pp. 1–36). Hershey, PA: IGI Global. doi:10.4018/978-1-4666-6551-4.ch001

Lederer, M., Kurz, M., & Lazarov, P. (2017). Usage and Suitability of Methods for Strategic Business Process Initiatives: A Multi Case Study Research. *International Journal of Productivity Management and Assessment Technologies*, *5*(1), 40–51. doi:10.4018/IJPMAT.2017010103

Lee, I. (2017). A Social Enterprise Business Model and a Case Study of Pacific Community Ventures (PCV). In V. Potocan, M. Üngan, & Z. Nedelko (Eds.), *Handbook of Research on Managerial Solutions in Non-Profit Organizations* (pp. 182–204). Hershey, PA: IGI Global. doi:10.4018/978-1-5225-0731-4.ch009

León, C., Pérez, J., & Renneboog, L. (2016). A Multi-Layer Network of the Colombian Sovereign Securities Market. In M. Diehl, B. Alexandrova-Kabadjova, R. Heuver, & S. Martínez-Jaramillo (Eds.), *Analyzing the Economics of Financial Market Infrastructures* (pp. 124–149). Hershey, PA: IGI Global. doi:10.4018/978-1-4666-8745-5.ch007

Lewandowski, M. (2017). Public Organizations and Business Model Innovation: The Role of Public Service Design. In M. Lewandowski & B. Kożuch (Eds.), *Public Sector Entrepreneurship and the Integration of Innovative Business Models* (pp. 47–72). Hershey, PA: IGI Global. doi:10.4018/978-1-5225-2215-7.ch003

Liu, H., Ke, W., Wei, K. K., & Lu, Y. (2016). The Effects of Social Capital on Firm Substantive and Symbolic Performance: In the Context of E-Business. *Journal of Global Information Management*, *24*(1), 61–85. doi:10.4018/JGIM.2016010104

Related Readings

Magala, S. J. (2017). Between Davos and Porto Alegre: Democratic Entrepreneurship as Crowdsourcing for Ideas. In M. Lewandowski & B. Kożuch (Eds.), *Public Sector Entrepreneurship and the Integration of Innovative Business Models* (pp. 1–9). Hershey, PA: IGI Global. doi:10.4018/978-1-5225-2215-7.ch001

Mandal, R., & Nath, H. K. (2017). Services Trade in Emerging Market Economies. In Rajagopal, & R. Behl (Eds.), Business Analytics and Cyber Security Management in Organizations (pp. 64-83). Hershey, PA: IGI Global. doi:10.4018/978-1-5225-0902-8.ch006

Mangalaraj, G., & Amaravadi, C. S. (2016). The B2B Market Place: A Review and a Typology. In I. Lee (Ed.), *Encyclopedia of E-Commerce Development, Implementation, and Management* (pp. 905–915). Hershey, PA: IGI Global. doi:10.4018/978-1-4666-9787-4.ch064

Martinez-Jaramillo, S., Molina-Borboa, J. L., & Bravo-Benitez, B. (2016). The role of Financial Market Infrastructures in Financial Stability: An Overview. In M. Diehl, B. Alexandrova-Kabadjova, R. Heuver, & S. Martínez-Jaramillo (Eds.), *Analyzing the Economics of Financial Market Infrastructures* (pp. 20–40). Hershey, PA: IGI Global. doi:10.4018/978-1-4666-8745-5.ch002

Massarenti, M. (2016). Undressing the Global Derivatives Market: Trade Repositories: Past, Present and Future. In M. Diehl, B. Alexandrova-Kabadjova, R. Heuver, & S. Martínez-Jaramillo (Eds.), *Analyzing the Economics of Financial Market Infrastructures* (pp. 359–368). Hershey, PA: IGI Global. doi:10.4018/978-1-4666-8745-5.ch018

McAvoy, D. (2017). Institutional Entrepreneurship in Defence Acquisition: What Don't We Understand? In K. Burgess & P. Antill (Eds.), *Emerging Strategies in Defense Acquisitions and Military Procurement* (pp. 222–241). Hershey, PA: IGI Global. doi:10.4018/978-1-5225-0599-0.ch013

Milne, A. (2016). Central Securities Depositories and Securities Clearing and Settlement: Business Practice and Public Policy Concerns. In M. Diehl, B. Alexandrova-Kabadjova, R. Heuver, & S. Martínez-Jaramillo (Eds.), *Analyzing the Economics of Financial Market Infrastructures* (pp. 334–358). Hershey, PA: IGI Global. doi:10.4018/978-1-4666-8745-5.ch017

Mohanty, S. K. (2017). Globalization, Innovation, and Marketing Philosophy: A Critical Assessment of Role of Technology in Defining New Dimensions. In Rajagopal, & R. Behl (Eds.), Business Analytics and Cyber Security Management in Organizations (pp. 48-63). Hershey, PA: IGI Global. doi:10.4018/978-1-5225-0902-8.ch005

Moreira, A. C., & Alves, C. B. (2016). Commitment-Trust Dynamics in the Internationalization Process: A Case Study of Market Entry in the Brazilian Market. In M. Garita & J. Godinez (Eds.), *Business Development Opportunities and Market Entry Challenges in Latin America* (pp. 224–255). Hershey, PA: IGI Global. doi:10.4018/978-1-4666-8820-9.ch011

Munkata, A. S., Anin, E. K., Essuman, D., & Ataburo, H. (2017). Pursuing Supply Chain Integration: Roles of Resources, Competences, Experience, and Industry-type. *International Journal of Business Analytics*, 4(1), 87–103. doi:10.4018/IJBAN.2017010105

Nekaj, E. L. (2017). The Crowd Economy: From the Crowd to Businesses to Public Administrations and Multinational Companies. In W. Vassallo (Ed.), *Crowdfunding for Sustainable Entrepreneurship and Innovation* (pp. 1–19). Hershey, PA: IGI Global. doi:10.4018/978-1-5225-0568-6.ch001

Nunez, S., & Castaño, R. (2017). Building Brands in Emerging Economies: A Consumer-Oriented Approach. In Rajagopal, & R. Behl (Eds.), Business Analytics and Cyber Security Management in Organizations (pp. 183-194). Hershey, PA: IGI Global. doi:10.4018/978-1-5225-0902-8.ch013

Nunez-Zabaleta, A., Olabarri, E., & Monge-Benito, S. (2017). Getting New Business Contacts in Foreign Markets through Social Networking Sites: Perspectives from Professionals of Basque Region in SPAIN. In V. Benson, R. Tuninga, & G. Saridakis (Eds.), *Analyzing the Strategic Role of Social Networking in Firm Growth and Productivity* (pp. 334–351). Hershey, PA: IGI Global. doi:10.4018/978-1-5225-0559-4.ch018

Ogrean, C., & Herciu, M. (2016). CSR Strategies in Emerging Markets: Socially Responsible Decision Making Processes and Business Practices for Sustainability. In M. Al-Shammari & H. Masri (Eds.), *Ethical and Social Perspectives on Global Business Interaction in Emerging Markets* (pp. 1–24). Hershey, PA: IGI Global. doi:10.4018/978-1-4666-9864-2.ch001

Oju, O. (2017). Impact of Innovation on the Entrepreneurial Success in Selected Business Enterprises in South-West Nigeria. In I. Oncioiu (Ed.), *Driving Innovation and Business Success in the Digital Economy* (pp. 16–25). Hershey, PA: IGI Global. doi:10.4018/978-1-5225-1779-5.ch002

Okoya, J. (2017). Interfacing with Diaspora/Ethnic Entrepreneurship: A Case of Getting the Right Balance in the HRM Ethnic Marketing Nexus. In S. Ojo (Ed.), *Diasporas and Transnational Entrepreneurship in Global Contexts* (pp. 173–187). Hershey, PA: IGI Global. doi:10.4018/978-1-5225-1991-1.ch010

Related Readings

Pandit, S., Milman, I., Oberhofer, M., & Zhou, Y. (2017). Principled Reference Data Management for Big Data and Business Intelligence. *International Journal of Organizational and Collective Intelligence*, 7(1), 47–66. doi:10.4018/IJOCI.2017010104

Paudel, N. P. (2016). Financial Market in Nepal: Challenges of the Financial Sector Development in Nepal. In A. Kashyap & A. Tomar (Eds.), *Financial Market Regulations and Legal Challenges in South Asia* (pp. 146–194). Hershey, PA: IGI Global. doi:10.4018/978-1-5225-0004-9.ch009

Pawliczek, A., & Rössler, M. (2017). Knowledge of Management Tools and Systems in SMEs: Knowledge Transfer in Management. In A. Bencsik (Ed.), *Knowledge Management Initiatives and Strategies in Small and Medium Enterprises* (pp. 180–203). Hershey, PA: IGI Global. doi:10.4018/978-1-5225-1642-2.ch009

Prokop, J. (2017). Firm Performance and Research and Development. In A. Vlachvei, O. Notta, K. Karantininis, & N. Tsounis (Eds.), *Factors Affecting Firm Competitiveness and Performance in the Modern Business World* (pp. 108–128). Hershey, PA: IGI Global. doi:10.4018/978-1-5225-0843-4.ch004

Qi, A., & Zheng, L. (2016). Project Risk Management: A Chinese Perspective. In C. Bodea, A. Purnus, M. Huemann, & M. Hajdu (Eds.), *Managing Project Risks for Competitive Advantage in Changing Business Environments* (pp. 45–69). Hershey, PA: IGI Global. doi:10.4018/978-1-5225-0335-4.ch003

Rao, N. R. (2017). Social Media: An Enabler in Developing Business Models for Enterprises. In N. Rao (Ed.), *Social Media Listening and Monitoring for Business Applications* (pp. 165–173). Hershey, PA: IGI Global. doi:10.4018/978-1-5225-0846-5.ch009

Raue, S., & Klein, L. (2016). Systemic Risk Management: A Practice Approach to the Systemic Management of Project Risk. In C. Bodea, A. Purnus, M. Huemann, & M. Hajdu (Eds.), *Managing Project Risks for Competitive Advantage in Changing Business Environments* (pp. 70–85). Hershey, PA: IGI Global. doi:10.4018/978-1-5225-0335-4.ch004

Reyes-Mercado, P. (2017). A Readiness Index for Marketing Analytics: A Resource-Based View Conceptualization for the Implementation Stage. In Rajagopal, & R. Behl (Eds.), Business Analytics and Cyber Security Management in Organizations (pp. 38-46). Hershey, PA: IGI Global. doi:10.4018/978-1-5225-0902-8.ch004

Rosenzweig, E. D., & Bendoly, E. (2017). An Investigation of Competitor Networks in Manufacturing Strategy and Implications for Performance. In A. Vlachvei, O. Notta, K. Karantininis, & N. Tsounis (Eds.), *Factors Affecting Firm Competitiveness and Performance in the Modern Business World* (pp. 43–82). Hershey, PA: IGI Global. doi:10.4018/978-1-5225-0843-4.ch002

Rossetti di Valdalbero, D., & Birnbaum, B. (2017). Towards a New Economy: Co-Creation and Open Innovation in a Trustworthy Europe. In W. Vassallo (Ed.), *Crowdfunding for Sustainable Entrepreneurship and Innovation* (pp. 20–36). Hershey, PA: IGI Global. doi:10.4018/978-1-5225-0568-6.ch002

Ruizalba, J., & Soares, A. (2016). Internal Market Orientation and Strategy Implementation. In A. Casademunt (Ed.), *Strategic Labor Relations Management in Modern Organizations* (pp. 183–194). Hershey, PA: IGI Global. doi:10.4018/978-1-5225-0356-9.ch011

Rusko, R. (2017). Strategic Turning Points in ICT Business: The Business Development, Transformation, and Evolution in the Case of Nokia. In I. Oncioiu (Ed.), *Driving Innovation and Business Success in the Digital Economy* (pp. 1–15). Hershey, PA: IGI Global. doi:10.4018/978-1-5225-1779-5.ch001

Rusko, R., Hietanen, L., Kohtakangas, K., Kemppainen-Koivisto, R., Siltavirta, K., & Järvi, T. (2017). Educational and Business Co-Operatives: The Channels for Collective Creativity and Entrepreneurial Teams. In Z. Fields (Ed.), *Collective Creativity for Responsible and Sustainable Business Practice* (pp. 242–259). Hershey, PA: IGI Global. doi:10.4018/978-1-5225-1823-5.ch013

Saini, D. (2017). Relevance of Teaching Values and Ethics in Management Education. In N. Baporikar (Ed.), *Management Education for Global Leadership* (pp. 90–111). Hershey, PA: IGI Global. doi:10.4018/978-1-5225-1013-0.ch005

Saiz-Alvarez, J. M., Muñiz-Ávila, E., & Huezo-Ponce, D. L. (2017). Informational Competencies Entrepreneurship and Integral Values in Higher Education. In N. Baporikar (Ed.), *Innovation and Shifting Perspectives in Management Education* (pp. 79–100). Hershey, PA: IGI Global. doi:10.4018/978-1-5225-1019-2.ch004

Shaikh, F. (2017). The Benefits of New Online (Digital) Technologies on Business: Understanding the Impact of Digital on Different Aspects of the Business. In I. Hosu & I. Iancu (Eds.), *Digital Entrepreneurship and Global Innovation* (pp. 1–17). Hershey, PA: IGI Global. doi:10.4018/978-1-5225-0953-0.ch001

Silvius, G. (2016). Integrating Sustainability into Project Risk Management. In C. Bodea, A. Purnus, M. Huemann, & M. Hajdu (Eds.), *Managing Project Risks for Competitive Advantage in Changing Business Environments* (pp. 23–44). Hershey, PA: IGI Global. doi:10.4018/978-1-5225-0335-4.ch002

Soares, E. R., & Zaidan, F. H. (2017). Composition of the Financial Logistic Costs of the IT Organizations Linked to the Financial Market: Financial Indicators of the Software Development Project. In G. Jamil, A. Soares, & C. Pessoa (Eds.), *Handbook of Research on Information Management for Effective Logistics and Supply Chains* (pp. 255–272). Hershey, PA: IGI Global. doi:10.4018/978-1-5225-0973-8.ch014

Soliman, F. (2015). Could Cultural Sustainability Improve Organisational Sustainability in Cloud Environments? In F. Soliman (Ed.), *Business Transformation and Sustainability through Cloud System Implementation* (pp. 1–15). Hershey, PA: IGI Global. doi:10.4018/978-1-4666-6445-6.ch001

Soliman, F. (2015). Sustainable Business Transformation in Supply Chains. In F. Soliman (Ed.), *Business Transformation and Sustainability through Cloud System Implementation* (pp. 16–31). Hershey, PA: IGI Global. doi:10.4018/978-1-4666-6445-6.ch002

Solomon, T., & Peter, R. (2017). The Emergence of Social Media as a Contemporary Marketing Practice. In V. Benson, R. Tuninga, & G. Saridakis (Eds.), *Analyzing the Strategic Role of Social Networking in Firm Growth and Productivity* (pp. 314–333). Hershey, PA: IGI Global. doi:10.4018/978-1-5225-0559-4.ch017

Sorooshian, S. (2017). Structural Equation Modeling Algorithm and Its Application in Business Analytics. In M. Tavana, K. Szabat, & K. Puranam (Eds.), *Organizational Productivity and Performance Measurements Using Predictive Modeling and Analytics* (pp. 17–39). Hershey, PA: IGI Global. doi:10.4018/978-1-5225-0654-6.ch002

Sousa, J. C., & Gaspar, J. (2016). Start-Up: A New Conceptual Approach of Innovation Process. In A. Goel & P. Singhal (Eds.), *Product Innovation through Knowledge Management and Social Media Strategies* (pp. 291–316). Hershey, PA: IGI Global. doi:10.4018/978-1-4666-9607-5.ch013

Stancu, S., Bodea, C., Naghi, L. E., Popescu, O. M., & Neamtu, A. (2017). Use of New Innovative Technologies in Business by All Age Groups. In I. Hosu & I. Iancu (Eds.), *Digital Entrepreneurship and Global Innovation* (pp. 79–103). Hershey, PA: IGI Global. doi:10.4018/978-1-5225-0953-0.ch005

Staszewska, B. M. (2017). Local Public Enterprise Business Model as Multiple Value Creation System. In M. Lewandowski & B. Kożuch (Eds.), *Public Sector Entrepreneurship and the Integration of Innovative Business Models* (pp. 188–213). Hershey, PA: IGI Global. doi:10.4018/978-1-5225-2215-7.ch008

Sula, O., & Elenurm, T. (2017). Strategic Role of Social Networking and Personal Knowledge Management Competencies for Future Entrepreneurs. In V. Benson, R. Tuninga, & G. Saridakis (Eds.), *Analyzing the Strategic Role of Social Networking in Firm Growth and Productivity* (pp. 248–266). Hershey, PA: IGI Global. doi:10.4018/978-1-5225-0559-4.ch014

Taminiau, J., Nyangon, J., Lewis, A. S., & Byrne, J. (2017). Sustainable Business Model Innovation: Using Polycentric and Creative Climate Change Governance. In Z. Fields (Ed.), *Collective Creativity for Responsible and Sustainable Business Practice* (pp. 140–159). Hershey, PA: IGI Global. doi:10.4018/978-1-5225-1823-5.ch008

Teixeira, N., Rafael, B., & Pardal, P. (2016). Internationalization and Financial Performance: A success case in Portugal. In L. Carvalho (Ed.), *Handbook of Research on Entrepreneurial Success and its Impact on Regional Development* (pp. 88–121). Hershey, PA: IGI Global. doi:10.4018/978-1-4666-9567-2.ch005

Triandini, E., Djunaidy, A., & Siahaan, D. (2017). A Maturity Model for E-Commerce Adoption By Small And Medium Enterprises In Indonesia. *Journal of Electronic Commerce in Organizations*, *15*(1), 44–58. doi:10.4018/JECO.2017010103

Tsironis, L. K. (2016). Business Process Improvement through Data Mining Techniques: An Experimental Approach. In P. Papajorgji, F. Pinet, A. Guimarães, & J. Papathanasiou (Eds.), *Automated Enterprise Systems for Maximizing Business Performance* (pp. 150–169). Hershey, PA: IGI Global. doi:10.4018/978-1-4666-8841-4.ch009

Unterman, A. (2016). Regulating Global FMIs: Achieving Stability and Efficiency across Borders. In M. Diehl, B. Alexandrova-Kabadjova, R. Heuver, & S. Martínez-Jaramillo (Eds.), *Analyzing the Economics of Financial Market Infrastructures* (pp. 41–70). Hershey, PA: IGI Global. doi:10.4018/978-1-4666-8745-5.ch003

Van der Westhuizen, T. (2017). A Systemic Approach towards Responsible and Sustainable Economic Development: Entrepreneurship, Systems Theory, and Socio-Economic Momentum. In Z. Fields (Ed.), *Collective Creativity for Responsible and Sustainable Business Practice* (pp. 208–227). Hershey, PA: IGI Global. doi:10.4018/978-1-5225-1823-5.ch011

Related Readings

Vargas-Hernández, J. G., Ioannis, A. I., & González-Armenta, L. (2017). Joint Venture Efficiency through Skills Complementarity or by Reducing Transaction Costs?: A Case Study of an Apparel Company in an Emerging Market. In A. Vlachvei, O. Notta, K. Karantininis, & N. Tsounis (Eds.), *Factors Affecting Firm Competitiveness and Performance in the Modern Business World* (pp. 162–190). Hershey, PA: IGI Global. doi:10.4018/978-1-5225-0843-4.ch006

Vasudeva, S., & Singh, G. (2017). Impact of E-Core Service Quality Dimensions on Perceived Value of M-Banking in Case of Three Socio-Economic Variables. *International Journal of Technology and Human Interaction*, *13*(1), 1–20. doi:10.4018/IJTHI.2017010101

Vecchi, A., & Brennan, L. (2015). Leveraging Business Model Innovation in the International Space Industry. In B. Christiansen (Ed.), *Handbook of Research on Global Business Opportunities* (pp. 131–149). Hershey, PA: IGI Global. doi:10.4018/978-1-4666-6551-4.ch006

Vlachvei, A., & Notta, O. (2017). Firm Competitiveness: Theories, Evidence, and Measurement. In A. Vlachvei, O. Notta, K. Karantininis, & N. Tsounis (Eds.), *Factors Affecting Firm Competitiveness and Performance in the Modern Business World* (pp. 1–42). Hershey, PA: IGI Global. doi:10.4018/978-1-5225-0843-4.ch001

Wang, F., Raisinghani, M. S., Mora, M., & Wang, X. (2016). Strategic E-Business Management through a Balanced Scored Card Approach. In I. Lee (Ed.), *Encyclopedia of E-Commerce Development, Implementation, and Management* (pp. 361–386). Hershey, PA: IGI Global. doi:10.4018/978-1-4666-9787-4.ch027

Wronka-Pośpiech, M. (2017). Applying Business Solutions to Social Problems: Social Co-Operative and Its Business Model – Evidence from Poland. In M. Lewandowski & B. Kożuch (Eds.), *Public Sector Entrepreneurship and the Integration of Innovative Business Models* (pp. 139–164). Hershey, PA: IGI Global. doi:10.4018/978-1-5225-2215-7.ch006

Yama, H. (2016). A Perspective of Cross-Cultural Psychological Studies for Global Business. In N. Zakaria, A. Abdul-Talib, & N. Osman (Eds.), *Handbook of Research on Impacts of International Business and Political Affairs on the Global Economy* (pp. 185–206). Hershey, PA: IGI Global. doi:10.4018/978-1-4666-9806-2.ch010

Yang, J. G. (2016). Potentials and Perils of E-Business in China. In I. Lee (Ed.), *Encyclopedia of E-Commerce Development, Implementation, and Management* (pp. 1250–1262). Hershey, PA: IGI Global. doi:10.4018/978-1-4666-9787-4.ch090

Yaokumah, W., Kumah, P., & Okai, E. S. (2017). Demographic Influences on E-Payment Services. *International Journal of E-Business Research*, *13*(1), 44–65. doi:10.4018/IJEBR.2017010103

Zhang, L. Z. (2015). Investment Strategies for Implementing Cloud Systems in Supply Chains. In F. Soliman (Ed.), *Business Transformation and Sustainability through Cloud System Implementation* (pp. 32–43). Hershey, PA: IGI Global. doi:10.4018/978-1-4666-6445-6.ch003

Zuber, C., & Pfohl, H. (2015). Cultural Management for Multinational Enterprises. In B. Christiansen (Ed.), *Handbook of Research on Global Business Opportunities* (pp. 71–102). Hershey, PA: IGI Global. doi:10.4018/978-1-4666-6551-4.ch004

Index

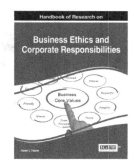

Stay Current on the Latest Emerging Research Developments

Become an IGI Global Reviewer for Authored Book Projects

Premier Reference Source

Solutions for High-Touch Communications in a High-Tech World

Premier Reference Source

Advanced Research on Biologically Inspired Cognitive Architectures

Premier Reference Source

Workforce Development Theory and Practice in the Mental Health Sector

Premier Reference Source

Resource Management and Efficiency in Cloud Computing Environments

The overall success of an authored book project is dependent on quality and timely reviews.

In this competitive age of scholarly publishing, constructive and timely feedback significantly decreases the turnaround time of manuscripts from submission to acceptance, allowing the publication and discovery of progressive research at a much more expeditious rate. Several IGI Global authored book projects are currently seeking highly qualified experts in the field to fill vacancies on their respective editorial review boards:

Applications may be sent to:
development@igi-global.com

Applicants must have a doctorate (or an equivalent degree) as well as publishing and reviewing experience. Reviewers are asked to write reviews in a timely, collegial, and constructive manner. All reviewers will begin their role on an ad-hoc basis for a period of one year, and upon successful completion of this term can be considered for full editorial review board status, with the potential for a subsequent promotion to Associate Editor.

If you have a colleague that may be interested in this opportunity, we encourage you to share this information with them.

IGI Global
Proudly Partners with

eContent Pro

---

eContent Pro specializes in the following areas:

Academic Copy Editing
Our expert copy editors will conduct a full copy editing procedure on your manuscript and will also address your preferred reference style to make sure your paper meets the standards of the style of your choice.

Expert Translation
Our expert translators will work to ensure a clear cut and accurate translation of your document, ensuring that your research is flawlessly communicated to your audience.

Professional Proofreading
Our editors will conduct a comprehensive assessment of your content and address all shortcomings of the paper in terms of grammar, language structures, spelling, and formatting.

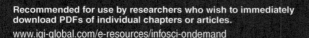

Printed in the United States
By Bookmasters